Intermediate Perl

Other Perl resources from O'Reilly

Related titles

Learning Perl
Programming Perl
Advanced Perl Programming

Perl Best Practices
Perl Testing: A Developer's Notebook™
Perl CD Bookshelf

Hacks Series Home

hacks.oreilly.com is a community site for developers and power users of all stripes. Readers learn from each other as they share their favorite tips and tools for Mac OS X, Linux, Google, Windows XP, and more.

Perl Books Resource Center

perl.oreilly.com is a complete catalog of O'Reilly's books on Perl and related technologies, including sample chapters and code examples.

Perl.com is the central web site for the Perl community. It is the perfect starting place for finding out everything there is to know about Perl.

Conferences

O'Reilly brings diverse innovators together to nurture the ideas that spark revolutionary industries. We specialize in documenting the latest tools and systems, translating the innovator's knowledge into useful skills for those in the trenches. Visit *conferences.oreilly.com* for our upcoming events.

Safari Bookshelf (*safari.oreilly.com*) is the premier online reference library for programmers and IT professionals. Conduct searches across more than 1,000 books. Subscribers can zero in on answers to time-critical questions in a matter of seconds. Read the books on your Bookshelf from cover to cover or simply flip to the page you need. Try it today for free.

Intermediate Perl

Randal L. Schwartz, brian d foy, and Tom Phoenix

O'REILLY®

Beijing · Cambridge · Farnham · Köln · Paris · Sebastopol · Taipei · Tokyo

Intermediate Perl
by Randal L. Schwartz, brian d foy, and Tom Phoenix

Copyright © 2006, 2003 O'Reilly Media, Inc. All rights reserved.
Printed in the United States of America.

Published by O'Reilly Media, Inc., 1005 Gravenstein Highway North, Sebastopol, CA 95472.

O'Reilly books may be purchased for educational, business, or sales promotional use. Online editions
are also available for most titles (*safari.oreilly.com*). For more information, contact our
corporate/institutional sales department: (800) 998-9938 or *corporate@oreilly.com*.

Editors: Allison Randal and Tatiana Apandi
Production Editor: Darren Kelly
Copyeditor: Chris Downey
Proofreader: Nancy Reinhardt

Indexer: Angela Howard
Cover Designer: Karen Montgomery
Interior Designer: David Futato
Illustrators: Robert Romano, Jessamyn Read,
and Lesley Borash

Printing History:

June 2003:	First Edition, published as *Learning Perl Objects, References & Modules*.
March 2006:	Second Edition.

 This book uses RepKover™, a durable and flexible lay-flat binding.

ISBN-10: 0-596-10206-2
ISBN-13: 978-0-596-10206-7
[M]   [10/07]

Table of Contents

Foreword

Perl's object-oriented (OO) mechanism is classic prestidigitation. It takes a collection of Perl's existing non-OO features, such as packages, references, hashes, arrays, subroutines, and modules, and then—with nothing up its sleeve—manages to conjure up fully functional objects, classes, and methods, seemingly out of nowhere.

That's a great trick. It means you can build on your existing Perl knowledge and ease your way into OO Perl development, without first needing to conquer a mountain of new syntax or navigate an ocean of new techniques. It also means you can progressively fine-tune OO Perl to meet your own needs, by selecting from the existing constructs the one that best suits your task.

But there's a problem. Since Perl co-opts packages, references, hashes, arrays, subroutines, and modules as the basis for its OO mechanism, to use OO Perl you already need to understand packages, references, hashes, arrays, subroutines, and modules.

And there's the rub. The learning curve hasn't been eliminated; it's merely been pushed back half a dozen steps.

So then, how are you going to learn everything you need to know about non-OO Perl so you can start to learn everything you need to know about OO Perl?

This book is the answer. In the following pages, Randal draws on two decades of using Perl, and four decades of watching *Gilligan's Island* and *Mr. Ed*, to explain each of the components of Perl that collectively underpin its OO features. And, better still, he then goes on to show exactly how to combine those components to create useful classes and objects.

So if you still feel like Gilligan when it comes to Perl's objects, references, and modules, this book is just what the Professor ordered.

And that's straight from the horse's mouth.

—Damian Conway, May 2003

Preface

Over a decade ago (nearly eternity in Internet Time), Randal Schwartz wrote the first edition of *Learning Perl*. In the intervening years, Perl itself has grown substantially from a "cool" scripting language used primarily by Unix system administrators to a robust object-oriented programming (OOP) language that runs on practically every computing platform known to mankind.

Throughout its four editions, *Learning Perl* remained the same size (about 300 pages) and continued to cover much of the same material to remain compact and accessible to the beginning programmer. But there is much more to learn about Perl now than when that first book was written.

Randal called the first edition of this book *Learning Perl Objects, References, and Modules,* and now it's *Intermediate Perl,* but we like to think of it as just *Learning More Perl.** This is the book that picks up where *Learning Perl* leaves off. We show you how to use Perl to write larger programs.

As in *Learning Perl*, we designed each chapter to be small enough to read in just an hour or so. Each chapter ends with a series of exercises to help you practice what you've just learned, and the answers are in the appendix for your reference. And like *Learning Perl*, we've developed the material in this book for a teaching environment and used it in that setting, including for our own use at Stonehenge Consulting Services, as we conduct on-site and open-enrollment trainings.

You don't have to be a Unix guru, or even a Unix user, to benefit from this book. Unless otherwise noted, everything in this book applies equally well to Windows ActivePerl from ActiveState and all other modern implementations of Perl. To use this book, you just need to be familiar with the material in *Learning Perl* and have the ambition to go further.

---

* Don't ask why it isn't called that. We must have had 300 emails on the subject. Okay, ask, since we know you're going to anyway. You never really stop learning Perl, so *Learning More Perl* doesn't really tell you much about the book. Our editor chose the name, which tells you what to expect.

Structure of This Book

You should read this book from front to back, stopping to do the exercises. Each chapter builds on preceding chapters, and we'll assume that you know the material from those chapters as we discuss new topics.

Chapter 1, *Introduction*
> An introduction to the material.

Chapter 2, *Intermediate Foundations*
> Pick up some intermediate Perl skills you'll need for the rest of the book.

Chapter 3, *Using Modules*
> Use Perl's core modules, as well as modules from other people. We're going to show you how to create your own modules later in the book, but until we do, you can still use modules you already have.

Chapter 4, *Introduction to References*
> Introduce a level of redirection to allow the same code to operate on different sets of data.

Chapter 5, *References and Scoping*
> Learn how Perl manages to keep track of pointers to data, and an introduction to anonymous data structures and autovivification.

Chapter 6, *Manipulating Complex Data Structures*
> Create, access, and print arbitrarily deep and nested data structures, including arrays of arrays and hashes of hashes.

Chapter 7, *Subroutine References*
> Capture behavior as an anonymous subroutine that you create dynamically and execute later.

Chapter 8, *Filehandle References*
> Store filehandles in scalar variables that you can easily pass around your program or store in data structures.

Chapter 9, *Practical Reference Tricks*
> Sorting complex operations, the *Schwartzian Transform*, and working with recursively defined data.

Chapter 10, *Building Larger Programs*
> Build larger programs by separating code into separate files and namespaces.

Chapter 11, *Introduction to Objects*
> Work with classes, method calls, inheritance, and overriding.

Chapter 12, *Objects with Data*
> Add per-instance data, including constructors, getters, and setters.

Chapter 13, *Object Destruction*
> Add behavior to an object that is going away, including object persistence.

Chapter 14, *Some Advanced Object Topics*
Use multiple inheritance, automatic methods, and references to filehandles.

Chapter 15, *Exporter*
How use works, how we can decide what to export, and how we can create our own import routines.

Chapter 16, *Writing a Distribution*
Package a module for sharing, including portable installation instructions.

Chapter 17, *Essential Testing*
Test your code to ensure it does what you want it to do.

Chapter 18, *Advanced Testing*
Test complex aspects of code and meta-code things such as documentation and test coverage.

Chapter 19, *Contributing to CPAN*
Share your work with the world by uploading it to CPAN.

Appendix, *Answers to Exercises*
Where to go to get answers.

Conventions Used in This Book

The following typographic conventions are used in this book:

Constant width
Used for function names, module names, filenames, environment variables, code snippets, and other literal text

Italics
Used for emphasis and for new terms where they are defined

Using Code Examples

This book is here to help you get your job done. In general, you may use the code in this book in your programs and documentation. You do not need to contact O'Reilly for permission unless you're reproducing a significant portion of the code. For example, writing a program that uses several chunks of code from this book does not require permission. Selling or distributing a CD-ROM of examples from O'Reilly books *does* require permission. Answering a question by citing this book and quoting example code does not require permission. Incorporating a significant amount of example code from this book into your product's documentation *does* require permission.

We appreciate, but do not require, attribution. An attribution usually includes the title, author, publisher, and ISBN. For example: *Intermediate Perl,* by Randal L. Schwartz, brian d foy, and Tom Phoenix. Copyright 2006 O'Reilly Media, Inc., 0-596-10206-2.

If you feel your use of code examples falls outside fair use or the permission given above, feel free to contact us at *permissions@oreilly.com*.

Comments and Questions

Please address comments and questions concerning this book to the publisher:

O'Reilly Media
1005 Gravenstein Highway North
Sebastopol, CA 95472
(800) 998-9938 (in the United States or Canada)
(707) 829-0515 (international/local)
(707) 829-0104 (fax)

The web page for this book, which lists errata, examples, or any additional information, can be found at:

> *http://www.oreilly.com/catalog/intermediateperl*

To comment or ask technical questions about this book, send email to:

> *bookquestions@oreilly.com*

For more information about books, conferences, Resource Centers, and the O'Reilly Network, see the O'Reilly web site at:

> *http://www.oreilly.com*

Safari® Enabled

 When you see a Safari® Enabled icon on the cover of your favorite technology book, it means the book is available online through the O'Reilly Network Safari Bookshelf.

Safari offers a solution that's better than e-books. It's a virtual library that lets you easily search thousands of top technology books, cut and paste code samples, download chapters, and find quick answers when you need the most accurate, current information. Try it for free at *http://safari.oreilly.com*.

Acknowledgments

From Randal. In the preface of the first edition of *Learning Perl*, I acknowledged the Beaverton McMenamin's Cedar Hills Pub* just down the street from my house for the

---

* *http://www.mcmenamins.com/*

"rent-free booth-office space" while I wrote most of the draft on my Powerbook 140. Well, like wearing your lucky socks every day when your favorite team is in the play-offs, I wrote nearly all of this book (including these words) at the same brewpub, in hopes that the light of success of the first book will shine on me twice. (As I update this preface for the second edition, I can see that my lucky socks do indeed work!)

This McM's has the same great local microbrew beer and greasy sandwiches, but they've gotten rid of my favorite pizza bread, replacing it with new items like marion-berry cobbler (a local treat) and spicy jambalaya. (And they added two booths and put in some pool tables.) Also, instead of the Powerbook 140, I'm using a Titanium Powerbook, with 1,000 times more disk, 500 times more memory, and a 200-times-faster CPU running a real Unix-based operating system (OS X) instead of the limited Mac OS. I also uploaded all of the draft sections (including this one) over my 144K cell-phone modem and emailed them directly to the reviewers, instead of having to wait to rush home to my 9600-baud external modem and phone line. How times have changed!

So, thanks once again to the staff of the McMenamin's Cedar Hills Pub for the booth space and hospitality.

Like the fourth edition of *Learning Perl*, I also owe much of what I'm saying here and how I'm saying it to the students of Stonehenge Consulting Services, who have given me immediate, precise feedback (by their glazed eyes and awkwardly constructed questions) when I was exceeding the "huh?" factor threshold. With that feedback over many dozens of presentations, I was able to keep refining and refactoring the materials that paved the way for this book.

Speaking of which, those materials started as a half-day "What's new in Perl 5?" summary commissioned by Margie Levine of Silicon Graphics, in addition to my fre-quently presented on-site, four-day Llama course (targeted primarily for Perl Version 4 at the time). Eventually, I got the idea to beef up those notes into a full course and enlisted fellow Stonehenge presenter Joseph Hall for the task. (He's the one who selected the universe from which the examples are drawn.) Joseph developed a two-day course for Stonehenge in parallel with his excellent *Effective Perl Programming* book, which we then used as the course textbook (until now).

Other Stonehenge instructors have also dabbled a bit in the "Packages, References, Objects, and Modules" course over the years, including Chip Salzenberg and Tad McClellan. But the bulk of the recent changes have been the responsibility of my senior trainer, Tom Phoenix, who has been "Stonehenge employee of the month" so often that I may have to finally give up my preferred parking space. Tom manages the materials (just as Tad manages operations) so I can focus on being the president and the janitor of Stonehenge.

Tom Phoenix contributed most exercises in this book and a timely set of review notes during my writing process, including entire paragraphs for me to just insert in place of the drivel I had written. We work well as a team, both in the classroom and in our joint writing efforts. It is for this effort that we've acknowledged Tom as a coauthor, but I'll take direct blame for any parts of the book you end up hating: none of that could have possibly been Tom's fault.

And last but not least, a special thanks to my business partner, brian d foy, who herded this book into its second revision and wrote most of the changes between the previous edition and this edition.

Of course, a book is nothing without a subject and a distribution channel, and for that I must acknowledge longtime associates Larry Wall and Tim O'Reilly. Thanks, guys, for creating an industry that has paid for my essentials, discretionary purchases, and dreams for nearly 15 years.

And, as always, a special thanks to Lyle and Jack for teaching me nearly everything I know about writing and convincing me that I was much more than a programmer who might learn to write: I was also a writer who happened to know how to program. Thank you.

And to you, the reader of this book, for whom I toiled away the countless hours while sipping a cold microbrew and scarfing down a piece of incredible cheesecake, trying to avoid spilling on my laptop keyboard: thank you for reading what I've written. I sincerely hope I've contributed (in at least a small way) to your Perl proficiency. If you ever meet me on the street, please say "Hi."* I'd like that. Thank you.

From brian. I have to thank Randal first, since I learned Perl from the first edition of *Learning Perl*, and learned the rest teaching the Llama and Alpaca courses for Stonehenge Consulting. Teaching is often the best way to learn.

I convinced Randal that we should update *Learning Perl*, and when we got done with that, I told him it was time to update this book. Our editor, Allison Randal, agreed and did the best she could to keep us on schedule.

Special non-Perl thanks to Stacey, Buster, Mimi, Roscoe, Amelia, Lila, and everyone else who tried to distract me while I was busy but still talked to me, even though I couldn't come out to play.

From Both of Us. Thanks to our reviewers, David H. Adler, Stephen Jenkins, Kevin Meltzer, Matthew Musgrove, Andrew Savige, and Ricardo Signes, for providing comments on the draft of this book.

Thanks also to our many students who have let us know what parts of the course material have needed improvement over the years. It's because of you that we're all so proud of it today.

---

* And yes, you can ask a Perl question at the same time. I don't mind.

Thanks to the many Perl Mongers who have made us feel at home as we've visited your cities. Let's do it again sometime.

And finally, our sincerest thanks to our friend Larry Wall, for having the wisdom to share his really cool and powerful toys with the rest of the world so that we can all get our work done just a little bit faster, easier, and with more fun.

## CHAPTER 1

Introduction

Welcome to the next step in your understanding of Perl. You're probably here either because you want to learn to write programs that are more than 100 lines long or because your boss has told you to do so.

See, our *Learning Perl* book was great because it introduced the use of Perl for short and medium programs (which is most of the programming done in Perl, we've observed). But, to avoid having "the Llama book" be big and intimidating, we left a lot of information out, deliberately and carefully.

In the pages that follow, you can get "the rest of the story" in the same style as our friendly Llama book. It covers what you need to write programs that are 100 to 10,000 lines long.

For example, you'll learn how to work with multiple programmers on the same project. This is great, because unless you work 35 hours each day, you'll need some help with larger tasks. You'll also need to ensure that all your code fits with the other code as you develop it for the final application.

This book will also show you how to deal with larger and more complex data structures, such as what we might casually call a "hash of hashes" or an "array of arrays of hashes of arrays." Once you know a little about references, you're on your way to arbitrarily complex data structures.

And then there's the buzzworthy notion of object-oriented programming (OOP), which allows parts of your code (or hopefully code from others) to be reused with minor or major variations within the same program. The book will cover that as well, even if you've never seen objects before.

An important aspect of working in teams is having a release cycle and tests for unit and integration testing. You'll learn the basics of packaging your code as a distribution and providing unit tests for that distribution, both for development and for verifying that your code works in the ultimate end environment.

And, just as was promised and delivered in *Learning Perl*, we'll entertain you along the way with interesting examples and bad puns. (We've sent Fred, Barney, Betty, and Wilma home, though. A new cast of characters will take the starring roles.)

What Should You Know Already?

We'll presume that you've already read *Learning Perl*, or at least pretend you have, and that you've played enough with Perl to already have those basics down. For example, you won't see an explanation in this book that shows how to access the elements of an array or return a value from a subroutine.

Make sure you know the following things:

- How to run a Perl program on your system
- The three basic Perl variable types: scalars, arrays, and hashes
- Control structures such as while, if, for, and foreach
- Subroutines
- Perl operators such as grep, map, sort, and print
- File manipulation such as open, file reading, and -X (file tests)

You might pick up deeper insight into these topics in this book, but we're going to presume you know the basics.

What About All Those Footnotes?

Like *Learning Perl*, this book relegates some of the more esoteric items out of the way for the first reading and places those items in footnotes.* You should skip those the first time through and pick them up on a rereading. You will not find anything in a footnote that you'll need to understand any of the material we present later.

What's with the Exercises?

Hands-on training gets the job done better. The best way to provide this training is with a series of exercises after every half-hour to hour of presentation. Of course, if you're a speed reader, the end of the chapter may come a bit sooner than a half hour. Slow down, take a breather, and do the exercises!

Each exercise has a "minutes to complete" rating. We intend for this rating to hit the midpoint of the bell curve, but don't feel bad if you take significantly longer or

---

* Like this.

shorter. Sometimes it's just a matter of how many times you've faced similar programming tasks in your studies or jobs. Use the numbers merely as a guideline.

Every exercise has its answer in the Appendix. Again, try not to peek; you'll ruin the value of the exercise.

What If I'm a Perl Course Instructor?

If you're a Perl instructor who has decided to use this as your textbook, you should know that each set of exercises is short enough for most students to complete in 45 minutes to an hour, with a little time left over for a break. Some chapters' exercises should be quicker, and some may take longer. That's because once all those little numbers in square brackets were written, we discovered that we didn't know how to add.

So let's get started. Class begins after you turn the page....

## CHAPTER 2

Intermediate Foundations

Before we get started on the meat of the book, we want to introduce some intermediate-level Perl idioms that we use throughout the book. These are the things that typically set apart the beginning and intermediate Perl programmers. Along the way, we'll also introduce you to the cast of characters that we'll use in the examples throughout the book.

List Operators

You already know about several list operators in Perl, but you may not have thought of them as working with lists. The most common list operator is probably print. We give it one or more arguments, and it puts them together for us.

```
print 'Two castaways are ', 'Gilligan', ' and ', 'Skipper', "\n";
```

There are several other list operators that you already know about from *Learning Perl*. The sort operator puts its input list in order. In their theme song, the castaways don't come in alphabetical order, but sort can fix that for us.

```
my @castaways = sort qw(Gilligan Skipper Ginger Professor Mary-Ann);
```

The reverse operator returns a list in the opposite order.

```
my @castaways = reverse qw(Gilligan Skipper Ginger Professor Mary-Ann);
```

Perl has many other operators that work with lists, and, once you get used to them, you'll find yourself typing less and expressing your intent more clearly.

List Filtering with grep

The grep operator takes a list of values and a "testing expression." It takes one item after another in the list and places it into the $_ variable. It then evaluates the testing expression in a scalar context. If the expression evaluates to a true value, grep passes $_ on to the output list.

```
my @lunch_choices = grep &is_edible($_), @gilligans_posessions.
```

In a list context, the grep operator returns a list of all such selected items. In a scalar context, grep returns the number of selected items.

```perl
my @results = grep EXPR, @input_list;
my $count   = grep EXPR, @input_list;
```

Here, *EXPR* stands in for any scalar expression that should refer to $_ (explicitly or implicitly). For example, to find all the numbers greater than 10, in our grep expression we check if $_ is greater than 10.

```perl
my @input_numbers = (1, 2, 4, 8, 16, 32, 64);
my @bigger_than_10 = grep $_ > 10, @input_numbers;
```

The result is just 16, 32, and 64. This uses an explicit reference to $_. Here's an example of an implicit reference to $_ from the pattern match operator:

```perl
my @end_in_4 = grep /4$/, @input_numbers;
```

And now we get just 4 and 64.

While the grep is running, it shadows any existing value in $_, which is to say that grep borrows the use of this variable but puts the original value back when it's done. The variable $_ isn't a mere copy of the data item, though; it is an alias for the actual data element, similar to the control variable in a foreach loop.

If the testing expression is complex, we can hide it in a subroutine:

```perl
my @odd_digit_sum = grep digit_sum_is_odd($_), @input_numbers;

sub digit_sum_is_odd {
        my $input = shift;
        my @digits = split //, $input;  # Assume no nondigit characters
        my $sum;
        $sum += $_ for @digits;
        return $sum % 2;
}
```

Now we get back the list of 1, 16, and 32. These numbers have a digit sum with a remainder of "1" in the last line of the subroutine, which counts as true.

The syntax comes in two forms, though: we just showed you the expression form, and now here's the block form. Rather than define an explicit subroutine that we'd use for only a single test, we can put the body of a subroutine directly in line in the grep operator, using the block forms:*

```perl
my @results = grep {
  block;
  of;
  code;
} @input_list;
```

---

* In the block form of grep, there's no comma between the block and the input list. In the expression form of grep, there must be a comma between the expression and the list.

```
my $count = grep {
  block;
  of;
  code;
} @input_list;
```

Just like the expression form, grep temporarily places each element of the input list into $_. Next, it evaluates the entire block of code. The last evaluated expression in the block is the testing expression. (And like all testing expressions, it's evaluated in a scalar context.) Because it's a full block, we can introduce variables that are scoped to the block. Let's rewrite that last example to use the block form:

```
my @odd_digit_sum = grep {
  my $input = $_;
  my @digits = split //, $input;   # Assume no nondigit characters
  my $sum;
  $sum += $_ for @digits;
  $sum % 2;
} @input_numbers;
```

Note the two changes: the input value comes in via $_ rather than an argument list, and we removed the keyword return. In fact, we would have been wrong to keep the return because we're no longer in a separate subroutine: just a block of code.* Of course, we can optimize a few things out of that routine since we don't need the intermediate variables:

```
my @odd_digit_sum = grep {
  my $sum;
  $sum += $_ for split //;
  $sum % 2;
} @input_numbers;
```

Feel free to crank up the explicitness if it helps you and your coworkers understand and maintain the code. That's the main thing that matters.

Transforming Lists with map

The map operator has a very similar syntax to the grep operator and shares a lot of the same operational steps. For example, it temporarily places items from a list into $_ one at a time, and the syntax allows both the expression block forms.

However, the testing expression becomes a mapping expression. The map operator evaluates the expression in a list context (not a scalar context like grep). Each evaluation of the expression gives a portion of the many results. The overall result is the list concatenation of all individual results. In a scalar context, map returns the number of

---

* The return would have exited the subroutine that contains this entire section of code. And yes, some of us have been bitten by that mistake in real, live coding on the first draft.

elements that are returned in a list context. But map should rarely, if ever, be used in anything but a list context.

Let's start with a simple example:

```
my @input_numbers = (1, 2, 4, 8, 16, 32, 64);
my @result = map $_ + 100, @input_numbers;
```

For each of the seven items map places into $_, we get a single output result: the number that is 100 greater than the input number. So the value of @result is 101, 102, 104, 108, 116, 132, and 164.

But we're not limited to having only one output for each input. Let's see what happens when each input produces two output items:

```
my @result = map { $_, 3 * $_ } @input_numbers;
```

Now there are two items for each input item: 1, 3, 2, 6, 4, 12, 8, 24, 16, 48, 32, 96, 64, and 192. We can store those pairs in a hash, if we need a hash showing what number is three times a small power of two:

```
my %hash = @result;
```

Or, without using the intermediate array from the map:

```
my %hash = map { $_, 3 * $_ } @input_numbers;
```

You can see that map is pretty versatile; we can produce any number of output items for each input item. And we don't always need to produce the same number of output items. Let's see what happens when we break apart the digits:

```
my @result = map { split //, $_ } @input_numbers;
```

The inline block of code splits each number into its individual digits. For 1, 2, 4, and 8, we get a single result. For 16, 32, and 64, we get two results per number. When map concatenates the results lists, we end up with 1, 2, 4, 8, 1, 6, 3, 2, 6, and 4.

If a particular invocation results in an empty list, map concatenates that empty result into the larger list, contributing nothing to the list. We can use this feature to select and reject items. For example, suppose we want only the split digits of numbers ending in 4:

```
my @result = map {
        my @digits = split //, $_;
        if ($digits[-1] == 4) {
          @digits;
        } else {
          ( );
        }
} @input_numbers;
```

If the last digit is 4, we return the digits themselves by evaluating @digits (which is in list context). If the last digit is not 4, we return an empty list, effectively removing results for that particular item. Thus, we can always use a map in place of a grep, but not vice versa.

Of course, everything we can do with map and grep, we can also do with explicit foreach loops. But then again, we can also code in assembler or by toggling bits into a front panel.* The point is that proper application of grep and map can help reduce the complexity of the program, allowing us to concentrate on high-level issues rather than details.

Trapping Errors with eval

Many lines of ordinary code have the potential to terminate a program prematurely if something goes wrong.

```
my $average = $total / $count;                # divide by zero?
print "okay\n" unless /$match/;               # illegal pattern?

open MINNOW, '>ship.txt'
or die "Can't create 'ship.txt': $!";         # user-defined die?

&implement($_) foreach @rescue_scheme;        # die inside sub?
```

But just because something has gone wrong with one part of our code, that doesn't mean that we want everything to crash. Perl uses the eval operator as its error-trapping mechanism.

```
eval { $average = $total / $count } ;
```

If an error happens while running code inside an eval block, the block is done executing. But even though the code inside the block is finished, Perl continues running the code just after the eval. It's most common after an eval to immediately check $@, which will either be empty (meaning that there was no error) or the dying words Perl had from the code that failed, perhaps something like "divide by zero" or a longer error message.

```
eval { $average = $total / $count } ;
print "Continuing after error: $@" if $@;

eval { &rescue_scheme_42 } ;
print "Continuing after error: $@" if $@;
```

The semicolon is needed after the eval block because eval is a function (not a control structure, such as if or while). But the block is a true block and may include lexical variables ("my" variables) and any other arbitrary statements. As a function, eval has a return value much like a subroutine's (the last expression evaluated, or a value returned early by the return keyword). Of course, if the code in the block fails, no value is returned; this gives undef in a scalar context, or an empty list in a list context. Thus, another way to calculate an average safely looks like this:

```
my $average = eval { $total / $count } ;
```

---

* If you're old enough to remember those front panels.

Now $average is either the quotient or undef, depending upon whether the operation completed successfully or not.

Perl even supports nested eval blocks. The power of an eval block to trap errors extends for as long as it's executing, so it catches errors deep within nested subroutine calls. eval can't trap the most serious of errors, though: the ones in which Perl itself stops running. These include things such as an uncaught signal, running out of memory, and other catastrophes. eval doesn't catch syntax errors, either; because Perl compiles the eval block with the rest of the code, it catches syntax errors at compile time, not at runtime. It doesn't catch warnings either (although Perl does provide a way to intercept warning messages; see $SIG{__WARN__}).

Dynamic Code with eval

There's also a second form of eval, whose parameter is a string expression instead of a block. It compiles and executes code from a string at runtime. While this is useful and supported, it is also dangerous if any untrustworthy data has gotten into the string. With a few notable exceptions, we recommend you avoid eval on a string. We'll use it a bit later, and you might see it in other people's code, so we'll show you how it works anyway.

```
eval '$sum = 2 + 2';
print "The sum is $sum\n";
```

Perl executes that code in the lexical context of the code around it, meaning that it's virtually as if we had typed that code right there. The result of the eval is the last evaluated expression, so we really don't need the entire statement inside the eval.

```
#!/usr/bin/perl

foreach my $operator ( qw(+ - * /) ) {
        my $result = eval "2 $operator 2";
        print "2 $operator 2 is $result\n";
        }
```

Here, we go through the operators + - * / and use each of those inside our eval code. In the string we give to eval, we interpolate the value of $operator into the string. The eval executes the code that the string represents and returns the last evaluated expression, which we assign it to $result.

If eval can't properly compile and run the Perl code we hand it, it sets $@ just like in its block form. In this example, we want to trap any divide-by-zero errors, but we don't divide by anything (another sort of error).

```
print 'The quotient is ', eval '5 /', "\n";
warn $@ if $@;
```

The eval catches the syntax error and puts the message in $@, which we check immediately after calling eval.

```
The quotient is
syntax error at (eval 1) line 2, at EOF
```

Later, in Chapters 10, 17, and 18, we'll use this to optionally load modules. If we can't load the module, Perl normally would stop the program. We'll catch the error and recover on our own when this happens.

In case you didn't catch our warning before, we'll say it again: be very careful with this form of eval. If you can find another way to do what you need, try that first. We'll use it later, in Chapter 10 to load code from an external file, but then we'll also show you a much better way to do that too.

Exercises

You can find the answers to these exercises in "Answers for Chapter 2" in the Appendix.

Exercise 1 [15 min]

Write a program that takes a list of filenames on the command line and uses grep to select the ones whose size in bytes is less than 1000. Use map to transform the strings in this list, putting four space characters in front of each and a newline character after. Print the resulting list.

Exercise 2 [25 min]

Write a program that asks the user to enter a pattern (regular expression). Read this as data from the keyboard; don't get it from the command-line arguments. Report a list of files in some hardcoded directory (such as "/etc" or 'C:\\Windows') whose names match the pattern. Repeat this until the user enters an empty string instead of a pattern. The user should not type the forward slashes that are traditionally used to delimit pattern matches in Perl; the input pattern is delimited by the trailing newline. Ensure that a faulty pattern, such as one with unbalanced parentheses, doesn't crash the program.

## CHAPTER 3

Using Modules

Modules are the building blocks for our programs. They provide reusable subroutines, variables, and even object-oriented classes. On our way to building our own modules, we'll show you some of those you might be interested in. We'll also look at the basics of using modules that others have already written.

The Standard Distribution

Perl comes with many of the popular modules already. Indeed, most of the 50+ MB of the most recent distribution are from modules. In October 1996, Perl 5.003_07 had 98 modules. Today, at the beginning of 2006, Perl 5.8.8 has 359.* Indeed, this is one of the advantages of Perl: it already comes with a lot of stuff that you need to make useful and complex programs without doing a lot of work yourself.

Throughout this book, we'll try to identify which modules comes with Perl (and in most cases, with which version they started coming with Perl). We'll call these "core modules" or note that they're in "the standard distribution." If you have Perl, you should have these modules. Since we're using Perl 5.8.7 as we write this, we'll assume that's the current version of Perl.

As you develop your code, you may want to consider if you want to use only core modules, so that you can be sure that anyone with Perl will have that module as long as they have at least the same version as you.† We'll avoid that debate here, mostly because we love CPAN too much to do without it.

---

* After you make it through this book, you should be able to use Module::CoreList to discover that count for yourself. That's what we did to get those numbers, after all.

† Although we don't go into it here, the Module::CoreList module has the lists of which modules came with which versions of Perl, along with other historical data.

Using Modules

Almost every Perl module comes with documentation, and even though we might not know how all of the behind-the-scenes magic works, we really don't have to worry about that stuff if we know how to use the interface. That's why the interface is there, after all: to hide the details.

On our local machine, we can read the module documentation with the `perldoc` command. We give it the module name we're interested in, and it prints out its documentation.

```
$ perldoc File::Basename
```

```
NAME
        fileparse - split a pathname into pieces

        basename - extract just the filename from a path

        dirname - extract just the directory from a path

SYNOPSIS
                use File::Basename;

                ($name,$path,$suffix) = fileparse($fullname,@suffixlist)
                fileparse_set_fstype($os_string);
                $basename = basename($fullname,@suffixlist);
                $dirname = dirname($fullname);
```

We've included the top portion of the documentation to show you the most important section (at least, the most important when you're starting). Module documentation typically follows the old Unix manpage format, which starts with a NAME and SYNOPSIS section.

The synopsis gives us examples of the module's use, and if we can suspend understanding for a bit and follow the example, we can use the module. That is to say, it may be that you're not yet familiar with some of the Perl techniques and syntax in the synopsis, but you can generally just follow the example and make everything work.

Now, since Perl is a mix of procedural, functional, object-oriented, and other sorts of language types, Perl modules come in a variety of different interfaces. We'll employ these modules in slightly different fashions, but as long as we can check the documentation, we shouldn't have a problem.

Functional Interfaces

To load a module, we use the Perl built-in use. We're not going to go into all of the details here, but we'll get to those in Chapters 10 and 15. At the moment, we just want to use the module. Let's start with File::Basename, that same module from the core distribution. To load it into our script, we say:

```
use File::Basename;
```

When we do this, File::Basename introduces three subroutines, fileparse, basename, and dirname,* into our script.† From this point forward, we can say:

```
my $basename = basename( $some_full_path );
my $dirname  = dirname( $some_full_path );
```

as if we had written the basename and dirname subroutines ourselves, or (nearly) as if they were built-in Perl functions. These routines pick out the filename and the directory parts of a pathname. For example, if $some_full_path were D:\Projects\Island Rescue\plan7.rtf (presumably, the program is running on a Windows machine), then $basename would be plan7.rtf and the $dirname would be D:\Projects\Island Rescue.

The File::Basename module knows what sort of system it's on, and thus its functions figure out how to correctly parse the strings for the different delimiters we might encounter.

However, suppose we already had a dirname subroutine. We've now overwritten it with the definition provided by File::Basename! If we had turned on warnings, we would have seen a message stating that; but otherwise, Perl really doesn't care.

Selecting What to Import

Fortunately, we can tell the use operation to limit its actions by specifying a list of subroutine names following the module name, called the *import list*:

```
use File::Basename ('fileparse', 'basename');
```

Now the module only gives us those two subroutines and leaves our own dirname alone. Of course, this is awkward to type, so more often we'll see this written with the quotewords operator:

```
use File::Basename qw( fileparse basename );
```

In fact, even if there's only one item, we tend to write it with a qw( ) list for consistency and maintenance; often we'll go back to say "give me another one from here," and it's simpler if it's already a qw( ) list.

We've protected the local dirname routine, but what if we still want the functionality provided by File::Basename's dirname? No problem. We just spell it out with its full package specification:

```
my $dirname = File::Basename::dirname($some_path);
```

---

* As well as a utility routine, fileparse_set_fstype.

† Actually, it imports them into the current package, but we haven't told you about those yet.

The list of names following use doesn't change which subroutines are defined in the module's package (in this case, File::Basename). We can always use the full name regardless of the import list, as in:[*]

```
my $basename = File::Basename::basename($some_path);
```

In an extreme (but extremely useful) case, we can specify an empty list for the import list, as in:

```
use File::Basename ( );          # no import
my $base = File::Basename::basename($some_path);
```

An empty list is different from an absent list. An empty list says "don't give me anything," while an absent list says "give me the defaults." If the module's author has done her job well, the default will probably be exactly what we want.

Object-Oriented Interfaces

Contrast the subroutines imported by File::Basename with what another core module has by looking at File::Spec. The File::Spec module is designed to support operations commonly performed on file specifications. (A file specification is usually a file or directory name, but it may be a name of a file that doesn't exist—in which case, it's not really a filename, is it?)

Unlike the File::Basename module, the File::Spec module has a primarily object-oriented interface. We load the module with use, as we did before.

```
use File::Spec;
```

However, since this module has an object-oriented interface,[†] it doesn't import any subroutines. Instead, the interface tells us to access the functionality of the module using its class methods. The catfile method joins a list of strings with the appropriate directory separator:

```
my $filespec = File::Spec->catfile( $homedir{gilligan},
        'web_docs', 'photos', 'USS_Minnow.gif' );
```

This calls the class method catfile of the File::Spec class, which builds a path appropriate for the local operating system and returns a single string.[‡] This is similar in syntax to the nearly two dozen other operations provided by File::Spec.

---

[*] You don't need the ampersand in front of any of these subroutine invocations, because the subroutine name is already known to the compiler following use.

[†] We can use File::Spec::Functions if we want a functional interface.

[‡] That string might be something like /home/gilligan/web_docs/photos/USS_Minnow.gif on a Unix system. On a Windows system, it would typically use backslashes as directory separators. This module lets us write portable code easily, at least where file specs are concerned.

The File::Spec module provides several other methods for dealing with file paths in a portable manner. You can read more about portability issues in the *perlport* documentation.

A More Typical Object-Oriented Module: Math::BigInt

So as not to get dismayed about how "un-OO" the File::Spec module seems since it doesn't have objects, let's look at yet another core module, Math::BigInt, which can handle integers beyond Perl's native reach.[*]

```
use Math::BigInt;

my $value = Math::BigInt->new(2);  # start with 2

$value->bpow(1000);                # take 2**1000

print $value->bstr( ), "\n";       # print it out
```

As before, this module imports nothing. Its entire interface uses class methods, such as new, against the class name to create instances, and then calls instance methods, such as bpow and bstr, against those instances.

The Comprehensive Perl Archive Network

CPAN is the result of many volunteers working together, many of whom were originally operating their own little (or big) Perl FTP sites back before that Web thing came along. They coordinated their efforts on the *perl-packrats* mailing list in late 1993 and decided that disk space was getting cheap enough that the same information should be replicated on all sites rather than having specialization on each site. The idea took about a year to ferment, and Jarkko Hietaniemi established the Finnish FTP site as the CPAN mothership from which all other mirrors could draw their daily or hourly updates.

Part of the work involved rearranging and organizing the separate archives. Places were established for Perl binaries for non-Unix architectures, scripts, and Perl's source code itself. However, the modules portion has come to be the largest and most interesting part of the CPAN.

The modules in CPAN are organized as a symbolic-link tree in hierarchical functional categories, pointing to author directories where the actual files are located. The modules area also contains indices that are generally in easy-to-parse-with-Perl formats, such as the Data::Dumper output for the detailed module index. Of course, these indices are all derived automatically from databases at the master server using

---

[*] Behind the scenes, Perl is limited by the architecture it's on. It's one of the few places where the hardware shows through.

other Perl programs. Often, the mirroring of the CPAN from one server to another is done with a now-ancient Perl program called `mirror.pl`.

From its small start of a few mirror machines, CPAN has now grown to over 200 public archives in all corners of the Net, all churning away, updating at least daily, sometimes as frequently as hourly. No matter where we are in the world, we can find a nearby CPAN mirror from which to pull the latest goodies.

The incredibly useful CPAN Search (*http://search.cpan.org*) will probably become your favorite interface. From that web site, you can search for modules, look at their documentation, browse through their distributions, inspect their CPAN Testers reports, and do many other things.

Installing Modules from CPAN

Installing a simple module from CPAN can be straightforward: we download the module distribution archive, unpack it, and change into its directory. We use `wget` here, but it doesn't matter which tool you use.

```
$ wget http://www.cpan.org/.../HTTP-Cookies-Safari-1.10.tar.gz
$ tar -xzf HTTP-Cookies-Safari-1.10.tar.gz
$ cd HTTP-Cookies-Safari-1.10s
```

From there we go one of two ways (which we'll explain in detail in Chapter 16). If we find a file named `Makefile.PL`, we run this series of commands to build, test, and finally install the source:

```
$ perl Makefile.PL
$ make
$ make test
$ make install
```

If we don't have permission to install modules in the system-wide directories,[*] we can tell Perl to install them under another path by using the `PREFIX` argument:

```
$ perl Makefile.PL PREFIX=/Users/home/Ginger
```

To make Perl look in that directory for modules, we can set the `PERL5LIB` environment variable. Perl adds those directories to its module directory search list.

```
$ export PERL5LIB=/Users/home/Ginger
```

We can also use the `lib` pragma to add to the module search path, although this is not as friendly, since we have to change the code, but also because it might not be the same directory on other machines where we want to run the code.

```
#!/usr/bin/perl
use lib qw(/Users/home/Ginger);
```

---

[*] These directories were set when the administrator installed Perl, and we can see them with `perl -V`.

Backing up for a minute, if we found a Build.PL file instead of a Makefile.PL, the process is the same. These distributions use Module::Build to build and install code. Since Module::Build is not a core Perl module,* we have to install it before we can install the distribution that needs it.

```
$ perl Build.PL
$ perl Build
$ perl Build test
$ perl Build install
```

To install into our private directories using Module::Build, we add the --install_ base parameter. We tell Perl how to find modules the same way we did before.

```
$ perl Build.PL --install_base /Users/home/Ginger
```

Sometimes we find both Makefile.PL and Build.PL in a distribution. What do we do then? We can use either one. Play favorites, if you like.

Setting the Path at the Right Time

Perl finds modules by looking through the directories in the special Perl array, @INC. The use statement executes at compile time, so it looks at the module search path, @INC, at compile time. That can break our program in hard-to-understand ways unless we take @INC into consideration.

For example, suppose we have our own directory under /home/gilligan/lib, and we place our own Navigation::SeatOfPants module in /home/gilligan/lib/Navigation/ SeatOfPants.pm. When we load our module, Perl won't find it.

```
use Navigation::SeatOfPants;
```

Perl complains to us that it can't find the module in @INC and shows us all of the directories it has in that array.

```
Can't locate Navigation/SeatofPants.pm in @INC (@INC contains: ...)
```

You might think that we should just add our module directory to @INC before we call the use. However, even adding:

```
unshift @INC, '/home/gilligan/lib';   # broken
use Navigation::SeatOfPants;
```

doesn't work. Why? Because the unshift happens at runtime, long after the use was attempted at compile time. The two statements are lexically adjacent but not temporally adjacent. Just because we wrote them next to each other doesn't mean they execute in that order. We want to change @INC before the use executes. One way to fix this is to add a BEGIN block around the unshift:

```
BEGIN { unshift @INC, '/home/gilligan/lib'; }
use Navigation::SeatOfPants;
```

---

* At least not yet. It should be part of Perl 5.10, though.

Now the BEGIN block compiles and executes at compile time, setting up the proper path for the following use.

However, this is noisy and prone to require far more explanation than you might be comfortable with, especially for the maintenance programmer who has to edit your code later. Let's replace all that clutter with that simple pragma we used before:

```
use lib '/home/gilligan/lib';
use Navigation::SeatOfPants;
```

Here, the lib pragma takes one or more arguments and adds them at the beginning of the @INC array, just like unshift did before.* It works because it executes at compile time, not runtime. Hence, it's ready in time for the use immediately following.

Because a use lib pragma will pretty much always have a site-dependent pathname, it is traditional and we encourage you to put it near the top of the file. This makes it easier to find and update when we need to move the file to a new system or when the lib directory's name changes. (Of course, we can eliminate use lib entirely if we can install our modules in standard @INC locations, but that's not always practical.)

Think of use lib as not "use this library" but rather "use this path to find my libraries (and modules)." Too often, we see code written like:

```
use lib '/home/gilligan/lib/Navigation/SeatOfPants.pm'; # WRONG
```

and then the programmer wonders why it didn't pull in the definitions. Be aware that use lib indeed runs at compile time, so this also doesn't work:

```
my $LIB_DIR = '/home/gilligan/lib';
...
use lib $LIB_DIR;      # BROKEN
use Navigation::SeatOfPants;
```

Certainly, Perl establishes the declaration of the $LIB_DIR variable at compile time (so we won't get an error with use strict, although the actual use lib should complain), but the actual assignment of the /home/gilligan/lib/ value doesn't happen until runtime. Oops, too late again!

At this point, we need to put something inside a BEGIN block or perhaps rely on yet another compile-time operation: setting a constant with use constant:

```
use constant LIB_DIR => '/home/gilligan/lib';
...
use lib LIB_DIR;
use Navigation::SeatOfPants;
```

There. Fixed again. That is, until we need the library to depend on the result of a calculation. (Where will it all end? Somebody stop the madness!) This should handle about 99 percent of our needs.

---

* use lib also unshifts an architecture-dependent library below the requested library, making it more valuable than the explicit counterpart presented earlier.

Handling Module Dependencies

We just saw that if we try to install a module that uses `Module::Build`, we have to install `Module::Build` first. That's a mild case of the general dependency headache, and all the coconuts on our castaways' island aren't going to fix it. We might have to install several other modules too, each of which, in turn, depends on even more modules.

Fortunately, we have tools to help us. The `CPAN.pm` module has been part of the core distribution since Perl 5.004. It gives us an interactive module installation shell.

```
$ perl -MCPAN -e shell
cpan shell -- CPAN exploration and modules installation (v1.7601)
ReadLine support available (try 'install Bundle::CPAN')

cpan>
```

To install a module along with its dependencies, we issue the `install` command with the name of the module. Now, `CPAN.pm` handles all the work of downloading, unpacking, building, testing, and installing the module, and it does so recursively for all its dependencies.

```
cpan> install CGI::Prototype
```

That's a bit too much work, though, so brian created the cpan script, which also comes with Perl. We simply list the modules we want to install, and it handles it for us.

```
$ cpan CGI::Prototype HTTP::Cookies::Safari Test::Pod
```

Another tool, `CPANPLUS`, is a complete rewrite of `CPAN.pm`, but it isn't part of the core distribution as we write this.

```
$ perl -MCPANPLUS -e shell
CPANPLUS::Shell::Default -- CPAN exploration and modules installation (v0.03)
*** Please report bugs to <cpanplus-bugs@lists.sourceforge.net>.
*** Using CPANPLUS::Backend v0.049.
*** ReadLine support available (try 'i Term::ReadLine::Perl').

CPAN Terminal>
```

To install a module, we use the `i` command.

```
CPAN Terminal> i CGI::Prototype
```

The `CPANPLUS` module also comes with a convenience script, called cpanp. If we give it the `i` switch and a list of modules, it installs them just like before.

```
$ cpanp i CGI::Prototype HTTP::Cookies::Safari Test::Pod
```

Exercises

You can find the answers to these exercises in "Answers for Chapter 3" in the Appendix.

Exercise 1 [25 min]

Read the list of files in the current directory and convert the names to their full path specification. Don't use the shell or an external program to get the current directory. The File::Spec and Cwd modules, both of which come with Perl, should help. Print each path with four spaces before it and a newline after it, just like you did for Exercise 1 of Chapter 2. Can you reuse part of that answer for this problem?

Exercise 2 [35 min]

Parse the International Standard Book Number from the back of this book (0596102062). Install the Business::ISBN module from CPAN and use it to extract the country code and the publisher code from the number.

## CHAPTER 4

Introduction to References

References are the basis for complex data structures, object-oriented programming (OOP), and fancy subroutine magic. They're the magic that was added between Perl version 4 and version 5 to make it all possible.

A Perl scalar variable holds a single value. An array holds an ordered list of one or more scalars. A hash holds a collection of scalars as values, keyed by other scalars. Although a scalar can be an arbitrary string, which allows complex data to be encoded into an array or hash, none of the three data types are well suited to complex data interrelationships. This is a job for the reference. Let's look at the importance of references by starting with an example.

Performing the Same Task on Many Arrays

Before the *Minnow* can leave on an excursion (for example, a three-hour tour), we should check every passenger and crew member to ensure they have all the required trip items in their possession. Let's say that, for maritime safety, every person onboard the Minnow needs to have a life preserver, some sunscreen, a water bottle, and a rain jacket. We can write a bit of code to check for the Skipper's supplies:

```
my @required = qw(preserver sunscreen water_bottle jacket);
my @skipper  = qw(blue_shirt hat jacket preserver sunscreen);

for my $item (@required) {
  unless (grep $item eq $_, @skipper) { # not found in list?
    print "skipper is missing $item.\n";
  }
}
```

The grep in a scalar context returns the number of times the expression $item eq $_ returns true, which is 1 if the item is in the list and 0 if not.* If the value is 0, it's false, and we print the message.

Of course, if we want to check on Gilligan and the Professor, we might write the following code:

```
my @gilligan = qw(red_shirt hat lucky_socks water_bottle);
for my $item (@required) {
  unless (grep $item eq $_, @gilligan) { # not found in list?
    print "gilligan is missing $item.\n";
  }
}

my @professor = qw(sunscreen water_bottle slide_rule batteries radio);
for my $item (@required) {
  unless (grep $item eq $_, @professor) { # not found in list?
    print "professor is missing $item.\n";
  }
}
```

You may start to notice a lot of repeated code here and think that we should refactor that into a common subroutine that we can reuse (and you'd be right):

```
sub check_required_items {
  my $who = shift;
  my @required = qw(preserver sunscreen water_bottle jacket);
  for my $item (@required) {
    unless (grep $item eq $_, @_) { # not found in list?
      print "$who is missing $item.\n";
    }
  }
}

my @gilligan = qw(red_shirt hat lucky_socks water_bottle);
check_required_items('gilligan', @gilligan);
```

Perl gives the subroutine five items in its @_ array initially: the name gilligan and the four items belonging to Gilligan. After the shift, @_ only has the items. Thus, the grep checks each required item against the list.

So far, so good. We can check the Skipper and the Professor with just a bit more code:

```
my @skipper   = qw(blue_shirt hat jacket preserver sunscreen);
my @professor = qw(sunscreen water_bottle slide_rule batteries radio);
check_required_items('skipper', @skipper);
check_required_items('professor', @professor);
```

---

* There are more efficient ways to check list membership for large lists, but for a few items, this is probably the easiest way to do so with just a few lines of code.

And for the other passengers, we repeat as needed. Although this code meets the initial requirements, we've got two problems to deal with:

- To create @_, Perl copies the entire contents of the array to be scanned. This is fine for a few items, but if the array is large, it seems a bit wasteful to copy the data just to pass it into a subroutine.

- Suppose we want to modify the original array to force the provisions list to include the mandatory items. Because we have a copy in the subroutine ("pass by value"), any changes we make to @_ aren't reflected automatically in the corresponding provisions array.*

To solve either or both of these problems, we need pass by reference rather than pass by value. And that's just what the doctor (or Professor) ordered.

Taking a Reference to an Array

Among its many other meanings, the backslash (\) character is also the "take a reference to" operator. When we use it in front of an array name, e.g., \@skipper, the result is a *reference* to that array. A reference to the array is like a pointer: it points at the array, but it is not the array itself.

A reference fits wherever a scalar fits. It can go into an element of an array or a hash, or into a plain scalar variable, like this:

```
my $reference_to_skipper = \@skipper;
```

The reference can be copied:

```
my $second_reference_to_skipper = $reference_to_skipper;
```

or even:

```
my $third_reference_to_skipper = \@skipper;
```

We can interchange all three references. We can even say they're identical, because, in fact, they are the same thing.

```
if ($reference_to_skipper == $second_reference_to_skipper) {
  print "They are identical references.\n";
}
```

This equality compares the numeric forms of the two references. The numeric form of the reference is the unique memory address of the @skipper internal data structure, unchanging during the life of the variable. If we look at the string form instead, with eq or print, we get a debugging string:

```
ARRAY(0x1a2b3c)
```

---

* Actually, assigning new scalars to elements of @_ after the shift modifies the corresponding variable being passed, but that still wouldn't let us extend the array with additional mandatory provisions.

which again is unique for this array because it includes the hexadecimal (base 16) representation of the array's unique memory address. The debugging string also notes that this is an array reference. Of course, if we ever see something like this in our output, it almost certainly means we have a bug; users of our program have little interest in hex dumps of storage addresses!

Because we can copy a reference, and passing an argument to a subroutine is really just copying, we can use this code to pass a reference to the array into the subroutine:

```
my @skipper = qw(blue_shirt hat jacket preserver sunscreen);
check_required_items("The Skipper", \@skipper);

sub check_required_items {
  my $who = shift;
  my $items = shift;
  my @required = qw(preserver sunscreen water_bottle jacket);
  ...
}
```

Now $items in the subroutine is a reference to the array of @skipper. But how do we get from a reference back into the original array? We *dereference* the reference, of course.

Dereferencing the Array Reference

If you look at @skipper, you'll see that it consists of two parts: the @ symbol and the name of the array. Similarly, the syntax $skipper[1] consists of the name of the array in the middle and some syntax around the outside to get at the second element of the array (index value 1 is the second element because index values start at 0).

Here's the trick: we can place any reference to an array in curly braces in place of the name of an array, ending up with a method to access the original array. That is, wherever we write skipper to name the array, we use the reference inside curly braces: { $items }. For example, both of these lines refer to the entire array:

```
@  skipper
@{ $items }
```

whereas both of these refer to the second item of the array:[*]

```
$  skipper [1]
${ $items }[1]
```

By using the reference form, we've decoupled the code and the method of array access from the actual array. Let's see how that changes the rest of this subroutine:

---

[*] Note that we added whitespace in these two displays to make the similar parts line up. This whitespace is legal in a program, even though most programs won't use it.

```
sub check_required_items {
  my $who   = shift;
  my $items = shift;

  my @required = qw(preserver sunscreen water_bottle jacket);
  for my $item (@required) {
    unless (grep $item eq $_, @{$items}) { # not found in list?
      print "$who is missing $item.\n";
    }
  }
}
```

All we did was replace @_ (the copy of the provisions list) with @{$items}, a dereferencing of the reference to the original provisions array. Now we can call the subroutine a few times, as before:

```
my @skipper = qw(blue_shirt hat jacket preserver sunscreen);
check_required_items('The Skipper', \@skipper);

my @professor = qw(sunscreen water_bottle slide_rule batteries radio);
check_required_items('Professor', \@professor);

my @gilligan = qw(red_shirt hat lucky_socks water_bottle);
check_required_items('Gilligan', \@gilligan);
```

In each case, $items points to a different array, so the same code applies to different arrays each time we invoke it. This is one of the most important uses of references: decoupling the code from the data structure on which it operates so we can reuse the code more readily.

Passing the array by reference fixes the first of the two problems we mentioned earlier. Now, instead of copying the entire provision list into the @_ array, we get a single element of a reference to that provisions array.

Could we have eliminated the two shifts at the beginning of the subroutine? Sure, but we sacrifice clarity:

```
sub check_required_items {
  my @required = qw(preserver sunscreen water_bottle jacket);
  for my $item (@required) {
    unless (grep $item eq $_, @{$_[1]}) { # not found in list?
      print "$_[0] is missing $item.\n";
    }
  }
}
```

We still have two elements in @_. The first element is the passenger or crew member name, which we use in the error message. The second element is a reference to the correct provisions array, which we use in the grep expression.

Getting Our Braces Off

Most of the time, the array reference we want to dereference is a simple scalar variable, such as @{$items} or ${$items}[1]. In those cases, we can drop the curly braces, unambiguously forming @$items or $$items[1].

However, we cannot drop the braces if the value within the braces is not a simple scalar variable. For example, for @{$_[1]} from that last subroutine rewrite, we can't remove the braces. That's a single element access to an array, not a scalar variable.

This rule also means that it's easy to see where the "missing" braces need to go. When we see $$items[1], a pretty noisy piece of syntax, we can tell that the curly braces must belong around the simple scalar variable, $items. Therefore, $items must be a reference to an array.

Thus, an easier-on-the-eyes version of that subroutine might be:

```
sub check_required_items {
  my $who   = shift;
  my $items = shift;

  my @required = qw(preserver sunscreen water_bottle jacket);
  for my $item (@required) {
    unless (grep $item eq $_, @$items) { # not found in list?
      print "$who is missing $item.\n";
    }
  }
}
```

The only difference here is that we removed the braces around @$items.

Modifying the Array

You've seen how to solve the excessive copying problem with an array reference. Now let's look at modifying the original array.

For every missing provision, we push that provision onto an array, forcing the passenger to consider the item:

```
sub check_required_items {
  my $who   = shift;
  my $items = shift;

  my @required = qw(preserver sunscreen water_bottle jacket);
  my @missing = (  );

  for my $item (@required) {
    unless (grep $item eq $_, @$items) { # not found in list?
      print "$who is missing $item.\n";
      push @missing, $item;
    }
  }
```

```
    if (@missing) {
      print "Adding @missing to @$items for $who.\n";
      push @$items, @missing;
    }
  }
```

Note the addition of the @missing array. If we find any items missing during the scan, we push them into @missing. If there's anything there at the end of the scan, we add it to the original provision list.

The key is in the last line of that subroutine. We're dereferencing the $items array reference, accessing the original array, and adding the elements from @missing. Without passing by reference, we'd modify only a local copy of the data, which has no effect on the original array.

Also, @$items (and its more generic form, @{$items}) works within a double-quoted string. We can't include any whitespace between the @ and the immediately following character, although we can include nearly arbitrary whitespace within the curly braces as if it were normal Perl code.

Nested Data Structures

In this example, the array @_ contains two elements, one of which is also an array. What if we take a reference to an array that also contains a reference to an array? We end up with a complex data structure, which can be quite useful.

For example, we can iterate over the data for the Skipper, Gilligan, and the Professor by first building a larger data structure holding the entire list of provision lists:

```
my @skipper = qw(blue_shirt hat jacket preserver sunscreen);
my @skipper_with_name = ('Skipper', \@skipper);
my @professor = qw(sunscreen water_bottle slide_rule batteries radio);
my @professor_with_name = ('Professor', \@professor);
my @gilligan = qw(red_shirt hat lucky_socks water_bottle);
my @gilligan_with_name = ('Gilligan', \@gilligan);
```

At this point, @skipper_with_name has two elements, the second of which is an array reference similar to what we passed to the subroutine. Now we group them all:

```
my @all_with_names = (
  \@skipper_with_name,
  \@professor_with_name,
  \@gilligan_with_name,
);
```

Note that we have just three elements, each of which is a reference to an array that has two elements: the name and its corresponding initial provisions. A picture of that is in Figure 4-1.

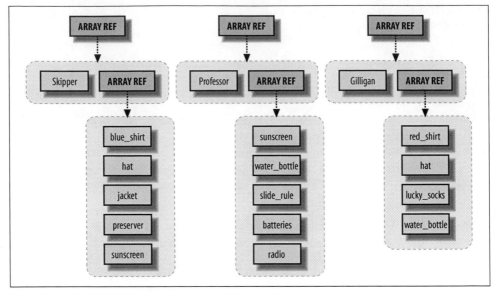

Figure 4-1. The array @all_with_names holds a multilevel data structure containing strings and references to arrays

Therefore, $all_with_names[2] will be the array reference for the Gilligan's data. If you dereference it as @{$all_with_names[2]}, you get a two-element array, "Gilligan" and another array reference.

How do we access that array reference? Using our rules again, it's ${$all_with_names[2]}[1]. In other words, taking $all_with_names[2], we dereference it in an expression that would be something like $DUMMY[1] as an ordinary array, so we'll place {$all_with_names[2]} in place of DUMMY.

How do we call the existing check_required_items( ) with this data structure? The following code is easy enough.

```
for my $person (@all_with_names) {
  my $who = $$person[0];
  my $provisions_reference = $$person[1];
  check_required_items($who, $provisions_reference);
}
```

This requires no changes to the subroutine. The control variable $person will be each of $all_with_names[0], $all_with_names[1], and $all_with_names[2], as the loop progresses. When we dereference $$person[0], we get "Skipper," "Professor," and "Gilligan," respectively. $$person[1] is the corresponding array reference of provisions for that person.

Of course, we can shorten this as well, since the entire dereferenced array matches the argument list precisely:

```
for my $person (@all_with_names) {
  check_required_items(@$person);
}
```

or even:

```
check_required_items(@$_) for @all_with_names;
```

As you can see, various levels of optimization can lead to obfuscation. Be sure to consider where your head will be a month from now when you have to reread your own code. If that's not enough, consider the new person who will take over your job after you have left.*

Simplifying Nested Element References with Arrows

Look at the curly-brace dereferencing again. As in our earlier example, the array reference for Gilligan's provision list is ${$all_with_names[2]}[1]. Now, what if we want to know Gilligan's first provision? We need to dereference *this* item one more level, so it's yet another layer of braces: ${${$all_with_names[2]}[1]}[0]. That's a really noisy piece of syntax. Can we shorten that? Yes!

Everywhere we write ${DUMMY}[$y], we can write DUMMY->[$y] instead. In other words, we can dereference an array reference, picking out a particular element of that array by simply following the expression defining the array reference with an arrow and a square-bracketed subscript.

For this example, this means we can pick out the array reference for Gilligan with a simple $all_with_names[2]->[1], and Gilligan's first provision with $all_with_names[2]->[1]->[0]. Wow, that's definitely easier on the eyes.

If *that* weren't already simple enough, there's one more rule: if the arrow ends up between "subscripty kinds of things," such as square brackets, we can also drop the arrow. $all_with_names[2]->[1]->[0] becomes $all_with_names[2][1][0]. Now it's looking even easier on the eyes.

The arrow has to be *between* non-subscripty things. Why wouldn't it be between subscripty things? Well, imagine a reference to the array @all_with_names:

```
my $root = \@all_with_names;
```

Now how do we get to Gilligan's first item?

```
$root -> [2] -> [1] -> [0]
```

More simply, using the "drop arrow" rule, we can use:

```
$root -> [2][1][0]
```

---

* O'Reilly Media has a great book to help you be nice to the next guy. *Perl Best Practices* by Damian Conway has 256 tips on writing more readable and maintainable Perl code.

We cannot drop the first arrow, however, because that would mean an array @root's third element, an entirely unrelated data structure. Let's compare this to the full curly-brace form again:

```
${${${$root}[2]}[1]}[0]
```

It looks much better with the arrow. Note, however, that no shortcut gets the entire array from an array reference. If we want all of Gilligan's provisions, we say:

```
@{$root->[2][1]}
```

Reading this from the inside out, we can think of it like this:

- Take $root.
- Dereference it as an array reference, taking the third element of that array (index number 2).
- Dereference that as an array reference, taking the second element of that array (index number 1).
- Dereference that as an array reference, taking the entire array.

The last step doesn't have a shortcut arrow form. Oh well.*

References to Hashes

Just as we can take a reference to an array, we can also take a reference to a hash. Once again, we use the backslash as the "take a reference to" operator:

```
my %gilligan_info = (
  name     => 'Gilligan',
  hat      => 'White',
  shirt    => 'Red',
  position => 'First Mate',
);
my $hash_ref = \%gilligan_info;
```

We can dereference a hash reference to get back to the original data. The strategy is similar to dereferencing an array reference. We write the hash syntax as we would have without references and then replace the name of the hash with a pair of curly braces surrounding the thing holding the reference. For example, to pick a particular value for a given key, we do this:

```
my $name = $ gilligan_info { 'name' };
my $name = $ { $hash_ref } { 'name' };
```

---

* It's not that it hasn't been discussed repeatedly by the Perl developers; it's just that nobody has come up with a nice backward-compatible syntax with universal appeal.

In this case, the curly braces have two different meanings. The first pair denotes the expression returning a reference, while the second pair delimits the expression for the hash key.

To perform an operation on the entire hash, we proceed similarly:

```
my @keys = keys % gilligan_info;
my @keys = keys % { $hash_ref };
```

As with array references, we can use shortcuts to replace the complex curly-braced forms under some circumstances. For example, if the only thing inside the curly braces is a simple scalar variable (as shown in these examples so far), we can drop the curly braces:

```
my $name = $$hash_ref{'name'};
my @keys = keys %$hash_ref;
```

Like an array reference, when referring to a specific hash element, we can use an arrow form:

```
my $name = $hash_ref->{'name'};
```

Because a hash reference fits wherever a scalar fits, we can create an array of hash references:

```
my %gilligan_info = (
  name     => 'Gilligan',
  hat      => 'White',
  shirt    => 'Red',
  position => 'First Mate',
);
my %skipper_info = (
  name     => 'Skipper',
  hat      => 'Black',
  shirt    => 'Blue',
  position => 'Captain',
);
my @crew = (\%gilligan_info, \%skipper_info);
```

Thus, $crew[0] is a hash reference to the information about Gilligan. We can get to Gilligan's name via any one of:

```
${ $crew[0] } { 'name' }
my $ref = $crew[0]; $$ref{'name'}
$crew[0]->{'name'}
$crew[0]{'name'}
```

On that last one, we can still drop the arrow between "subscripty kinds of things," even though one is an array bracket and one is a hash brace.

Let's print a crew roster:

```
my %gilligan_info = (
  name     => 'Gilligan',
  hat      => 'White',
  shirt    => 'Red',
```

```
    position => 'First Mate',
);
my %skipper_info = (
  name     => 'Skipper',
  hat      => 'Black',
  shirt    => 'Blue',
  position => 'Captain',
);
my @crew = (\%gilligan_info, \%skipper_info);

my $format = "%-15s %-7s %-7s %-15s\n";
printf $format, qw(Name Shirt Hat Position);
for my $crewmember (@crew) {
  printf $format,
    $crewmember->{'name'},
    $crewmember->{'shirt'},
    $crewmember->{'hat'},
    $crewmember->{'position'};
}
```

That last part looks very repetitive. We can shorten it with a hash slice. Again, if the original syntax is:

```
@ gilligan_info { qw(name position) }
```

the hash slice notation from a reference looks like:

```
@ { $hash_ref } { qw(name position) }
```

We can drop the first brace pair because the only thing within is a simple scalar value, yielding:

```
@ $hash_ref { qw(name position) }
```

Thus, we can replace that final loop with:

```
for my $crewmember (@crew) {
  printf $format, @$crewmember{qw(name shirt hat position)};
}
```

There is no shortcut form with an arrow (->) for array slices or hash slices, just as there is no shortcut for entire arrays or hashes.

A hash reference prints as a string that looks like HASH(0x1a2b3c), showing the hexadecimal memory address of the hash. That's not very useful to an end user and only barely more usable to the programmer, except as an indication of the lack of appropriate dereferencing.

Exercises

You can find the answers to these exercises in "Answers for Chapter 4" in the Appendix.

Exercise 1 [5 min]

How many different things do these expressions refer to?

```
$ginger->[2][1]
${$ginger[2]}[1]
$ginger->[2]->[1]
${$ginger->[2]}[1]
```

Exercise 2 [30 min]

Using the final version of check_required_items, write a subroutine check_items_for_all that takes a hash reference as its only parameter, pointing at a hash whose keys are the people aboard the *Minnow* and whose corresponding values are array references of the things they intend to bring onboard.

For example, the hash reference might be constructed like so:

```
my @gilligan  = ... gilligan items ...;
my @skipper   = ... skipper items ...;
my @professor = ... professor items ...;
my %all = (
  Gilligan  => \@gilligan,
  Skipper   => \@skipper,
  Professor => \@professor,
);
check_items_for_all(\%all);
```

The newly constructed subroutine should call check_required_items for each person in the hash, updating their provisions list to include the required items.

CHAPTER 5

References and Scoping

We can copy and pass around references like any other scalar. At any given time, Perl knows the number of references to a particular data item. Perl can also create references to *anonymous data structures* (structures that do not have explicit names) and create references automatically as needed to fulfill certain kinds of operations. Let's look at copying references and how it affects scoping and memory usage.

More Than One Reference to Data

Chapter 4 explored how to take a reference to an array @skipper and place it into a new scalar variable:

```
my @skipper = qw(blue_shirt hat jacket preserver sunscreen);
my $reference_to_skipper = \@skipper;
```

We can then copy the reference or take additional references, and they'll all refer to the same thing and are interchangeable:

```
my $second_reference_to_skipper = $reference_to_skipper;
my $third_reference_to_skipper  = \@skipper;
```

At this point, we have four different ways to access the data contained in @skipper:

```
@skipper
@$reference_to_skipper
@$second_reference_to_skipper
@$third_reference_to_skipper
```

Perl tracks how many ways it can access the data through a mechanism called *reference counting*. The original name counts as one, and each additional reference that we create (including copies of references) also counts as one. The total number of references to the array of provisions is now four.

We can add and remove references as we wish, and as long as the reference count doesn't hit zero, Perl maintains the array in memory and it is still accessible via any of the other access paths. For example, we might have a temporary reference:

```
check_provisions_list(\@skipper)
```

When this subroutine executes, Perl creates a fifth reference to the data and copies it into @_ for the subroutine. The subroutine is free to create additional copies of that reference, which Perl notes as needed. Typically, when the subroutine returns, Perl discards all such references automatically, and you're back to four references again.

We can kill off each reference by using the variable for something other than a reference to the value of @skipper. For example, we can assign undef to the variable:

```
$reference_to_skipper = undef;
```

Or, maybe we just let the variable go out of scope:

```
my @skipper = ...;

{ # naked block
...
my $ref = \@skipper;
...
...
} # $ref goes out of scope at this point
```

In particular, a reference held in a subroutine's private (lexical) variable goes away at the end of the subroutine.

Whether we change the value, or the variable itself goes away, Perl notes it as an appropriate reduction in the number of references to the data.

Perl recycles the memory for the array only when all references (including the name of the array) go away. In this case, Perl only reclaims memory when @skipper and all the references we created to it disappear.

Such memory is available to Perl for other data later in this program invocation, and generally Perl doesn't give it back to the operating system.

What If That Was the Name?

Typically, all references to a variable are gone before the variable itself. But what if one of the references outlives the variable name? For example, consider this code:

```
my $ref;

{
  my @skipper = qw(blue_shirt hat jacket preserver sunscreen);
  $ref        = \@skipper;

  print "$ref->[2]\n"; # prints jacket\n
}

print "$ref->[2]\n"; # still prints jacket\n
```

Immediately after we declare the @skipper array, we have one reference to the five-element list. After $ref is initialized, we'll have two, down to the end of the block.

When the block ends, the @skipper name disappears. However, this was only one of the two ways to access the data! Thus, the five-element list is still in memory, and $ref still points to that data.

At this point, the five-element list is in an *anonymous array*, which is a fancy term for an array without a name.

Until the value of $ref changes, or $ref itself disappears, we can still use all the dereferencing strategies we used prior to when the name of the array disappeared. In fact, it's still a fully functional array that we can shrink or grow just as we do any other Perl array:

```
push @$ref, 'sextant'; # add a new provision
print "$ref->[-1]\n"; # prints sextant\n
```

We can even increase the reference count at this point:

```
my $copy_of_ref = $ref;
```

or equivalently:

```
my $copy_of_ref = \@$ref;
```

The data stays alive until we destroy the last reference:

```
$ref = undef; # not yet...
$copy_of_ref = undef; # poof!
```

Reference Counting and Nested Data Structures

The data remains alive until we destroy the last reference, even if that reference lives within a larger active data structure. Suppose an array element is itself a reference. Recall the example from Chapter 4:

```
my @skipper = qw(blue_shirt hat jacket preserver sunscreen);
my @skipper_with_name   = ('The Skipper', \@skipper);

my @professor = qw(sunscreen water_bottle slide_rule batteries radio);
my @professor_with_name = ('The Professor', \@professor);

my @gilligan = qw(red_shirt hat lucky_socks water_bottle);
my @gilligan_with_name   = ('Gilligan', \@gilligan);

my @all_with_names = (
        \@skipper_with_name,
        \@professor_with_name,
        \@gilligan_with_name,
        );
```

Imagine for a moment that the intermediate variables are all part of a subroutine:

```
my @all_with_names;

sub initialize_provisions_list {
  my @skipper = qw(blue_shirt hat jacket preserver sunscreen);
  my @skipper_with_name = ('The Skipper', \@skipper);
```

```
    my @professor = qw(sunscreen water_bottle slide_rule batteries radio);
  my @professor_with_name = ('The Professor', \@professor);

  my @gilligan = qw(red_shirt hat lucky_socks water_bottle);
  my @gilligan_with_name = ('Gilligan', \@gilligan);

  @all_with_names = ( # set global
    \@skipper_with_name,
    \@professor_with_name,
    \@gilligan_with_name,
  );
}

initialize_provisions_list( );
```

We set the value of @all_with_names to contain three references. Inside the subroutine we have named arrays with references to arrays first placed into other named arrays. Eventually, the values end up in the global @all_with_names. However, as the subroutine returns, the names for the six arrays disappear. Each array has had one other reference taken to it, making the reference count temporarily two, and then back to one as the name disappears. Because the reference count is not yet zero, the data continues to live on, although it is now referenced only by elements of @all_with_names.

Rather than assign the global variable, we can rewrite this without @all_with_names and return the list directly:

```
sub get_provisions_list {
  my @skipper = qw(blue_shirt hat jacket preserver sunscreen);
  my @skipper_with_name = ('The Skipper', \@skipper);

  my @professor = qw(sunscreen water_bottle slide_rule batteries radio);
  my @professor_with_name = ('The Professor', \@professor);

  my @gilligan = qw(red_shirt hat lucky_socks water_bottle);
  my @gilligan_with_name = ('Gilligan', \@gilligan);

  return (
    \@skipper_with_name,
    \@professor_with_name,
    \@gilligan_with_name,
  );
}

my @all_with_names = get_provisions_list( );
```

Here, we create the value that we'll eventually store in @all_with_names as the last expression evaluated in the subroutine. The subroutine returns a three-element list. As long as the named arrays within the subroutine have had at least one reference taken of them, and it is still part of the return value, the data remains alive.* If we alter or discard the references in @all_with_names, Perl reduces the reference count for the corresponding arrays. If that means the reference count has become zero (as in this example), Perl also eliminates the arrays themselves. Because the arrays inside @all_with_names also contain a reference (such as the reference to @skipper), Perl reduces that reference count by one. Again, that reduces the reference count to zero, freeing that memory as well, in a cascading effect.

Removing the top of a tree of data generally removes all the data contained within. The exception is when we make additional copies of the references of the nested data. For example, if we copy Gilligan's provisions:

```
my $gilligan_stuff = $all_with_names[2][1];
```

then when we remove @all_with_names, we still have one live reference to what was formerly @gilligan, and the data from there downward remain alive.

The bottom line is simply: Perl does the right thing. If we still have a reference to data, we still have the data.

When Reference Counting Goes Bad

Reference counting as a way to manage memory has been around for a long time. A really long time. The downside of reference counting is that it breaks when the data structure is not a *directed graph*—that is, when some parts of the structure point back in to other parts in a looping way. For example, suppose each of two data structures contains a reference to the other (see Figure 5-1):

```
my @data1 = qw(one won);
my @data2 = qw(two too to);

push @data2, \@data1;
push @data1, \@data2;
```

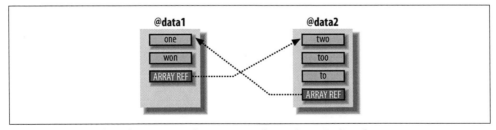

Figure 5-1. When the references in a data structure form a loop, Perl's reference-counting system may not be able to recognize and recycle the no-longer-needed memory space

---

* Compare this with having to return an array from a C function. We must either return a pointer to a static memory space, making the subroutine nonreentrant, or we must malloc new memory space, requiring the caller to know to free the data. Perl just does the right thing.

At this point, we have two names for the data in @data1: @data1 itself and @{$data2[3]}, and two names for the data in @data2: @data2 itself and @{$data1[2]}. We've created a loop. In fact, we can access won with an infinite number of names, such as $data1[2][3][2][3][2][3][1].

What happens when these two array names go out of scope? Well, the reference count for the two arrays goes down from two to one, but not zero. And because it's not zero, Perl thinks there might still be a way to get to the data, even though there isn't! Thus, we've created a *memory leak*. A memory leak in a program causes the program to consume more and more memory over time. Ugh.

At this point, you're right to think that example is contrived. Of course we would never make a looped data structure in a real program! Actually, programmers often make these loops as part of doubly linked lists, linked rings, or a number of other data structures. The key is that Perl programmers rarely do so because the most important reasons to use those data structures don't apply in Perl. Most of that deals with managing memory and connecting discontiguous memory blocks, which Perl does for us. If you've used other languages, you may have noticed programming tasks that are comparatively easy in Perl. For example, it's easy to sort a list of items or to add or remove items, even in the middle of the list. Those tasks are difficult in some other languages, and using a looped data structure is a common way to get around the language's limitations.

Why mention it here? Well, even Perl programmers sometimes copy an algorithm from another programming language. There's nothing inherently wrong with doing this, although it would be better to decide why the original author used a "loopy" data structure and then recode the algorithm to use Perl's strengths. Perhaps you should use a hash instead, or perhaps the data should go into an array that will be sorted later.

Some upcoming version of Perl is likely to use *garbage collection* in addition to, or instead of, referencing counting.[*] Until then, we must be careful not to create circular references or, if we do, break the circle before the variables go out of scope. For example, the following code doesn't leak:

```
{
  my @data1 = qw(one won);
  my @data2 = qw(two too to);
  push @data2, \@data1;
  push @data1, \@data2;
  ... use @data1, @data2 ...
  # at the end:
  @data1 = (  );
  @data2 = (  );
}
```

_____

[*] Just don't ask us about it. We wrote this book a long time before you got a chance to read it, so we didn't exactly know the details back then.

We eliminated the reference to @data2 from within @data1, and vice versa. Now the data have only one reference each, which all go to zero references at the end of the block. In fact, we can clear out either one and not the other, and it still works nicely. Chapter 13 shows how to create weak references, which can help with many of these problems.

Creating an Anonymous Array Directly

In the get_provisions_list routine earlier, we created a half dozen array names that we used only so that we could take a reference to them immediately afterward. When the subroutine exited, the array names all went away, but the references remained.

While creating temporarily named arrays would work in the simplest cases, creating such names becomes more complicated as the data structures become more detailed. We'd have to keep thinking of names of arrays just so we could forget them shortly thereafter.

We can reduce the namespace clutter by narrowing down the scope of the various array names. Rather than declaring them within the scope of the subroutine, we can create a temporary block:

```
my @skipper_with_name;
{
  my @skipper = qw(blue_shirt hat jacket preserver sunscreen);
  @skipper_with_name = ('The Skipper', \@skipper);
}
```

At this point, the second element of @skipper_with_name is a reference to the array formerly known as @skipper. However, that name is no longer relevant.

This is a lot of typing to simply say "the second element should be a reference to an array containing these elements." We can create such a value directly using the *anonymous array constructor*, which is yet another use for square brackets:

```
my $ref_to_skipper_provisions =
  [ qw(blue_shirt hat jacket preserver sunscreen) ];
```

The square brackets take the value within (evaluated in a list context); establish a new, anonymous array initialized to those values; and (here's the important part) return a reference to that array. It's as if we had said:

```
my $ref_to_skipper_provisions;
{
  my @temporary_name =
  ( qw(blue_shirt hat jacket preserver sunscreen) );
  $ref_to_skipper_provisions = \@temporary_name;
}
```

Here we don't need to come up with a temporary name, and we don't need the extra noise of the temporary block. The result of a square-bracketed anonymous array constructor is an array reference, which fits wherever a scalar variable fits.

Now we can use it to construct the larger list:

```
my $ref_to_skipper_provisions =
  [ qw(blue_shirt hat jacket preserver sunscreen) ];
my @skipper_with_name = ('The Skipper', $ref_to_skipper_provisions);
```

Of course, we didn't actually need that scalar temporary, either. We can put a scalar reference to an array as part of a larger list:

```
my @skipper_with_name = (
  'The Skipper',
  [ qw(blue_shirt hat jacket preserver sunscreen) ]
);
```

Now let's walk through this. We've declared @skipper_with_name, the first element of which is the Skipper's name string, and the second element is an array reference, obtained by placing the five provisions into an array and taking a reference to it. So @skipper_with_name is only two elements long, just as before.

Don't confuse the square brackets with the parentheses here. They each have their distinct purpose. If we replace the square brackets with parentheses, we end up with a six-element list. If we replace the outer parentheses (on the first and last lines) with square brackets, we construct an anonymous array that's two elements long and then take the reference to that array as the only element of the ultimate @skipper_with_name array.* So, in summary, if we have this syntax:

```
my $fruits;
{
  my @secret_variable = ('pineapple', 'papaya', 'mango');
  $fruits = \@secret_variable;
}
```

we can replace it with:

```
my $fruits = ['pineapple', 'papaya', 'mango'];
```

Does this work for more complicated structures? Yes! Anytime we need an element of a list to be a reference to an array, we can create that reference with an anonymous array constructor. In fact, we can also nest them in our provisions list:

```
sub get_provisions_list {
  return (
    ['The Skipper',   [qw(blue_shirt hat jacket preserver sunscreen)] ],
    ['The Professor', [qw(sunscreen water_bottle slide_rule batteries radio)  ] ],
    ['Gilligan',      [qw(red_shirt hat lucky_socks water_bottle)       ] ],
  );
}

my @all_with_names = get_provisions_list(  );
```

---

* In classrooms, we've seen that too much indirection (or not enough indirection) tends to contribute to the most common mistakes made when working with references.

Walking through this from the outside in, we have a return value of three elements. Each element is an array reference, pointing to an anonymous two-element array. The first element of each array is a name string, while the second element is a reference to an anonymous array of varying lengths naming the provisions—all without having to come up with temporary names for any of the intermediate layers.

To the caller of this subroutine, the return value is identical to the previous version. However, from a maintenance point of view, the reduced clutter of not having all the intermediate names saves screen and brain space.

We can show a reference to an empty anonymous array using an empty anonymous array constructor. For example, if we add one "Mrs. Howell" to that travel list, as someone who has packed rather light, we'd simply insert:

```
['Mrs. Howell',
  [  ]
],
```

This is a single element of the larger list. This item is a reference to an array with two elements, the first of which is the name string, and the second of which is itself a reference to an empty anonymous array. The array is empty because Mrs. Howell hasn't packed anything for this trip.

Creating an Anonymous Hash

Similar to creating an anonymous array, you can also create an anonymous hash. Consider the crew roster from Chapter 4:

```
my %gilligan_info = (
  name     => 'Gilligan',
  hat      => 'White',
  shirt    => 'Red',
  position => 'First Mate',
);

my %skipper_info = (
  name     => 'Skipper',
  hat      => 'Black',
  shirt    => 'Blue',
  position => 'Captain',
);

my @crew = (\%gilligan_info, \%skipper_info);
```

The variables %gilligan_info and %skipper_info are just temporaries we needed to create the hashes for the final data structure. We can construct the reference directly with the *anonymous hash constructor*, which is yet another meaning for curly braces, as we'll see. We can replace this:

```
my $ref_to_gilligan_info;

{
  my %gilligan_info = (
    name     => 'Gilligan',
    hat      => 'White',
    shirt    => 'Red',
    position => 'First Mate',
  );
  $ref_to_gilligan_info = \%gilligan_info;
}
```

with the anonymous hash constructor:

```
my $ref_to_gilligan_info = {
  name     => 'Gilligan',
  hat      => 'White',
  shirt    => 'Red',
  position => 'First Mate',
};
```

The value between the open and closing curly braces is an eight-element list. The eight-element list becomes a four-element anonymous hash (four key/value pairs). Perl takes a reference to this hash and returns as a single scalar value, which we assign to the scalar variable. Thus, we can rewrite the roster creation as:

```
my $ref_to_gilligan_info = {
  name     => 'Gilligan',
  hat      => 'White',
  shirt    => 'Red',
  position => 'First Mate',
};

my $ref_to_skipper_info = {
  name     => 'Skipper',
  hat      => 'Black',
  shirt    => 'Blue',
  position => 'Captain',
};

my @crew = ($ref_to_gilligan_info, $ref_to_skipper_info);
```

As before, we can now avoid the temporary variables and insert the values directly into the top-level list:

```
my @crew = (
  {
    name     => 'Gilligan',
    hat      => 'White',
    shirt    => 'Red',
    position => 'First Mate',
  },
```

```
  {
    name     => 'Skipper',
    hat      => 'Black',
    shirt    => 'Blue',
    position => 'Captain',
  },
);
```

Note we use trailing commas on the lists when the element is not immediately next to the closing brace, bracket, or parenthesis. This is a nice style element to adopt because it allows for easy maintenance. We can add or rearrange lines quickly, or comment out lines without destroying the integrity of our list.

Now @crew is identical to the value it had before, but we no longer need to invent names for the intermediate data structures. As before, the @crew variable contains two elements, each of which is a reference to a hash containing keyword-based information about a particular crew member.

The anonymous hash constructor always evaluates its contents in a list context and then constructs a hash from key/value pairs, just as if we had assigned that list to a named hash. Perl returns a reference to that hash as a single value that fits wherever a scalar fits.

Now, a word from our parser: because blocks and anonymous hash constructors both use curly braces in roughly the same places in the syntax tree, the compiler has to make ad hoc determinations about which of the two you mean. If the compiler ever decides incorrectly, you might need to provide a hint to get what you want. To show the compiler that you want an anonymous hash constructor, put a plus sign before the opening curly brace: +{ ... }. To be sure to get a block of code, just put a semicolon (representing an empty statement) at the beginning of the block: {; ... }.

Autovivification

Let's look again at the provisions list. Suppose we were reading the data from a file, in this format:

```
The Skipper
  blue_shirt
  hat
  jacket
  preserver
  sunscreen
Professor
  sunscreen
  water_bottle
  slide_rule
Gilligan
  red_shirt
  hat
  lucky_socks
  water_bottle
```

We indent provisions with some whitespace, following a non-indented line with the person's name. Let's construct a hash of provisions. The keys of the hash will be the person's name, and the value will be an array reference to an array containing a list of provisions.

Initially, we might gather the data using a simple loop:

```
my %provisions;
my $person;

while (<>) {
  if (/^(\S.*)/) { # a person's name (no leading whitespace)
    $person = $1;
    $provisions{$person} = [  ] unless exists $provisions{$person};
  } elsif (/^\s+(\S.*)/) { # a provision
    die 'No person yet!' unless defined $person;
    push @{ $provisions{$person} }, $1;
  } else {
    die "I don't understand: $_";
  }
}
```

First, we declare the variables for the resulting hash of provisions and the current person. For each line that we read, we determine if it's a person or a provision. If it's a person, we remember the name and create the hash element for that person. The unless exists test ensures that we won't delete someone's provision list if his list is split in two places in the datafile.

For example, suppose that "The Skipper" and " sextant" (note the leading whitespace) are at the end of the datafile in order to list an additional data item.

The key is the person's name, and the value is initially a reference to an empty anonymous array. If the line is a provision, push it to the end of the correct array, using the array reference.

This code works fine, but it actually says more than it needs to. Why? Because we can leave out the line that initializes the hash element's value to a reference to an empty array:

```
my %provisions;
my $person;

while (<>) {
  if (/^(\S.*)/) { # a person's name (no leading whitespace)
    $person = $1;
    ## $provisions{$person} = [  ] unless exists $provisions{$person};
  } elsif (/^\s+(\S.*)/) { # a provision
    die 'No person yet!' unless defined $person;
    push @{ $provisions{$person} }, $1;
  } else {
    die "I don't understand: $_";
  }
}
```

What happens when we try to store that blue shirt for the Skipper? While looking at the second line of input, we'll end up with this effect:

```
push @{ $provisions{'The Skipper'} }, "blue_shirt";
```

At this point, $provisions{"The Skipper"} doesn't exist, but we're trying to use it as an array reference. To resolve the situation, Perl automatically inserts a reference to a new empty anonymous array into the variable and continues the operation. In this case, the reference to the newly created empty array is dereferenced, and we push the blue shirt to the provisions list.

This process is called *autovivification*. Any nonexistent variable, or a variable containing undef, which we dereference while looking for a variable location (technically called an *lvalue context*), is automatically stuffed with the appropriate reference to an empty item, and Perl allows the operation to proceed.

This is actually the same behavior we've probably been using in Perl all along. Perl creates new variables as needed. Before that statement, $provisions{"The Skipper"} didn't exist, so Perl created it. Then @{ $provisions{"The Skipper"} } didn't exist, so Perl created it as well.

For example, this works:

```
my $not_yet;              # new undefined variable
@$not_yet = (1, 2, 3);
```

Here, we dereference the value $not_yet as if it were an array reference. But since it's initially undef, Perl acts as if we had said:

```
my $not_yet;
$not_yet = [  ]; # inserted through autovivification
@$not_yet = (1, 2, 3);
```

In other words, an initially empty array becomes an array of three elements.

This autovivification also works for multiple levels of assignment:

```
my $top;
$top->[2]->[4] = 'lee-lou';
```

Initially, $top contains undef, but because we dereference it as if it were an array reference, Perl inserts a reference to an empty anonymous array into $top. Perl then accesses the third element (index value 2), which causes Perl to grow the array to be three elements long. That element is also undef, so Perl stuffs it with a reference to another empty anonymous array. We then spin out along that newly created array, setting the fifth element to lee-lou.

Autovivification and Hashes

Autovivification also works for hash references. If we dereference a variable containing undef as if it were a hash reference, a reference to an empty anonymous hash is inserted, and the operation continues.

One place this comes in very handy is in a typical data reduction task. For example, let's say the Professor gets an island-area network up and running (perhaps using Coco-Net or maybe Vines) and now wants to track the traffic from host to host. He begins logging the number of bytes transferred to a log file, giving the source host, the destination host, and the number of transferred bytes:

```
professor.hut gilligan.crew.hut 1250
professor.hut lovey.howell.hut 910
thurston.howell.hut lovey.howell.hut 1250
professor.hut lovey.howell.hut 450
professor.hut laser3.copyroom.hut 2924
ginger.girl.hut professor.hut 1218
ginger.girl.hut maryann.girl.hut 199
...
```

Now the Professor wants to produce a summary of the source host, the destination host, and the total number of transferred bytes for the day. Tabulating the data is as simple as:

```
my %total_bytes;
while (<>) {
  my ($source, $destination, $bytes) = split;
  $total_bytes{$source}{$destination} += $bytes;
}
```

Let's see how this works on the first line of data. We'll be executing:

```
$total_bytes{'professor.hut'}{'gilligan.crew.hut'} += 1250;
```

Because %total_bytes is initially empty, Perl doesn't find the first key of professor. hut, but it establishes an undef value for the dereferencing as a hash reference. (Keep in mind that an implicit arrow is between the two sets of curly braces here.) Perl sticks a reference to an empty anonymous hash in that element, which it then immediately extends to include the element with a key of gilligan.crew.hut. Its initial value is undef, which acts like a zero when you add 1250 to it, and the result of 1250 is inserted back into the hash.

Any later data line that contains this same source host and destination host will reuse that same value, adding more bytes to the running total. But each new destination host extends a hash to include a new initially undef byte count, and each new source host uses autovivification to create a destination host hash. In other words, Perl does the right thing, as always.

Once we've processed the file, it's time to display the summary. First, we determine all the sources:

```
for my $source (keys %total_bytes) {
  ...
```

Now, we should get all destinations. The syntax for this is a bit tricky. We want all keys of the hash, resulting from dereferencing the value of the hash element, in the first structure:

```
for my $source (keys %total_bytes) {
  for my $destination (keys %{ $total_bytes{$source} }) {
    ....
```

For good measure, we should probably sort both lists to be consistent:

```
for my $source (sort keys %total_bytes) {
  for my $destination (sort keys %{ $total_bytes{$source} }) {
    print "$source => $destination:",
      " $total_bytes{$source}{$destination} bytes\n";
  }
  print "\n";
}
```

This is a typical data-reduction report generation strategy.[*] Simply create a hash-of-hashrefs (perhaps nested even deeper, as you'll see later), using autovivification to fill in the gaps in the upper data structures as needed, and then walk through the resulting data structure to display the results.

Exercises

You can find the answers to these exercises in "Answers for Chapter 5" in the Appendix.

Exercise 1 [5 min]

Without running it, can you see what's wrong with this piece of a program? If you can't see the problem after a minute or two, see whether trying to run it will give you a hint of how to fix it.

```
my %passenger_1 = {
  name       => 'Ginger',
  age        => 22,
  occupation => 'Movie Star',
  real_age   => 35,
  hat        => undef,
};
```

---

[*] You can read more examples in the *Perl Data Structures Cookbook*, the perldsc documentation page.

```
my %passenger_2 = {
  name          => 'Mary Ann',
  age           => 19,
  hat           => 'bonnet',
  favorite_food => 'corn',
};

my @passengers = (\%passenger_1, \%passenger_2);
```

Exercise 2 [40 min]

The Professor's datafile (mentioned earlier in this chapter) is available as coconet.dat in the files you can download from the O'Reilly web site. There may be comment lines (beginning with a pound sign); be sure to skip them. (That is, your program should skip them. You might find a helpful hint if *you* read them!)

Modify the code from this chapter so that each source machine's portion of the output shows the total number of bytes from that machine. List the source machines in order from most to least data transferred. Within each group, list the destination machines in order from most to least data transferred to that target from the source machine.

The result should be that the machine that sent the most data will be the first source machine in the list, and the first destination should be the machine to which it sent the most data. The Professor can use this printout to reconfigure the network for efficiency.

CHAPTER 6

Manipulating Complex Data Structures

Now that you've seen the basics of references, let's look at additional ways to manipulate complex data. We'll start by using the debugger to examine complex data structures and then use Data::Dumper to show the data under programmatic control. Next, you'll learn to store and retrieve complex data easily and quickly using Storable, and finally we'll wrap up with a review of grep and map and see how they apply to complex data.

Using the Debugger to View Complex Data

The Perl debugger can display complex data easily. For example, let's single-step through one version of the byte-counting program from Chapter 5:

```
my %total_bytes;
while (<>) {
  my ($source, $destination, $bytes) = split;
  $total_bytes{$source}{$destination} += $bytes;
}
for my $source (sort keys %total_bytes) {
  for my $destination (sort keys %{ $total_bytes{$source} }) {
    print "$source => $destination:",
      " $total_bytes{$source}{$destination} bytes\n";
  }
  print "\n";
}
```

Here's the data we'll use to test it:

```
professor.hut gilligan.crew.hut 1250
professor.hut lovey.howell.hut 910
thurston.howell.hut lovey.howell.hut 1250
professor.hut lovey.howell.hut 450
ginger.girl.hut professor.hut 1218
ginger.girl.hut maryann.girl.hut 199
```

We can do this a number of ways. One of the easiest is to invoke Perl with a `-d` switch on the command line:

```
myhost% perl -d bytecounts bytecounts-in

Loading DB routines from perl5db.pl version 1.19
Editor support available.

Enter h or `h h' for help, or `man perldebug' for more help.

main::(bytecounts:2):        my %total_bytes;
  DB<1> s
main::(bytecounts:3):        while (<>) {
  DB<1> s
main::(bytecounts:4):          my ($source, $destination, $bytes) = split;
  DB<1> s
main::(bytecounts:5):          $total_bytes{$source}{$destination} += $bytes;
  DB<1> x $source, $destination, $bytes
0  'professor.hut'
1  'gilligan.crew.hut'
2  1250
```

If you're playing along at home, be aware that each new release of the debugger works differently than any other, so your screen probably won't look exactly like ours. Also, if you get stuck at any time, type h for help or look at perldoc perldebug.

The debugger shows each line of code before it executes it. That means that, at this point, we're about to invoke the autovivification, and we've got our keys established. The s command single-steps the program, while the x command dumps a list of values in a nice format. We can see that $source, $destination, and $bytes are correct, and now it's time to update the data:

```
DB<2> s
  main::(bytecounts:3):        while (<>) {
```

We've created the hash entries through autovivification. Let's see what we've got:

```
DB<2> x \%total_bytes
  0  HASH(0x132dc)
'professor.hut' => HASH(0x37a34)
  'gilligan.crew.hut' => 1250
```

When we give x a hash reference, it dumps the entire contents of the hash, showing the key/value pairs. If any of the values are also hash references, it dumps those as well, recursively. What we'll see is that the %total_bytes hash has a single key of professor.hut, whose corresponding value is another hash reference. The referenced hash contains a single key of gilligan.crew.hut, with a value of 1250, as expected.

Let's see what happens just after the next assignment:

```
DB<3> s
  main::(bytecounts:4):        my ($source, $destination, $bytes) = split;
DB<3> s
  main::(bytecounts:5):        $total_bytes{$source}{$destination} += $bytes;
DB<3> x $source, $destination, $bytes
  0  'professor.hut'
  1  'lovey.howell.hut'
```

```
    2  910
DB<4> s
  main::(bytecounts:3):          while (<>) {
DB<4> x \%total_bytes
  0  HASH(0x132dc)
 'professor.hut' => HASH(0x37a34)
    'gilligan.crew.hut' => 1250
    'lovey.howell.hut' => 910
```

Now we've added bytes flowing from professor.hut to lovey.howell.hut. The top-level hash hasn't changed, but the second-level hash has added a new entry. Let's continue:

```
DB<5> s
  main::(bytecounts:4):          my ($source, $destination, $bytes) = split;
DB<6> s
  main::(bytecounts:5):          $total_bytes{$source}{$destination} += $bytes;
DB<6> x $source, $destination, $bytes
  0  'thurston.howell.hut'
  1  'lovey.howell.hut'
  2  1250
DB<7> s
  main::(bytecounts:3):          while (<>) {
DB<7> x \%total_bytes
  0  HASH(0x132dc)
 'professor.hut' => HASH(0x37a34)
    'gilligan.crew.hut' => 1250
    'lovey.howell.hut' => 910
 'thurston.howell.hut' => HASH(0x2f9538)
    'lovey.howell.hut' => 1250
```

Ah, now it's getting interesting. A new entry in the top-level hash has a key of thurston.howell.hut, and a new hash reference, autovivified initially to an empty hash. Immediately after the new empty hash was put in place, a new key/value pair was added, indicating 1250 bytes transferred from thurston.howell.hut to lovey.howell.hut. Let's step some more:

```
DB<8> s
  main::(bytecounts:4):          my ($source, $destination, $bytes) = split;
DB<8> s
  main::(bytecounts:5):          $total_bytes{$source}{$destination} += $bytes;
DB<8> x $source, $destination, $bytes
  0  'professor.hut'
  1  'lovey.howell.hut'
  2  450
DB<9> s
  main::(bytecounts:3):          while (<>) {
DB<9> x \%total_bytes
  0  HASH(0x132dc)
 'professor.hut' => HASH(0x37a34)
    'gilligan.crew.hut' => 1250
    'lovey.howell.hut' => 1360
 'thurston.howell.hut' => HASH(0x2f9538)
    'lovey.howell.hut' => 1250
```

Now we're adding in some more bytes from professor.hut to lovey.howell.hut, reusing the existing value place. Nothing too exciting there. Let's keep stepping:

```
DB<10> s
  main::(bytecounts:4):           my ($source, $destination, $bytes) = split;
DB<10> s
  main::(bytecounts:5):           $total_bytes{$source}{$destination} += $bytes;
DB<10> x $source, $destination, $bytes
  0  'ginger.girl.hut'
  1  'professor.hut'
  2  1218
DB<11> s
  main::(bytecounts:3):           while (<>) {
DB<11> x \%total_bytes
  0  HASH(0x132dc)
 'ginger.girl.hut' => HASH(0x297474)
    'professor.hut' => 1218
 'professor.hut' => HASH(0x37a34)
    'gilligan.crew.hut' => 1250
    'lovey.howell.hut' => 1360
 'thurston.howell.hut' => HASH(0x2f9538)
    'lovey.howell.hut' => 1250
```

This time, we added a new source, ginger.girl.hut. Notice that the top level hash now has three elements, and each element has a different hash reference value. Let's step some more:

```
DB<12> s
  main::(bytecounts:4):           my ($source, $destination, $bytes) = split;
DB<12> s
  main::(bytecounts:5):           $total_bytes{$source}{$destination} += $bytes;
DB<12> x $source, $destination, $bytes
  0  'ginger.girl.hut'
  1  'maryann.girl.hut'
  2  199
DB<13> s
  main::(bytecounts:3):           while (<>) {
DB<13> x \%total_bytes
  0  HASH(0x132dc)
 'ginger.girl.hut' => HASH(0x297474)
    'maryann.girl.hut' => 199
    'professor.hut' => 1218
 'professor.hut' => HASH(0x37a34)
    'gilligan.crew.hut' => 1250
    'lovey.howell.hut' => 1360
 'thurston.howell.hut' => HASH(0x2f9538)
    'lovey.howell.hut' => 1250
```

Now we've added a second destination to the hash that records information for all bytes originating at ginger.girl.hut. Because that was the final line of data (in this run), a step brings us down to the lower foreach loop:

```
DB<14> s
  main::(bytecounts:8):           for my $source (sort keys %total_bytes) {
```

Even though we can't directly examine the list value from inside those parentheses, we can display it:

```
DB<14> x sort keys %total_bytes
   0   'ginger.girl.hut'
   1   'professor.hut'
   2   'thurston.howell.hut'
```

This is the list the foreach now scans. These are all the sources for transferred bytes seen in this particular logfile. Here's what happens when we step into the inner loop:

```
DB<15> s
   main::(bytecounts:9):       for my $destination (sort keys %{ $total_bytes{$source}
}) {
```

At this point, we can determine from the inside out exactly what values will result from the list value from inside the parentheses. Let's look at them:

```
DB<15> x $source
   0   'ginger.girl.hut'
DB<16> x $total_bytes{$source}
   0   HASH(0x297474)
   'maryann.girl.hut' => 199
   'professor.hut' => 1218
DB<18> x keys %{ $total_bytes{$source } }
   0   'maryann.girl.hut'
   1   'professor.hut'
DB<19> x sort keys %{ $total_bytes{$source } }
   0   'maryann.girl.hut'
   1   'professor.hut'
```

Note that dumping $total_bytes{$source} shows that it was a hash reference. Also, the sort appears not to have done anything, but the output of keys is not necessarily in a sorted order. The next step finds the data:

```
DB<20> s
   main::(bytecounts:10):       print "$source => $destination:",
   main::(bytecounts:11):            " $total_bytes{$source}{$destination} bytes\n";
DB<20> x $source, $destination
   0   'ginger.girl.hut'
   1   'maryann.girl.hut'
DB<21> x $total_bytes{$source}{$destination}
   0   199
```

As we can see with the debugger, we can easily show the data, even structured data, to help us understand our program.

Viewing Complex Data with Data::Dumper

Another way to visualize a complex data structure rapidly is to *dump* it. A particularly nice dumping package is included in the Perl core distribution, called Data::Dumper. Let's replace the last half of the byte-counting program with a simple call to Data::Dumper:

```
use Data::Dumper;

my %total_bytes;
while (<>) {
  my ($source, $destination, $bytes) = split;
  $total_bytes{$source}{$destination} += $bytes;
}

print Dumper(\%total_bytes);
```

The Data::Dumper module defines the Dumper subroutine. This subroutine is similar to the x command in the debugger. We can give Dumper one or more values, and Dumper turns those values into a printable string. The difference between the debugger's x command and Dumper, however, is that the string generated by Dumper is Perl code:

```
myhost% perl bytecounts2 <bytecounts-in
$VAR1 = {
          'thurston.howell.hut' => {
                                     'lovey.howell.hut' => 1250
                                   },
          'ginger.girl.hut' => {
                                 'maryann.girl.hut' => 199,
                                 'professor.hut' => 1218
                               },
          'professor.hut' => {
                               'gilligan.crew.hut' => 1250,
                               'lovey.howell.hut' => 1360
                             }
        };
myhost%
```

The Perl code is fairly understandable; it shows that we have a reference to a hash of three elements, with each value of the hash being a reference to a nested hash. We can evaluate this code and get a hash that's equivalent to the original hash. However, if you're thinking about doing this in order to have a complex data structure persist from one program invocation to the next, please keep reading.

Data::Dumper, like the debugger's x command, handles shared data properly. For example, go back to that "leaking" data from Chapter 5:

```
use Data::Dumper;
$Data::Dumper::Purity = 1; # declare possibly self-referencing structures
my @data1 = qw(one won);
my @data2 = qw(two too to);
push @data2, \@data1;
push @data1, \@data2;
print Dumper(\@data1, \@data2);
```

Here's the output from this program:

```
$VAR1 = [
          'one',
          'won',
          [
```

```
                'two',
                'too',
                'to',
                [ ]
             ]
          ];
  $VAR1->[2][3] = $VAR1;
  $VAR2 = $VAR1->[2];
```

Notice how we've created two different variables now, since there are two parameters to Dumper. The element $VAR1 corresponds to a reference to @data1, while $VAR2 corresponds to a reference to @data2. The debugger shows the values similarly:

```
DB<1> x \@data1, \@data2
      0   ARRAY(0xf914)
   0   'one'
   1   'won'
   2   ARRAY(0x3122a8)
      0   'two'
      1   'too'
      2   'to'
      3   ARRAY(0xf914)
         -> REUSED_ADDRESS
   1   ARRAY(0x3122a8)
   -> REUSED_ADDRESS
```

Note that the phrase REUSED_ADDRESS indicates that some parts of the data are actually references we've already seen.

YAML

Data::Dumper is not the only game on the island, though. Brian Ingerson came up with Yet Another Markup Language (YAML) to provide a more readable (and more compact) dump. It works in the same way as Data::Dumper. We'll see more about YAML when we talk about modules later, so we won't say much about it here.

From the earlier example, we plug in YAML where we had Data::Dumper, and use Dump( ) where we had Dumper( ).

```
use YAML;

my %total_bytes;

while (<>) {
        my ($source, $destination, $bytes) = split;
        $total_bytes{$source}{$destination} += $bytes;
        }

print Dump(\%total_bytes);
```

When you use the same data from the earlier example, you get this output:

```
--- #YAML:1.0
ginger.girl.hut:
```

```
  maryann.girl.hut: 199
  professor.hut: 1218
professor.hut:
  gilligan.crew.hut: 1250
  lovey.howell.hut: 1360
thurston.howell.hut:
  lovey.howell.hut: 1250
```

That's a lot easier to read because it takes up less space on the screen, which can be really handy when you have deeply nested data structures.

Storing Complex Data with Storable

We can take the output of Data::Dumper's Dumper routine, place it into a file, and then load the file to a different program. When we evaluate the code as Perl code, we end up with two package variables, $VAR1 and $VAR2, that are equivalent to the original data. This is called *marshaling* the data: converting complex data into a form that we can write to a file as a stream of bytes for later reconstruction.

However, another Perl core module is much better suited for marshaling: Storable. It's better suited because compared to Data::Dumper, Storable produces smaller and faster-to-process files. (The Storable module is standard in recent versions of Perl, but you can always install it from the CPAN if it's missing.)

The interface is similar to using Data::Dumper, except we must put everything into one reference. For example, let's store the mutually referencing data structures:

```
use Storable;
my @data1 = qw(one won);
my @data2 = qw(two too to);
push @data2, \@data1;
push @data1, \@data2;
store [\@data1, \@data2], 'some_file';
```

The file produced by this step is under 100 bytes, which is quite a bit shorter than the equivalent Data::Dumper output. It's also much less readable for humans. It's easy for Storable to read, as you'll soon see.* Next, fetch the data, again using the Storable module. The result will be a single array reference. We dump the result to see if it stored the right values:

```
use Storable;
my $result = retrieve 'some_file';
use Data::Dumper;
$Data::Dumper::Purity = 1;
print Dumper($result);
```

---

* The format used by Storable is architecture byte-order dependent by default. Its documentation shows how to create byte-order-independent storage files.

Here's the result:

```
$VAR1 = [
          [
            'one',
            'won',
            [
              'two',
              'too',
              'to',
              [ ]
            ]
          ],
          [ ]
        ];
$VAR1->[0][2][3] = $VAR1->[0];
$VAR1->[1] = $VAR1->[0][2];
```

This is functionally the same as the original data structure. We're now looking at the two array references within one top-level array. To get something closer to what we saw before, we can be more explicit about the return value:

```
use Storable;
my ($arr1, $arr2) = @{ retrieve 'some_file' };
use Data::Dumper;
$Data::Dumper::Purity = 1;
print Dumper($arr1, $arr2);
```

or equivalently:

```
use Storable;
my $result = retrieve 'some_file';
use Data::Dumper;
$Data::Dumper::Purity = 1;
print Dumper(@$result);
```

and we'll get:

```
$VAR1 = [
          'one',
          'won',
          [
            'two',
            'too',
            'to',
            [ ]
          ]
        ];
$VAR1->[2][3] = $VAR1;
$VAR2 = $VAR1->[2];
```

just as we did in the original program. With Storable, we can store data and retrieve it later. More information on Storable can be found in perldoc Storable, as always.

Using the map and grep Operators

As the data structures become more complex, it helps to have higher-level constructs deal with common tasks such as selection and transformation. In this regard, Perl's grep and map operators are worth mastering.

Applying a Bit of Indirection

Some problems that may appear very complex are actually simple once we've seen a solution or two. For example, suppose we want to find the items in a list that have odd digit sums but don't want the items themselves. What we want to know is where they occurred in the original list.

All that's required is a bit of indirection.[*] First, we have a selection problem, so we use a grep. Let's not grep the values themselves but the index for each item:

```
my @input_numbers = (1, 2, 4, 8, 16, 32, 64);
my @indices_of_odd_digit_sums = grep {
  ...
} 0..$#input_numbers;
```

Here, the expression 0..$#input_numbers will be a list of indices for the array. Inside the block, $_ is a small integer, from 0 to 6 (seven items total). Now, we don't want to decide whether $_ has an odd digit sum. We want to know whether the array element at that index has an odd digit sum. Instead of using $_ to get the number of interest, use $input_numbers[$_]:

```
my @indices_of_odd_digit_sums = grep {
  my $number = $input_numbers[$_];
  my $sum;
  $sum += $_ for split //, $number;
  $sum % 2;
} 0..$#input_numbers;
```

The result will be the indices at which 1, 16, and 32 appear in the list: 0, 4, and 5. We could use these indices in an array slice to get the original values again:

```
my @odd_digit_sums = @input_numbers[ @indices_of_odd_digit_sums ];
```

The strategy here for an indirect grep or map is to think of the $_ values as identifying a particular item of interest, such as the key in a hash or the index of an array, and then use that identification within the block or expression to access the actual values.

---

[*] A famous computing maxim states that "there is no problem so complex that it cannot be solved with appropriate additional layers of indirection." Of course, with indirection comes obfuscation, so there's got to be a magic middle ground somewhere.

Here's another example: select the elements of @x that are larger than the corresponding value in @y. Again, we'll use the indices of @x as our $_ items:

```
my @bigger_indices = grep {
  if ($_ > $#y or $x[$_] > $y[$_]) {
    1; # yes, select it
  } else {
    0; # no, don't select it
  }
} 0..$#x;
my @bigger = @x[@bigger_indices];
```

In the grep, $_ varies from 0 to the highest index of @x. If that element is beyond the end of @y, we automatically select it. Otherwise, we look at the individual corresponding values of the two arrays, selecting only the ones that meet our match.

However, this is a bit more verbose than it needs to be. We could simply return the boolean expression rather than a separate 1 or 0:

```
my @bigger_indices = grep {
  $_ > $#y or $x[$_] > $y[$_];
} 0..$#x;
my @bigger = @x[@bigger_indices];
```

More easily, we can skip the step of building the intermediate array by simply returning the items of interest with a map:

```
my @bigger = map {
  if ($_ > $#y or $x[$_] > $y[$_]) {
    $x[$_];
  } else {
    ( );
  }
} 0..$#x;
```

If the index is good, return the resulting array value. If the index is bad, return an empty list, making that item disappear.

Selecting and Altering Complex Data

We can use these operators on more complex data. Taking the provisions list from Chapter 5:

```
my %provisions = (
  'The Skipper'   => [qw(blue_shirt hat jacket preserver sunscreen)],
  'The Professor' => [qw(sunscreen water_bottle slide_rule radio batteries) ],
  'Gilligan'      => [qw(red_shirt hat lucky_socks water_bottle) ],
);
```

In this case, $provisions{"The Professor"} gives an array reference of the provisions brought by the Professor, and $provisions{"Gilligan"}[-1] gives the last item Gilligan thought to bring.

We run a few queries against this data. Who brought fewer than five items?

```
my @packed_light = grep @{ $provisions{$_} } < 5, keys %provisions;
```

In this case, $_ is the name of a person. We take that name, look up the array refer-
ence of the provisions for that person, dereference that in a scalar context to get the
count of provisions, and then compare it to 5. And wouldn't you know it; the only
name is Gilligan.

Here's a trickier one. Who brought a water bottle?

```
my @all_wet = grep {
  my @items = @{ $provisions{$_} };
  grep $_ eq 'water_bottle', @items;
} keys %provisions;
```

Starting with the list of names again (keys %provisions), we pull up all the packed
items first and then use that list in an inner grep to count the number of those items
that equal water_bottle. If the count is 0, there's no bottle, so the result is false for
the outer grep. If the count is nonzero, we have a bottle, so the result is true for the
outer grep. Now we see that the Skipper will be a bit thirsty later, without any relief.

We can also perform transformations. For example, turn this hash into a list of array
references, with each array containing two items. The first is the original person's
name; the second is a reference to an array of the provisions for that person:

```
my @remapped_list = map {
  [ $_ => $provisions{$_} ];
} keys %provisions;
```

The keys of %provisions are names of the people. For each name, we construct a
two-element list of the name and the corresponding provisions array reference. This
list is inside an anonymous array constructor, so we get back a reference to a newly
created array for each person. Three names in; three references out.* Or, let's go a
different way. Turn the input hash into a series of references to arrays. Each array
will have a person's name and one of the items they brought:

```
my @person_item_pairs = map {
  my $person = $_;
  my @items = @{ $provisions{$person} };
  map [$person => $_], @items;
} keys %provisions;
```

Yes, a map within a map. The outer map selects one person at a time. We save this name
in $person, and then we extract the item list from the hash. The inner map walks over
this item list, executing the expression to construct an anonymous array reference for
each item. The anonymous array contains the person's name and the provision item.

---

* If we had left the inner brackets off, we'd end up with six items out. That's not very useful, unless we're creating a different hash from them.

We had to use $person here to hold the outer $_ temporarily. Otherwise, we can't refer to both temporary values for the outer map and the inner map.

Exercises

You can find the answers to these exercises in "Answers for Chapter 6" in the Appendix.

Exercise 1 [20 min]

The program from Exercise 2 in Chapter 5 needs to read the entire datafile each time it runs. However, the Professor has a new router logfile each day and doesn't want to keep all that data in one giant file that takes longer and longer to process.

Fix up that program to keep the running totals in a datafile so the Professor can simply run it on each day's logs to get the new totals.

Exercise 2 [5 min]

To make it really useful, what other features should be added to that program? You don't need to implement them!

## CHAPTER 7

Subroutine References

So far, you've seen references to three main Perl data types: scalars, arrays, and hashes. We can also take a reference to a *subroutine* (sometimes called a *coderef*).

Why would we want to do that? Well, in the same way that taking a reference to an array lets you have the same code work on different arrays at different times, taking a reference to a subroutine allows the same code to call different subroutines at different times. Also, references permit complex data structures. A reference to a subroutine allows a subroutine to effectively become part of that complex data structure.

Put another way, a variable or a complex data structure is a repository of values throughout the program. A reference to a subroutine can be thought of as a repository of *behavior* in a program. The examples in this section show how this works.

Referencing a Named Subroutine

The Skipper and Gilligan are having a conversation:

```
sub skipper_greets {
  my $person = shift;
  print "Skipper: Hey there, $person!\n";
}

sub gilligan_greets {
  my $person = shift;
  if ($person eq "Skipper") {
    print "Gilligan: Sir, yes, sir, $person!\n";
  } else {
    print "Gilligan: Hi, $person!\n";
  }
}

skipper_greets("Gilligan");
gilligan_greets("Skipper");
```

This results in:

```
Skipper: Hey there, Gilligan!
Gilligan: Sir, yes, sir, Skipper!
```

So far, nothing unusual has happened. Note, however, that Gilligan has two different behaviors, depending on whether he's addressing the Skipper or someone else.

Now, have the Professor walk into the hut. Both of the *Minnow* crew greet the newest participant:

```
skipper_greets('Professor');
gilligan_greets('Professor');
```

which results in:

```
Skipper: Hey there, Professor!
Gilligan: Hi, Professor!
```

Now the Professor feels obligated to respond:

```
sub professor_greets {
  my $person = shift;
  print "Professor: By my calculations, you must be $person!\n";
}

professor_greets('Gilligan');
professor_greets('Skipper');
```

resulting in:

```
Professor: By my calculations, you must be Gilligan!
Professor: By my calculations, you must be Skipper!
```

Whew! That's lot of typing and not very general. If each person's behavior is in a separate named subroutine, and a new person walks in the door, we have to figure out what other subroutines to call. We could certainly do it with enough hard-to-maintain code, but we can simplify the process by adding a bit of indirection, just as we did with arrays and hashes.

First, let's use the "take a reference to" operator. It actually needs no introduction because it's that very same backslash as before:

```
my $ref_to_greeter = \&skipper_greets;
```

We're taking a reference to the subroutine skipper_greets( ). Note that the preceding ampersand is mandatory here, and the lack of trailing parentheses is also intentional. Perl stores the reference to the subroutine (a coderef) within $ref_to_greeter, and, like all other references, it fits nearly anywhere a scalar fits.

There's only one reason to get back to the original subroutine by dereferencing the coderef: to invoke it. Dereferencing a code reference is similar to dereferencing other references. First, start with the way we would have written it before we heard of references (including the optional ampersand prefix):

```
& skipper_greets ( 'Gilligan' )
```

Next, we replace the name of the subroutine with curly braces around the thing holding the reference:

```
& { $ref_to_greeter } ( 'Gilligan' )
```

There we have it. This construct invokes the subroutine currently referenced by $ref_to_greeter, passing it the single Gilligan parameter.

But boy-oh-boy, is that ugly or what? Luckily, the same reference simplification rules apply. If the value inside the curly braces is a simple scalar variable, we can drop the braces:

```
& $ref_to_greeter ( 'Gilligan' )
```

We can also flip it around a bit with the arrow notation:

```
$ref_to_greeter -> ( 'Gilligan' )
```

That last form is particularly handy when the coderef is in a larger data structure, as you'll see in a moment.

To have both Gilligan and the Skipper greet the Professor, we merely need to iterate over all the subroutines:

```
for my $greet (\&skipper_greets, \&gilligan_greets) {
  $greet->('Professor');
}
```

First, inside the parentheses, we create a list of two items, each of which is a coderef. The coderefs are then individually dereferenced, invoking the corresponding subroutine and passing it the Professor string.

We've seen the coderefs in a scalar variable and as an element of a list. Can we put these coderefs into a larger data structure? Certainly. Create a table that maps people to the behavior they exhibit to greet others, and then rewrite that previous example using the table:

```
sub skipper_greets {
  my $person = shift;
  print "Skipper: Hey there, $person!\n";
}

sub gilligan_greets {
  my $person = shift;
  if ($person eq 'Skipper') {
    print "Gilligan: Sir, yes, sir, $person!\n";
  } else {
    print "Gilligan: Hi, $person!\n";
  }
}

sub professor_greets {
  my $person = shift;
  print "Professor: By my calculations, you must be $person!\n";
}
```

```
my %greets = (
  Gilligan  => \&gilligan_greets,
  Skipper   => \&skipper_greets,
  Professor => \&professor_greets,
);

for my $person (qw(Skipper Gilligan)) {
  $greets{$person}->('Professor');
}
```

Note that $person is a name, which we look up in the hash to get to a coderef. Then we dereference that coderef, passing it the name of the person being greeted, and we get the correct behavior, resulting in:

```
Skipper: Hey there, Professor!
Gilligan: Hi, Professor!
```

Now have everyone greet everyone, in a very friendly room:

```
sub skipper_greets {
  my $person = shift;
  print "Skipper: Hey there, $person!\n";
}

sub gilligan_greets {
  my $person = shift;
  if ($person eq 'Skipper') {
    print "Gilligan: Sir, yes, sir, $person!\n";
  } else {
    print "Gilligan: Hi, $person!\n";
  }
}

sub professor_greets {
  my $person = shift;
  print "Professor: By my calculations, you must be $person!\n";
}

my %greets = (
  Gilligan  => \&gilligan_greets,
  Skipper   => \&skipper_greets,
  Professor => \&professor_greets,
);

my @everyone = sort keys %greets;
for my $greeter (@everyone) {
  for my $greeted (@everyone) {
    $greets{$greeter}->($greeted)
      unless $greeter eq $greeted; # no talking to yourself
  }
}
```

This results in:

```
Gilligan: Hi, Professor!
Gilligan: Sir, yes, sir, Skipper!
Professor: By my calculations, you must be Gilligan!
Professor: By my calculations, you must be Skipper!
Skipper: Hey there, Gilligan!
Skipper: Hey there, Professor!
```

Hmm. That's a bit complex. Let's let them walk into the room one at a time:

```
sub skipper_greets {
  my $person = shift;
  print "Skipper: Hey there, $person!\n";
}

sub gilligan_greets {
  my $person = shift;
  if ($person eq 'Skipper') {
    print "Gilligan: Sir, yes, sir, $person!\n";
  } else {
    print "Gilligan: Hi, $person!\n";
  }
}

sub professor_greets {
  my $person = shift;
  print "Professor: By my calculations, you must be $person!\n";
}

my %greets = (
  Gilligan  => \&gilligan_greets,
  Skipper   => \&skipper_greets,
  Professor => \&professor_greets,
);

my @room; # initially empty
for my $person (qw(Gilligan Skipper Professor)) {
  print "\n";
  print "$person walks into the room.\n";
  for my $room_person (@room) {
    $greets{$person}->($room_person); # speaks
    $greets{$room_person}->($person); # gets reply
  }
  push @room, $person; # come in, get comfy
}
```

The result is a typical day on that tropical island:

```
Gilligan walks into the room.

Skipper walks into the room.
Skipper: Hey there, Gilligan!
Gilligan: Sir, yes, sir, Skipper!
```

```
Professor walks into the room.
Professor: By my calculations, you must be Gilligan!
Gilligan: Hi, Professor!
Professor: By my calculations, you must be Skipper!
Skipper: Hey there, Professor!
```

Anonymous Subroutines

In that last example, we never explicitly called subroutines such as professor_
greets( ), we only called them indirectly through the coderef. Thus, we wasted some
brain cells to come up with a name for the subroutine used only in one other place,
to initialize the data structure. But, just as we can create anonymous hashes and
arrays, we can create anonymous subroutines!

Let's add another island inhabitant: Ginger. But rather than define her greeting
behavior as a named subroutine, we create an anonymous subroutine:

```
my $ginger = sub {
  my $person = shift;
  print "Ginger: (in a sultry voice) Well hello, $person!\n";
};
$ginger->('Skipper');
```

An anonymous subroutine looks like an ordinary sub declaration, but there's no name
(or prototype) between sub and the block that follows. It's also part of a statement, so
we need a trailing semicolon or other expression separator after it in most cases.

```
sub { ... body of subroutine ... };
```

The value in $ginger is a coderef, just as if we had defined the following block as a
subroutine and then taken a reference to it. When we reach the last statement, we see:

```
Ginger: (in a sultry voice) Well hello, Skipper!
```

Although we kept the value in a scalar variable, we could have put that sub { ... }
construct directly into the initialization of the greetings hash:

```
my %greets = (

  Skipper => sub {
    my $person = shift;
    print "Skipper: Hey there, $person!\n";
  },

  Gilligan => sub {
    my $person = shift;
    if ($person eq 'Skipper') {
      print "Gilligan: Sir, yes, sir, $person!\n";
    } else {
      print "Gilligan: Hi, $person!\n";
    }
  },
```

```
  Professor => sub {
    my $person = shift;
    print "Professor: By my calculations, you must be $person!\n";
  },

  Ginger => sub {
    my $person = shift;
    print "Ginger: (in a sultry voice) Well hello, $person!\n";
  },

);

my @room; # initially empty
for my $person (qw(Gilligan Skipper Professor Ginger)) {
  print "\n";
  print "$person walks into the room.\n";
  for my $room_person (@room) {
    $greets{$person}->($room_person); # speaks
    $greets{$room_person}->($person); # gets reply
  }
  push @room, $person; # come in, get comfy
}
```

Notice how much it simplifies the code. The subroutine definitions are right within the only data structure that references them directly. The result is straightforward:

```
Gilligan walks into the room.

Skipper walks into the room.
Skipper: Hey there, Gilligan!
Gilligan: Sir, yes, sir, Skipper!

Professor walks into the room.
Professor: By my calculations, you must be Gilligan!
Gilligan: Hi, Professor!
Professor: By my calculations, you must be Skipper!
Skipper: Hey there, Professor!

Ginger walks into the room.
Ginger: (in a sultry voice) Well hello, Gilligan!
Gilligan: Hi, Ginger!
Ginger: (in a sultry voice) Well hello, Skipper!
Skipper: Hey there, Ginger!
Ginger: (in a sultry voice) Well hello, Professor!
Professor: By my calculations, you must be Ginger!
```

Adding a few more castaways is as simple as putting the entry for the greeting behavior into the hash and adding them into the list of people entering the room. We get this scaling of effort because we've preserved the behavior as data over which you can iterate and look up, thanks to your friendly subroutine references.

Callbacks

A subroutine reference is often used for a *callback*. A callback defines what to do when a subroutine reaches a particular place in an algorithm.

For example, the File::Find module exports a find subroutine that can efficiently walk through a given filesystem hierarchy in a fairly portable way. In its simplest form, we give the find subroutine two parameters: a starting directory and "what to do" for each file or directory name found recursively below that starting directory. The "what to do" is specified as a subroutine reference:

```
use File::Find;
sub what_to_do {
  print "$File::Find::name found\n";
}
my @starting_directories = qw(.);

find(\&what_to_do, @starting_directories);
```

find starts at the current directory (.) and locates each file or directory. For each item, we call the subroutine what_to_do( ), passing it a few documented values through global variables. In particular, the value of $File::Find::name is the item's full pathname (beginning with the starting directory).

In this case, we're passing both data (the list of starting directories) and *behavior* as parameters to the find routine.

It's a bit silly to invent a subroutine name to use the name only once, so we can write the previous code using an anonymous subroutine, such as:

```
use File::Find;
my @starting_directories = qw(.);

find(
  sub {
    print "$File::Find::name found\n";
  },
  @starting_directories,
);
```

Closures

We could also use File::Find to find out some other things about files, such as their size. For the callback's convenience, the current working directory is the item's containing directory, and the item's name within that directory is found in $_.

Maybe you have noticed that, in the previous code, we used $File::Find::name for the item's name. So which name is real, $_ or $File::Find::name? $File::Find::name gives the name relative to the starting directory, but during the callback, the working directory is the one that holds the item just found. For example, suppose that we want find to look for files in the current working directory, so we give it (".") as the list of directories to search. If we call find when the current working directory is /usr, find looks below that directory. When find locates /usr/bin/perl, the current working directory (during the callback) is /usr/bin. $_ holds *perl,* and $File::Find::name holds *./bin/perl,* which is the name relative to the directory in which you started the search.

All of this means that the file tests, such as -s, automatically report on the just-found item. Although this is convenient, the current directory inside the callback is different from the search's starting directory.

What if we want to use File::Find to accumulate the total size of all files seen? The callback subroutine cannot take arguments, and the caller discards its result. But that doesn't matter. When dereferenced, a subroutine reference can see all visible lexical variables when the reference to the subroutine is taken. For example:

```
use File::Find;

my $total_size = 0;
find(sub { $total_size += -s if -f }, '.');
print $total_size, "\n";
```

As before, we call the find routine with two parameters: a reference to an anonymous subroutine and the starting directory. When it finds names within that directory (and its subdirectories), it calls the anonymous subroutine.

Note that the subroutine accesses the $total_size variable. We declare this variable outside the scope of the subroutine but still visible to the subroutine. Thus, even though find invokes the callback subroutine (and would not have direct access to $total_size), the callback subroutine accesses and updates the variable.

The kind of subroutine that can access all lexical variables that existed at the time we declared it is called a *closure* (a term borrowed from the world of mathematics). In Perl terms, a closure is just a subroutine that references a lexical variable that has gone out of scope.

Furthermore, the access to the variable from within the closure ensures that the variable remains alive as long as the subroutine reference is alive. For example, let's number the output files:[*]

```
use File::Find;

my $callback;
{
  my $count = 0;
  $callback = sub { print ++$count, ": $File::Find::name\n" };
}
find($callback, '.');
```

---

[*] This code seems to have an extra semicolon at the end of the line that assigns to $callback, doesn't it? But remember, the construct sub { ... } is an expression. Its value (a coderef) is assigned to $callback, and there's a semicolon at the end of that statement. It's easy to forget to put the proper punctuation after the closing curly brace of an anonymous subroutine declaration.

Here, we declare a variable to hold the callback. We cannot declare this variable within the naked block (the block following that is not part of a larger Perl syntax construct), or Perl will recycle it at the end of that block. Next, the lexical $count variable is initialized to 0. We then declare an anonymous subroutine and place its reference into $callback. This subroutine is a closure because it refers to the lexical $count variable.

At the end of the naked block, the $count variable goes out of scope. However, because it is still referenced by subroutine in $callback, it stays alive as an anonymous scalar variable.* When the callback is invoked from find, the value of the variable formerly known as $count is incremented from 1 to 2 to 3, and so on.

Returning a Subroutine from a Subroutine

Although a naked block worked nicely to define the callback, having a subroutine return that subroutine reference instead might be more useful:

```
use File::Find;

sub create_find_callback_that_counts {
  my $count = 0;
  return sub { print ++$count, ": $File::Find::name\n" };
}

my $callback = create_find_callback_that_counts( );
find($callback, '.');
```

It's the same process here, just written a bit differently. When we invoke create_find_callback_that_counts( ), we initialize the lexical variable $count to 0. The return value from that subroutine is a reference to an anonymous subroutine that is also a closure because it accesses the $count variable. Even though $count goes out of scope at the end of the create_find_callback_that_counts( ) subroutine, there's still a binding between it and the returned subroutine reference, so the variable stays alive until the subroutine reference is finally discarded.

If we reuse the callback, the same variable still has its most recently used value. The initialization occurred in the original subroutine (create_find_callback_that_counts), not the callback (unnamed) subroutine:

```
use File::Find;

sub create_find_callback_that_counts {
  my $count = 0;
  return sub { print ++$count, ": $File::Find::name\n" };
}
```

---

* To be more accurate, the closure declaration increases the reference count of the referent, as if another reference had been taken explicitly. Just before the end of the naked block, the reference count of $count is two, but after the block has exited, the value still has a reference count of one. Although no other code may access $count, it will still be kept in memory as long as the reference to the sub is available in $callback or elsewhere.

```
my $callback = create_find_callback_that_counts( );
print "my bin:\n";
find($callback, 'bin');
print "my lib:\n";
find($callback, 'lib');
```

This example prints consecutive numbers starting at 1 for the entries below bin, but then continues the numbering when we start entries in lib. The same $count variable is used in both cases. However, if we invoke the create_find_callback_that_counts( ) twice, we get two different $count variables:

```
use File::Find;

sub create_find_callback_that_counts {
  my $count = 0;
  return sub { print ++$count, ": $File::Find::name\n" };
}

my $callback1 = create_find_callback_that_counts( );
my $callback2 = create_find_callback_that_counts( );
print "my bin:\n";
find($callback1, 'bin');
print "my lib:\n";
find($callback2, 'lib');
```

In this case, we have two separate $count variables, each accessed from within their own callback subroutine.

How would we get the total size of all found files from the callback? Earlier, we were able to do this by making $total_size visible. If we stick the definition of $total_size into the subroutine that returns the callback reference, we won't have access to the variable. But we can cheat a bit. For one thing, we can determine that we'll never call the callback subroutine with any parameters, so, if the subroutine receives a parameter, we make it return the total size:

```
use File::Find;

sub create_find_callback_that_sums_the_size {
  my $total_size = 0;
  return sub {
    if (@_) { # it's our dummy invocation
      return $total_size;
    } else { # it's a callback from File::Find:
      $total_size += -s if -f;
    }
  };
}

my $callback = create_find_callback_that_sums_the_size( );
find($callback, 'bin');
my $total_size = $callback->('dummy'); # dummy parameter to get size
print "total size of bin is $total_size\n";
```

Distinguishing actions by the presence or absence of parameters is not a universal solution. Fortunately, we can create more than one subroutine reference in create_find_callback_that_counts( ):

```
use File::Find;

sub create_find_callbacks_that_sum_the_size {
  my $total_size = 0;
  return(sub { $total_size += -s if -f }, sub { return $total_size });
}

my ($count_em, $get_results) = create_find_callbacks_that_sum_the_size( );
find($count_em, 'bin');
my $total_size = &$get_results( );
print "total size of bin is $total_size\n";
```

Because we created both subroutine references from the same scope, they both have access to the same $total_size variable. Even though the variable has gone out of scope before we call either subroutine, they still share the same heritage and can use the variable to communicate the result of the calculation.

Returning the two subroutine references from the creating subroutine does not invoke them. The references are just data at that point. It's not until we invoke them as a callback or an explicit subroutine dereferencing that they actually do their duty.

What if we invoke this new subroutine more than once?

```
use File::Find;

sub create_find_callbacks_that_sum_the_size {
  my $total_size = 0;
  return(sub { $total_size += -s if -f }, sub { return $total_size });
}

## set up the subroutines
my %subs;
foreach my $dir (qw(bin lib man)) {
  my ($callback, $getter) = create_find_callbacks_that_sum_the_size( );
  $subs{$dir}{CALLBACK}  = $callback;
  $subs{$dir}{GETTER}    = $getter;
}

## gather the data
for (keys %subs) {
  find($subs{$_}{CALLBACK}, $_);
}

## show the data
for (sort keys %subs) {
  my $sum = $subs{$_}{GETTER}->( );
  print "$_ has $sum bytes\n";
}
```

In the section to set up the subroutines, we create three instances of callback-and-getter pairs. Each callback has a corresponding subroutine to get the results. Next, in the section to gather the data, we call find three times with each corresponding callback subroutine reference. This updates the individual $total_size variables associated with each callback. Finally, in the section to show the data, we call the getter routines to fetch the results.

The six subroutines (and the three $total_size variables they share) are reference counted. When we modify %subs or it goes out of scope, the values have their reference counts reduced, recycling the contained data. (If that data also references further data, those reference counts are reduced appropriately.)

Closure Variables as Inputs

While the previous examples showed closure variables being modified, closure variables are also useful to provide initial or lasting input to the subroutine. For example, let's write a subroutine to create a File::Find callback that prints files exceeding a certain size:

```
use File::Find;

sub print_bigger_than {
  my $minimum_size = shift;
  return sub { print "$File::Find::name\n" if -f and -s >= $minimum_size };
}

my $bigger_than_1024 = print_bigger_than(1024);
find($bigger_than_1024, 'bin');
```

We pass the 1024 parameter into the print_bigger_than, which then gets shifted into the $minimum_size lexical variable. Because we access this variable within the subroutine referenced by the return value of the print_bigger_than variable, it becomes a closure variable, with a value that persists for the duration of that subroutine reference. Again, invoking this subroutine multiple times creates distinct "locked-in" values for $minimum_size, each bound to its corresponding subroutine reference.

Closures are "closed" only on lexical variables, since lexical variables eventually go out of scope. Because a package variable (which is a global) never goes out of scope, a closure never closes on a package variable. All subroutines refer to the same single instance of the global variable.

Closure Variables as Static Local Variables

A subroutine doesn't have to be an anonymous subroutine to be a closure. If a named subroutine accesses lexical variables, and those variables go out of scope, the named subroutine retains a reference to the lexicals, just as you saw with anonymous subroutines. For example, consider two routines that count coconuts for Gilligan:

```
{
  my $count;
  sub count_one { ++$count }
  sub count_so_far { return $count }
}
```

If we place this code at the beginning of the program, we declare the variable $count inside the naked block scope, and the two subroutines that reference the variable become closures. However, because they have a name, they will persist beyond the end of the scope (as do all named subroutines). Since the subroutines persist beyond the scope and access variables declared within that scope, they become closures and thus can continue to access $count throughout the lifetime of the program.

So, with a few calls, we can see an incremented count:

```
count_one( );
count_one( );
count_one( );
print 'we have seen ', count_so_far( ), " coconuts!\n";
```

$count retains its value between calls to count_one( ) or count_so_far( ), but no other section of code can access this $count at all.

In C, this is known as a *static local* variable: a variable that is visible to only a subset of the program's subroutines but persists throughout the life of the program, even between calls to those subroutines.

What if we wanted to count down? Something like this will do:

```
{
  my $countdown = 10;
  sub count_down { $countdown-- }
  sub count_remaining { $countdown }
}

count_down( );
count_down( );
count_down( );
print 'we're down to ', count_remaining( ), " coconuts!\n";
```

That is, it'll do as long as we put it near the beginning of the program, before any invocations of count_down( ) or count_remaining( ). Why?

This block doesn't work when you put it after those invocations because there are two functional parts to the first line:

```
my $countdown = 10;
```

One part is the declaration of $countdown as a lexical variable. That part is noticed and processed as the program is parsed during the *compile phase*. The second part is the assignment of 10 to the allocated storage. This is handled as Perl executes the code during the *run phase*. Unless Perl executes the run phase for this code, the variable has its initial undef value.

One practical solution to this problem is to change the block in which the static local appears into a BEGIN block:

```
BEGIN {
  my $countdown = 10;
  sub count_down { $countdown-- }
  sub count_remaining { $countdown }
}
```

The BEGIN keyword tells the Perl compiler that as soon as this block has been parsed successfully (during the compile phase), jump for a moment to run phase and run the block as well. Presuming the block doesn't cause a fatal error, compilation then continues with the text following the block. The block itself is also discarded, ensuring that the code within is executed precisely once in a program, even if it had appeared syntactically within a loop or subroutine.

Exercise

You can find the answer to this exercise in "Answer for Chapter 7" in the Appendix.

Exercise [50 min]

The Professor modified some files on Monday afternoon, and now he's forgotten which ones they were. This happens all the time. He wants you to make a subroutine called gather_mtime_between, which, given a starting and ending timestamp, returns a pair of coderefs. The first one will be used with File::Find to gather the names of only the items that were modified between those two times; the second one should return the list of items found.

Here's some code to try; it should list only items that were last modified on the most recent Monday, although you could easily change it to work with a different day. (You don't have to type all of this code. This program should be available as the file named ex6-1.plx in the downloadable files, available on the O'Reilly web site.)

Hint: you can find a file's timestamp (mtime) with code such as:

```
my $timestamp = (stat $file_name)[9];
```

Because it's a slice, remember that those parentheses are mandatory. Don't forget that the working directory inside the callback isn't necessarily the starting directory in which find was called.

```
use File::Find;
use Time::Local;

my $target_dow = 1;        # Sunday is 0, Monday is 1, ...
my @starting_directories = (".");

my $seconds_per_day = 24 * 60 * 60;
my($sec, $min, $hour, $day, $mon, $yr, $dow) = localtime;
```

```perl
  my $start = timelocal(0, 0, 0, $day, $mon, $yr);        # midnight today
  while ($dow != $target_dow) {
    # Back up one day
    $start -= $seconds_per_day;        # hope no DST! :-)
    if (--$dow < 0) {
      $dow += 7;
    }
  }
  my $stop = $start + $seconds_per_day;

  my($gather, $yield)  = gather_mtime_between($start, $stop);
  find($gather, @starting_directories);
  my @files = $yield->(  );

  for my $file (@files) {
    my $mtime = (stat $file)[9];        # mtime via slice
    my $when = localtime $mtime;
    print "$when: $file\n";
  }
```

Note the comment about DST. In many parts of the world, on the days when day-light savings time or summer time kicks in and out, the day is no longer 86,400 seconds long. The program glosses over this issue, but a more pedantic coder might take it into consideration appropriately.

Filehandle References

We've seen arrays, hashes, and subroutines passed around in references, permitting a level of indirection to solve certain types of problems. We can also store `filehandles` in references. Let's look at the old problems and the new solutions.

The Old Way

In the olden days, Perl used barewords for filehandle names. The filehandle is another Perl data type, although people don't talk about it too much since it doesn't get its own special sigil. You've probably already seen a lot of code that uses these bareword filehandles.

```
open LOG_FH, '>> castaways.log'
        or die "Could not open castaways.log: $!";
```

What happens if we want to pass around these filehandles so we could share them with other parts of our code, such as libraries? You've probably seen some tricky looking code that uses a typeglob or a reference to a typeglob.

```
log_message( *LOG_FH, 'The Globetrotters are stranded with us!' );

log_message( *LOG_FH, 'An astronaut passes overhead' );
```

In the `log_message()` routine, we take the first element off of the argument list and store it in another typeglob. Without going into too many details, a *typeglob* stores pointers to all the package variables of that name. When we assign one typeglob to another, we create aliases to the same data. We can now access the data, including the details of the filehandle, from another name. Then, when we use that name as a filehandle, Perl knows to look for the filehandle portion of the typeglob. We'd have a much easier time if filehandles had sigils!

```
sub log_message {
  local *FH = shift;

  print FH @_, "\n";
}
```

Notice the use of local there. A typeglob works with the symbol table, which means it's dealing with package variables. Package variables can't be lexical variables, so we can't use my. Since we don't want to stomp on anything else that might be named FH somewhere else in the script, we must use local to say that the name FH has a temporary value for the duration of the log_message subroutine and that when the subroutine finishes, Perl should restore any previous values to FH as if we were never there.

If all of that makes you nervous and wish that none of this stuff existed, that's good. Don't do this anymore! We put it in a section called "The Old Way" because there is a much better way to do it now. Pretend this section never existed and move on to the next one.

The Improved Way

Starting with Perl 5.6, open can create a filehandle reference in a normal scalar variable. Instead of using a bareword for the filehandle name, we use a scalar variable whose value is undef.

```
my $log_fh;
open $log_fh, '>> castaways.log'
        or die "Could not open castaways.log: $!";
```

If the scalar already has a value, this doesn't work because Perl won't stomp on our data. Perl tries to use the value in C<$log_fh> as a symbolic reference, so it tries to print to the filehandle named C<5>. Under C<use strict>, this is a fatal error.

```
my $log_fh = 5;
open $log_fh, '>> castaways.log'
        or die "Could not open castaways.log: $!";
print $log_fh "We need more coconuts!\n";   # doesn't work
```

However, the Perl idiom is to do everything in one step. We can declare the variable right in the open statement. It looks funny at first, but after doing it a couple (okay, maybe several) times, you'll get used to it and like it better.

```
open my $log_fh, '>> castaways.log'
        or die "Could not open castaways.log: $!";
```

When we want to print to the filehandle, we use the scalar variable instead of a bareword. Notice that there is still no comma after the filehandle.

```
print $log_fh "We have no bananas today!\n";
```

That syntax might look funny to you, though, and even if it doesn't look funny to you, it might look odd to the person who has to read your code later. In *Perl Best Practices*, Damian Conway recommends putting braces around the filehandle portion to explicitly state what you intend. This syntax makes it look more like grep and map with inline blocks.

```
print {$log_fh} "We have no bananas today!\n";
```

Now we treat the filehandle reference just like any other scalar. We don't have to do any tricky magic to make it work.

```
log_message( $log_fh, 'My name is Mr. Ed' );

sub log_message {
  my $fh = shift;

  print $fh @_, "\n";
}
```

We can also create filehandle references from which we can read. We simply put the right thing in the second argument.

```
open my $fh, "castaways.log"
        or die "Could not open castaways.log: $!";
```

Now we use the scalar variable in place of the bareword in the line input operator. Before, we would have seen the bareword between the angle brackets:

```
while( <LOG_FH> ) { ... }
```

And now we see the scalar variable in its place.

```
while( <$log_fh> ) { ... }
```

In general, where we've seen the bareword filehandle we can substitute the scalar variable filehandle reference.

In any of these forms, when the scalar variable goes out of scope (or we assign another value to it), Perl closes the file. We don't have to explicitly close the file ourselves.

The Even Better Way

So far, our examples have shown the two-argument form of open, but that actually has a catch: the open mode and the filename both live in the second argument. That means that we have to store two different things in one string, and we have to trust Perl to be able to figure it out.

To get around that, we break the second argument into two separate arguments.

```
open my $log_fh, '>>', 'castaways.log'
        or die "Could not open castaways.log: $!";
```

This three-argument form has the added advantage of access to the Perl IO filters. We won't go into too much detail here.* The open function's entry in perlfunc is over 400 lines, even though it has its own perldoc tutorial, perlopentut.

---

* Although brian does in "Get More Out of Open," *The Perl Journal*, October 31, 2005, *http://www.tpj.com/documents/s=9923/tpj1130955178261/bdf_open.htm.*

IO::Handle

Behind the scenes, Perl is really using the IO::Handle module to work this magic, so our filehandle scalar is really an object.* The IO::Handle package is a base class for input-output things, so it handles a lot more than just files.

Unless you're creating new IO modules, you probably shouldn't use IO::Handle directly. Instead, use some of the handy modules built on top of it. We haven't told you about object-oriented programming (OOP) yet (it's in Chapter 11, so we almost have), but in this case, you just have to follow the example in its documentation.

Some of these modules do some of the same things that we can already do with Perl's built-in open (depending on which version of Perl we have), but they can be handy when we want to decide as late as possible which module should handle input or output. Instead of using the built-in open, we use the module interface. To switch the behavior, we simply change the module name. Since we've set up our code to use a module interface, it's not that much work to switch modules.

IO::File

The IO::File module subclasses IO::Handle to work with files. It comes with the standard Perl distribution, so you should already have it. There are a variety of ways to create an IO::File object.

We can create the filehandle reference with the one-argument form of the constructor. We check the result of the operation by looking for a defined value in the filehandle reference variable.

```
use IO::File;

my $fh = IO::File->new( '> castaways.log' )
            or die "Could not create filehandle: $!";
```

If you don't like that (for the same reasons as regular open), use one of the other calling conventions. The optional second argument is the filehandle mode.†

```
my $read_fh  = IO::File->new( 'castaways.log', 'r' );

my $write_fh = IO::File->new( 'castaways.log', 'w' );
```

Using a bit mask as the mode allows for more granular control. The IO::File module supplies the constants.

```
my $append_fh = IO::File->new( 'castaways.log', O_WRONLY|O_APPEND );
```

---

* Have you ever wondered why there is no comma after the filehandle portion of the print? It's really the indirect object notation (which we haven't mentioned yet, unless you've read the whole book before you read the footnotes, like we told you to do in the preface!).

† These are the ANSI C fopen mode strings. You can also use these with the built-in open. Indeed, IO::File uses the built-in open behind the scenes.

Besides opening named files, we might want to open an anonymous temporary file. On systems that support this sort of thing, we simply create the new object to get a read-write filehandle.

```
my $temp_fh = IO::File->new_tmpfile;
```

As before, Perl closes these files when the scalar variable goes out of scope, but if that's not enough, we do it ourselves explicitly.

```
$temp_fh->close;
```

```
undef $append_fh;
```

Anonymous IO::File Objects

If we don't put our IO::File object in a simple scalar variable, some operations require a slightly modified syntax to work. For example, we want to copy every file matched by the glob pattern of *.input to a corresponding file whose suffix is .output, but do it in parallel. First, we open all the files, both inputs and outputs:

```
my @handlepairs;

foreach my $file ( glob( '*.input' ) ) {
        (my $out = $file) =~ s/\.input$/.output/;
        push @handlepairs, [
                (IO::File->new('<$file') || die),
                (IO::File->new('>$out') || die),
        ];
}
```

Now we have an array of references to arrays, each element of which is an IO::File object. Now, let's pump the data from the input files to the output files.

```
while (@handlepairs) {
  @handlepairs = grep {
    if (defined(my $line = $_->[0]->getline)) {
      print { $_->[1] } $line;
    } else {
      0;
    }
  } @handlepairs;
}
```

As long as we have pairs, we keep passing the list through the grep structure:

```
@handlepairs = grep { CONDITION } @handlepairs;
```

On each pass, only the handle pairs that evaluate as true in the grep CONDITION survive. Inside, we take the first element of each pair and try to read from it. If that's successful, write that line to the second element of the pair (the corresponding output handle). If the print is successful, it returns true, which lets grep know that we want to keep that pair. If either the print fails or the getline returns undef, the grep sees the false value as an indication to discard that pair. Discarding the pair automatically closes both filehandles. Cool!

Note that we can't use the more traditional filehandle read or filehandle print operations, because the reading and writing filehandles weren't in a simple scalar variable. We can rewrite that loop to see if copying the handles is easier:

```
while (@handlepairs) {
  @handlepairs = grep {
    my ($IN, $OUT) = @$_;
    if (defined(my $line = <$IN>)) {
      print $OUT $line;
    } else {
      0;
    }
  } @handlepairs;
}
```

This scenario is arguably better. Most of the time, simply copying the complexly referenced value into a simple scalar is easier on the eyes. In fact, another way to write that loop is to get rid of the ugly if structure:

```
while (@handlepairs) {
  @handlepairs = grep {
    my ($IN, $OUT) = @$_;
    my $line;
    defined($line = <IN>) and print $OUT $line;
  } @handlepairs;
}
```

As long as someone understands that and is a partial evaluator and that print returns true when everything is okay, this is a fine replacement. Remember the Perl motto: "There's more than one way to do it" (although not all of them are equally nice or legitimate).

IO::Scalar

Sometimes we don't want to print to a file and would rather build up the output in a string. Some module interfaces don't give us that option, so we have to make it look like we are printing to a file by using a filehandle. We might also want to build up our content before we write it to a file so we can encrypt it, compress it, or send it as email directly from your program.

The IO::Scalar module uses the magic of tie behind the scenes to give us a filehandle reference that appends to a scalar. This module doesn't come with the standard Perl distribution, so you'll have to install it yourself most likely.

```
use IO::Scalar;

my $string_log = '';
my $scalar_fh = IO::Scalar->new( \$string_log );

print $scalar_fh "The Howells' private beach club is closed\n";
```

Now our log message ends up in the scalar variable $string_log instead of a file. What if we want to read from our logfile, though? We do the same thing. In this example, we create $scalar_fh just as we did before, then read from it with the line input operator. In our while loop, we'll extract the log messages that contain Gilligan (which is probably most of them, since he's always part of the mess):

```
use IO::Scalar;

my $string_log = '';
my $scalar_fh = IO::Scalar->new( \$string_log );

while( <$scalar_fh> ) {
        next unless /Gilligan/;
        print;
        }
```

As of Perl version 5.8, we can do this directly in Perl without using IO::Scalar.

```
open( my $fh, '>>', \$string_log )
        or die "Could not append to string! $!";
```

IO::Tee

What if we want to send output to more than one place at a time? What if we want to send it to a file *and* save it in a string at the same time? Using what we know already, we'd have to do something like this:

```
my $string = '';

open my $log_fh, '>>', 'castaways.log'
        or die "Could not open castaways.log;
open my $scalar_fh, '>>', \$string;

my $log_message = "The Minnow is taking on water!\n"
print $log_fh    $log_message;
print $scalar_fh $log_message;
```

Of course, we could shorten that a bit so we only have one print statement. We use the foreach control structure to iterate through the filehandle references, store each in $fh in turn, and print to each one.

```
foreach my $fh ( $log_fh, $scalar_fh ) {
        print $fh $log_message;
        }
```

That's still a bit too much work. In the foreach, we had to decide which filehandles to include. What if we could just define a group of filehandles that answered to the same name? Well, that's what IO::Tee does for us. Imagine it like a tee connector on a bilge output pipe; when the water gets to the tee, it can flow it two different directions at the same time. When our output gets to IO::Tee, it can go to two (or more) different channels at the same time. That is, IO::Tee *multiplexes* output. In this example, the castaways' log message goes to both the logfile and the scalar variable.

```
use IO::Tee;

$tee_fh = IO::Tee->new( $log_fh, $scalar_fh );

print $tee_fh "The radio works in the middle of the ocean!\n";
```

That's not all, though. If the first argument to IO::Tee is an input filehandle (the succeeding arguments must be output filehandles), we can use the same teed filehandle to read from input and write to the output. The source and destination channels are different, but we get to treat them as a single filehandle.

```
use IO::Tee;

$tee_fh = IO::Tee->new( $read_fh, $log_fh, $scalar_fh );

# reads from $read_fh
my $message = <$tee_fh>;

# prints to $log_fh and $scalar_fh
print $tee_fh $message;
```

The $read_fh doesn't have to be connected to a file, either. It might also be connected to a socket, a scalar variable, an external command's output,* or anything else we can dream up.

Directory Handle References

In the same way that we can create references to filehandles, we can create directory handle references.

```
opendir my $dh, '.' or die "Could not open directory: $!";

foreach my $file ( readdir( $dh ) ) {
        print "Skipper, I found $file!\n";
        }
```

The directory handle reference obeys the same rules we laid out before. This only works if the scalar variable does not already have a value, and the handle automatically closes when the variable goes out of scope or we assign it a new value.

IO::Dir

We can use object-oriented interfaces for directory handles too. The IO::Dir module has been part of the standard Perl distribution since 5.6. It doesn't add interesting new features but wraps the Perl built-in functions.†

---

* You can create readable filehandles to external commands with IO::Pipe.

† For each IO::Dir method name, append "dir" and look at the documentation in perlfunc.

```
use IO::Dir;

my $dir_fh = IO::Dir->new( '.' ) || die "Could not open dirhandle! $!\n";

while( defined( my $file = $dir_fh->read ) ) {
        print "Skipper, I found $file!\n";
        }
```

We don't have to create a new directory handle if we decide we want to go through the list again (perhaps later in the program). We can rewind the directory handle to start over:

```
while( defined( my $file = $dir_fh->read ) ) {
        print "I found $file!\n";
        }

# time passes
$dir_fh->rewind;

while( defined( my $file = $dir_fh->read ) ) {
        print "I can still find $file!\n";
        }
```

Exercises

You can find the answers to these exercises in "Answers for Chapter 8" in the Appendix.

Exercise 1 [20 min]

Write a program that prints the date and the day of the week, but allow the user to choose to send the output either to a file, a scalar, or both at the same time. No matter which output channels the user selects, send the output with a single print statement. If the user chooses to send the output to a scalar, at the end of the program print the scalar's value to standard output.

Exercise 2 [30 min]

The Professor has to read a logfile that looks like:

```
Gilligan: 1 coconut
Skipper: 3 coconuts
Gilligan: 1 banana
Ginger: 2 papayas
Professor: 3 coconuts
MaryAnn: 2 papayas
...
```

He wants to write a series of files, called `gilligan.info`, `maryann.info`, and so on. Each file should contain all the lines that begin with that name. (Names are always delimited by the trailing colon.) At the end, `gilligan.info` should start with:

```
Gilligan: 1 coconut
Gilligan: 1 banana
```

Now the logfile is large, and the coconut-powered computer is not very fast, so he wants to process the input file in one pass and write all output files in parallel. How does he do it?

Hint: use a hash, keyed by the castaway name, holding `IO::File` objects for each output file. Create them as necessary.

Exercise 3 [15 min]

Write a program that takes in multiple directory names from the command line, then prints out their contents. Use a function that takes a directory handle reference that you made using `IO::Dir`.

## CHAPTER 9

Practical Reference Tricks

This chapter looks at optimizing sorting and dealing with recursively defined data.

Review of Sorting

Perl's built-in sort operator sorts text strings in their natural text order, by default.* This is fine if we want to sort text strings:

```
my @sorted = sort qw(Gilligan Skipper Professor Ginger Mary_Ann);
```

but gets pretty messy when we want to sort numbers:

```
my @wrongly_sorted = sort 1, 2, 4, 8, 16, 32;
```

The resulting list is 1, 16, 2, 32, 4, 8. Why didn't sort order these properly? It treats each item as a string and sorts them in string order. Any string that begins with 3 sorts before any string that begins with 4.

If we don't want the default sorting order, we don't need to write an entire sorting *algorithm*, which is good news since Perl already has a good one of those. But no matter what sorting algorithm we use, at some point we have to look at item A and item B and decide which one comes first. That's the part we'll write: code to handle just two items. Perl will do the rest.

By default, as Perl orders the items, it uses a string comparison. We can specify a new comparison using a *sort block* that we place between the sort keyword and the list of things to sort.† Within the sort block, $a and $b stand in for two of the items sort will compare. If we're sorting numbers, then $a and $b will be two numbers from our list.

The sort block must return a coded value to indicate the sort order. If $a comes before $b in our desired sorting order, it should return -1; it should return +1 if $b

---

* My friends call that the "ASCIIbetical" ordering. Normally, modern Perl doesn't use ASCII; instead, it uses a default sort order, depending on the current locale and character set. See the perllocale (not perllocal!) manpage.

† We can also used a name subroutine that sort invokes for each comparison.

comes before $a; if the order doesn't matter, it should return 0. The order might not matter, for example, if it's a case-insensitive sort comparing "FRED" to "Fred", or if it's a numeric sort comparing 42 to 42.*

For example, to sort those numbers in their proper order, we can use a sort block comparing $a and $b, like so:

```
my @numerically_sorted = sort {
  if ($a < $b)    { -1 }
  elsif ($a > $b) { +1 }
  else            {  0 }
} 1, 2, 4, 8, 16, 32;
```

Now we have a proper numeric comparison, so we have a proper numeric sort. Of course, this is far too much typing, so we can use the spaceship operator instead:

```
my @numerically_sorted = sort { $a <=> $b } 1, 2, 4, 8, 16, 32;
```

The spaceship operator returns -1, 0, and +1, according to the rules we laid out. A descending sort is simple in Perl:†

```
my @numerically_descending =
    reverse sort { $a <=> $b } 1, 2, 4, 8, 16, 32;
```

But there is more than one way to do it. The spaceship operator is nearsighted; and can't see which one of its parameters comes from $a and which from $b; it sees only which value is to its left and which is to its right. If we reverse the position of $a and $b, the spaceship will sort everything in the opposite order:

```
my @numerically_descending =
    sort { $b <=> $a } 1, 2, 4, 8, 16, 32;
```

In every place the previous sort expression returned -1, this expression returns +1, and vice versa. Thus, the sort is in the opposite order, and so it doesn't need a reverse. It's also easy to remember because if $a is to the left of $b, we get out the lower items first, just like a and b would be in the resulting list.

Which way is better? When should we use a reverse sort, and when should we switch $a and $b? Well, in most cases it shouldn't matter much for efficiency, so it's probably best to optimize for clarity and use reverse. For a more complex comparison, however, a single reverse may not be up to the task.

Like the spaceship operator, we can indicate a string sort with cmp, although this is rarely used alone because it is the default comparison. The cmp operator is most often used in more complex comparisons, as we'll show shortly.

---

* Actually, we can use any negative or positive number in place of -1 and +1, respectively. Recent Perl versions include a default sorting engine that is *stable*, so zero returns from the sort block cause the relative ordering of $a and $b to reflect their order in the original list. Older versions of Perl didn't guarantee such stability, and a future version might not use a stable sort, so don't rely on it.

† As of version 5.8.6, Perl recognizes the reverse sort and does it without generating the temporary, intermediate list.

Sorting with Indices

In the same way we used indices to solve a few problems with grep and map back in Chapter 2, we can also use indices with sort to get some interesting results. For example, let's sort the list of names from earlier:

```
my @sorted = sort qw(Gilligan Skipper Professor Ginger Mary_Ann);
print "@sorted\n";
```

which necessarily results in:

```
Gilligan Ginger Mary_Ann Professor Skipper
```

But what if we wanted to look at the original list and determine which element of the original list now appears as the first, second, third, and so on, element of the sorted list? For example, Ginger is the second element of the sorted list and was the fourth element of the original list. How do we determine that the second element of the final list was the fourth element of the original list?

Well, we can apply a bit of indirection. Let's not sort the actual names but rather the indices of each name:

```
my @input = qw(Gilligan Skipper Professor Ginger Mary_Ann);
my @sorted_positions = sort { $input[$a] cmp $input[$b] } 0..$#input;
print "@sorted_positions\n";
```

This time, $a and $b aren't the elements of the list, but the indices. So instead of comparing $a to $b, we use cmp to compare $input[$a] to $input[$b] as strings. The result of the sort are the indices, in an order defined by the corresponding elements of @input. This prints 0 3 4 2 1, which means that the first element of the sorted list is element 0 of the original list, Gilligan. The second element of the sorted list is element 3 of the original list, which is Ginger, and so on. Now we can rank information rather than just move the names around.

Actually, we have the inverse of the rank. We still don't know, for a given name in the original list, which position it occupies in the output list. But with a bit more magic, we can get there as well:

```
my @input = qw(Gilligan Skipper Professor Ginger Mary_Ann);
my @sorted_positions = sort { $input[$a] cmp $input[$b] } 0..$#input;
my @ranks;
@ranks[@sorted_positions] = (0..$#sorted_positions);
print "@ranks\n";
```

The code prints 0 4 3 1 2. This means that Gilligan is position 0 in the output list, Skipper is position 4, Professor is position 2, and so on. The positions here are 0-based, so add 1 to get "human" ordinal values. One way to cheat is to use 1..@sorted_positions instead of 0..$#sorted_positions, so a way to dump it all out looks like:

```
my @input = qw(Gilligan Skipper Professor Ginger Mary_Ann);
my @sorted_positions = sort { $input[$a] cmp $input[$b] } 0..$#input;
my @ranks;
```

```
@ranks[@sorted_positions] = (1..@sorted_positions);
for (0..$#ranks) {
  print "$input[$_] sorts into position $ranks[$_]\n";
}
```

This results in:

```
Gilligan sorts into position 1
Skipper sorts into position 5
Professor sorts into position 4
Ginger sorts into position 2
Mary_Ann sorts into position 3
```

This general technique can be convenient if we need to look at our data in more than one way. Perhaps we keep many records in order by a numeric code for efficiency reasons, but we occasionally want to view them in alphabetical order as well. Or maybe the data items themselves are impractical to sort, such as a month's worth of server logs.

Sorting Efficiently

As the Professor tries to maintain the community computing facility (built entirely out of bamboo, coconuts, and pineapples, and powered by a certified Perl-hacking monkey), he continues to discover that people are leaving entirely too much data on the single monkey-powered filesystem and decides to print a list of offenders.

The Professor has written a subroutine called ask_monkey_about( ), which, given a castaway's name, returns the number of pineapples of storage they use. We have to ask the monkey because he's in charge of the pineapples. An initial naive approach to find the offenders from greatest to least might be something like:

```
my @castaways =
  qw(Gilligan Skipper Professor Ginger Mary_Ann Thurston Lovey);
my @wasters = sort {
  ask_monkey_about($b) <=> ask_monkey_about($a)
} @castaways;
```

In theory, this would be fine. For the first pair of names (Gilligan and Skipper), we ask the monkey "How many pineapples does Gilligan have?" and "How many pineapples does Skipper have?" We get back two values from the monkey and use them to order Gilligan and Skipper in the final list.

However, at some point, we have to compare the number of pineapples that Gilligan has with another castaway as well. For example, suppose the pair is Ginger and Gilligan. We ask the monkey about Ginger, get a number back, and then ask the monkey about Gilligan…again. This will probably annoy the monkey a bit, since we already asked earlier. But we need to ask for each value two, three, or maybe even four times, just to put the seven values into order.

This can be a problem because it irritates the monkey.

How do we keep the number of monkey requests to a minimum? Well, we can build a table first. We use a map with seven inputs and seven outputs, turning each castaway item into a separate array reference, with each referenced array consisting of the castaway name and the pineapple count reported by the monkey:

```
my @names_and_pineapples = map {
  [ $_, ask_monkey_about($_) ]
} @castaways;
```

At this point, we asked the monkey seven questions in a row, but that's the last time we have to talk to the monkey! We now have everything we need to finish the task.

For the next step, we sort the arrayrefs, ordering them by the monkey-returned value:

```
my @sorted_names_and_pineapples = sort {
  $b->[1] <=> $a->[1];
} @names_and_pineapples;
```

In this subroutine, $a and $b are still two elements from the list of things to be sorted. When we're sorting numbers, $a and $b are numbers; when we're sorting references, $a and $b are references. We dereference them to get to the corresponding array itself, and pick out item 1 from the array (the monkey's pineapple value). Because $b appears to the left of $a, it'll be a descending sort as well. (We want a descending sort because the Professor wants the first name on the list to be the person who uses the most pineapples.)

We're almost done, but what if we just wanted the top names, rather than the names and pineapple counts? We merely need to perform another map to transform the references back to the original data:

```
my @names = map $_->[0], @sorted_names_and_pineapples;
```

Each element of the list ends up in $_, so we'll dereference that to pick out the element 0 of that array, which is just the name.

Now we have a list of names, ordered by their pineapple counts, and the monkey's off our backs, all in three easy steps.

The Schwartzian Transform

The intermediate variables between each of these steps were not necessary, except as input to the next step. We can save ourselves some brainpower by just stacking all the steps together:

```
my @names =
  map $_->[0],
  sort { $b->[1] <=> $a->[1] }
  map [ $_, ask_monkey_about($_) ],
  @castaways;
```

Because the `map` and `sort` operators are right to left, we have to read this construct from the bottom up. Take a list of `@castaways`, create some arrayrefs by asking the monkey a simple question, sort the list of arrayrefs, and then extract the names from each arrayref. This gives us the list of names in the desired order.

This construct is commonly called the *Schwartzian Transform*, which was named after Randal (but not by Randal), thanks to a Usenet posting he made many years ago. The Schwartzian Transform has since proven to be a very nice thing to have in our bag of sorting tricks.

If this transform looks like it might be too complex to memorize or come up with from first principles, it might help to look at the flexible and constant parts:

```
my @output_data =
  map $_->[0],
  sort { SORT COMPARISON USING $a->[1] AND $b->[1] }
  map [ $_, EXPENSIVE FUNCTION OF $_ ],
  @input_data;
```

The basic structure maps the original list into a list of arrayrefs, computing the expensive function only once for each; sorts those array refs, looking at the cached value of each expensive function invocation;[*] and then extracts the original values back out in the new order. All we have to do is plug in the proper two operations, and we're done. For example, to use the Schwartzian Transform to implement a case-insensitive sort, we could use code like this:[†]

```
my @output_data =
  map $_->[0],
  sort { $a->[1] cmp $b->[1] }
  map [ $_, "\U$_" ],
  @input_data;
```

Multi-Level Sort with the Schwartzian Transform

If we need to sort on more than one criterion, the Schwartzian Transform is still up to the task.

```
my @output_data =
  map $_->[0],
  sort { SORT COMPARISON USING $a->[1] AND $b->[1] or
          ANOTHER USING $a->[2] AND $b->[2] or
       YET ANOTHER USING $a->[3] AND $b->[3] }
  map [ $_, SOME FUNCTION OF $_, ANOTHER, YET ANOTHER ],
  @input_data;
```

---

[*] An *expensive* operation is one that takes a relatively long time or a relatively large amount of memory.

[†] This is an efficient way to do this only if the uppercasing operation is sufficiently expensive, which it might be if our strings tend to be very long or if we have a large enough number of them. For a small number of not-long strings, a simple `my @output_data = sort { "\U$a" cmp "\U$b"} @input_data` is probably more efficient. If in doubt, benchmark.

This code skeleton has a three-level sort comparison, using three computed values saved in the anonymous array (alongside the original data item to be sorted, which always comes first).

Recursively Defined Data

While the data we've processed with references up to this point has been rather fixed structure, sometimes we have to deal with hierarchical data, which is often defined recursively.

For Example One, consider an HTML table that has rows containing cells—and some of those cells may also contain entire tables. Example Two could be a visual representation of a filesystem consisting of directories containing files and other directories. Example Three is a company organization chart, which has managers with direct reports, some of whom may be managers themselves. And Example Four is a more complex organization chart, which can contain instances of the HTML tables of Example One, the filesystem representations of Example Two, or even entire organization charts....

We can use references to acquire, store, and process such hierarchical information. Frequently, the routines to manage the data structures end up as recursive subroutines.

Recursive algorithms deal with the unlimited complexity of their data by beginning with a base case and building upon that.[*] The base case considers what to do in the simplest case: when the leaf node has no branches, when the array is empty, when the counter is at zero. In fact, it's common to have more than one base case in various branches of a recursive algorithm. A recursive algorithm with no base case is an infinite loop.

A recursive subroutine has a branch from which it calls itself to handle a portion of the task, and a branch that doesn't call itself to handle the base cases. In Example One above, the base case could be a table cell that is empty. There could also be base cases for empty tables and table rows. In Example Two, base cases would be needed for files, and perhaps for empty directories.

For example, a recursive subroutine handling the factorial function, which is one of the simplest recursive functions, might look like:

```
sub factorial {
  my $n = shift;
  if ($n <= 1) {
    return 1;
  } else {
```

---

[*] Recursive functions should all have a base, or trivial case, where they don't need to recurse and that all other recursions can eventually reach. That is, unless we have a lot of time on our hands to let the function recurse forever.

```
        return $n * factorial($n - 1);
    }
}
```

Here we have a base case where $n is less than or equal to 1, which does not invoke the recursive instance, along with a recursive case for $n greater than 1, which calls the routine to handle a portion of the problem (i.e., compute the factorial of the next lower number).

This task would probably be solved better using iteration rather than recursion, even though the classic definition of factorial is often given as a recursive operation.

Building Recursively Defined Data

Suppose we wanted to capture information about a filesystem, including the filenames and directory names, and their included contents. Represent a directory as a hash, in which the keys are the names of the entries within the directory, and values are undef for plain files. A sample /bin directory looks like:

```
my $bin_directory = {
  cat  => undef,
  cp   => undef,
  date => undef,
  ... and so on ...
};
```

Similarly, the Skipper's home directory might also contain a personal *bin* directory (at something like *~skipper/bin*) that contains personal tools:

```
my $skipper_bin = {
  navigate           => undef,
  discipline_gilligan => undef,
  eat                => undef,
};
```

Nothing in either structure tells where the directory is located in the hierarchy. It just represents the contents of some directory.

Go up one level to the Skipper's home directory, which is likely to contain a few files along with the personal *bin* directory:

```
my $skipper_home = {
  '.cshrc'                     => undef,
    'Please_rescue_us.pdf'      => undef,
    'Things_I_should_have_packed' => undef,
  bin                          => $skipper_bin,
};
```

Ahh, notice that we have three files, but the fourth entry bin doesn't have undef for a value but rather the hash reference created earlier for the Skipper's personal *bin* directory. This is how we indicate subdirectories. If the value is undef, it's a plain file;

if it's a hash reference, we have a subdirectory, with its own files and subdirectories. Of course, we can have combined these two initializations:

```
my $skipper_home = {
  '.cshrc'                 => undef,
  Please_rescue_us.pdf     => undef,
  Things_I_should_have_packed => undef,

  bin => {
    navigate             => undef,
    discipline_gilligan  => undef,
    eat                  => undef,
  },
};
```

Now the hierarchical nature of the data starts to come into play.

Obviously, we don't want to create and maintain a data structure by changing literals in the program. We should fetch the data by using a subroutine. Write a subroutine that returns undef for a given pathname if the path is a file, or a hash reference of the directory contents if the path is a directory. The base case of looking at a file is the easiest, so let's write that:

```
sub data_for_path {
  my $path = shift;
  if (-f $path) {
    return undef;
  }
  if (-d $path) {
    ...
  }
  warn "$path is neither a file nor a directory\n";
  return undef;
}
```

If the Skipper calls this on *.cshrc*, he'll get back an undef value, indicating that a file was seen.

Now for the directory part. We need a hash reference, which we declare as a named hash inside the subroutine. For each element of the hash, we call ourselves to populate the value of that hash element. It goes something like this:

```
sub data_for_path {
  my $path = shift;
  if (-f $path or -l $path) {        # files or symbolic links
    return undef;
  }
  if (-d $path) {
    my %directory;
    opendir PATH, $path or die "Cannot opendir $path: $!";
    my @names = readdir PATH;
    closedir PATH;
    for my $name (@names) {
        next if $name eq '.' or $name eq '..';
```

```
        $directory{$name} = data_for_path("$path/$name");
      }
    return \%directory;
    }
  warn "$path is neither a file nor a directory\n";
  return undef;
}
```

The base cases in this recursive algorithm are the files and symbolic links. This algorithm wouldn't correctly traverse the filesystem if it followed symbolic links to directories as if they were true (hard) links, since it could end up in a circular loop if the symlink pointed to a directory that contained the symlink.* It would also fail to correctly traverse a malformed filesystem—that is, one in which the directories form a ring rather than a tree structure, say. Although malformed filesystems may not often be an issue, recursive algorithms in general are vulnerable to errors in the structure of the recursive data.

For each file within the directory being examined, the response from the recursive call to data_for_path is undef. This populates most elements of the hash. When the reference to the named hash is returned, the reference becomes a reference to an anonymous hash because the name immediately goes out of scope. (The data itself doesn't change, but the number of ways in which we can access the data changes.)

If there is a subdirectory, the nested subroutine call uses readdir to extract the contents of that directory and returns a hash reference, which is inserted into the hash structure created by the caller.

At first, it may look a bit mystifying, but if we walk through the code slowly, we'll see it's always doing the right thing. Test the results of this subroutine by calling it on . (the current directory) and inspecting the result:

```
use Data::Dumper;
print Dumper(data_for_path('.'));
```

Obviously, this will be more interesting if our current directory contains subdirectories.

Displaying Recursively Defined Data

The Dumper routine of Data::Dumper displays the output nicely, but what if we don't like the format being used? We can write a routine to display the data. Again, for recursively defined data, a recursive subroutine is usually the key.

To dump the data, we need to know the name of the directory at the top of the tree, because that's not stored within the structure:

```
sub dump_data_for_path {
        my $path = shift;
```

---

* Not that any of us have ever done that and wondered why the program took forever. The second time really wasn't our fault anyway, and the third time was just bad luck. That's our story and we're sticking to it.

```
        my $data = shift;

        if (not defined $data) { # plain file
                print "$path\n";
                return;
                }
        ...
        }
```

For a plain file, dump the pathname; for a directory, $data is a hash reference. Let's walk through the keys and dump the values:

```
sub dump_data_for_path {
        my $path = shift;
        my $data = shift;

        if (not defined $data) { # plain file
                print "$path\n";
                return;
        }

        my %directory = %$data;

        for (sort keys %directory) {
                dump_data_for_path("$path/$_", $directory{$_});
        }
}
```

For each element of the directory, we pass a path consisting of the incoming path followed by the current directory entry, and the data pointer is either undef for a file or a subdirectory hash reference for another directory. We can see the results by running:

```
dump_data_for_path('.', data_for_path('.'));
```

Again, this is more interesting in a directory that has subdirectories, but the output should be similar to:

```
find . -print
```

from the shell prompt.

Exercises

You can find the answers to these exercises in "Answers for Chapter 9" in the Appendix.

Exercise 1 [15 min]

Using the glob operator, a naive sort of every name in the */bin* directory by their relative sizes might be written as:

```
my @sorted = sort { -s $a <=> -s $b } glob "/bin/*";
```

Rewrite this using the Schwartzian Transform technique.

If you don't have many files in the */bin* directory, perhaps because you don't have a Unix machine, change the argument to glob as needed.

Exercise 2 [15 min]

Read up on the Benchmark module, included with Perl. Write a program that will answer the question "How much does using the Schwartzian Transform speed up the task of Exercise 1?"

Exercise 3 [10 min]

Using a Schwartzian Transform, read a list of words, and sort them in "dictionary order." Dictionary order ignores all capitalization and internal punctuation. Hint: the following transformation might be useful:

```
my $string = 'Mary-Ann';
$string =~ tr/A-Z/a-z/;      # force all lowercase
$string =~ tr/a-z//cd;       # strip all but a-z from the string
print $string;               # prints "maryann"
```

Be sure you don't mangle the data! If the input includes the Professor and the skipper, the output should have them listed in that order, with that capitalization.

Exercise 4 [20 min]

Modify the recursive directory dumping routine so it shows the nested directories through indentation. An empty directory should show up as:

```
sandbar, an empty directory
```

while a nonempty directory should appear with nested contents, indented two spaces:

```
uss_minnow, with contents:
  anchor
  broken_radio
  galley, with contents:
    captain_crunch_cereal
    gallon_of_milk
    tuna_fish_sandwich
  life_preservers
```

## CHAPTER 10

Building Larger Programs

This chapter looks at how to break up a program into pieces and includes some of the concerns that arise when we put those pieces back together again, or when many people work together on the same program.

The Cure for the Common Code

The Skipper writes many Perl programs to provide navigation for all the common ports of call for the *Minnow*. He finds himself cutting and pasting a very common routine into each program:

```perl
sub turn_toward_heading {
  my $new_heading = shift;
  my $current_heading = current_heading( );
  print "Current heading is ", $current_heading, ".\n";
  print "Come about to $new_heading ";
  my $direction = 'right';
  my $turn = ($new_heading - $current_heading) % 360;
  if ($turn > 180) { # long way around
    $turn = 360 - $turn;
    $direction = 'left';
  }
  print "by turning $direction $turn degrees.\n";
}
```

This routine gives the shortest turn to make from the current heading (returned by the subroutine current_heading( )) to a new heading (given as the first parameter to the subroutine).

The first line of this subroutine might have read instead:

```perl
my ($new_heading) = @_;
```

This is mostly a style call: in both cases, the first parameter ends up in $new_heading. However, we've seen that removing the items from @_ as they are identified does have some advantages. So, we stick (mostly) with the "shifting" style of argument parsing. Now back to the matter at hand....

After writing a dozen programs using this routine, the Skipper realizes that the output is excessively chatty when he's already taken the time to steer the proper course (or perhaps simply started drifting in the proper direction). After all, if the current heading is 234 degrees and he needs to turn to 234 degrees, we see:

```
Current heading is 234.
Come about to 234 by turning right 0 degrees.
```

How annoying! The Skipper decides to fix this problem by checking for a zero turn value:

```perl
sub turn_toward_heading {
  my $new_heading = shift;
  my $current_heading = current_heading( );
  print "Current heading is ", $current_heading, ".\n";
  my $direction = 'right';
  my $turn = ($new_heading - $current_heading) % 360;
  unless ($turn) {
    print "On course (good job!).\n";
    return;
  }
  print "Come about to $new_heading ";
  if ($turn > 180) { # long way around
    $turn = 360 - $turn;
    $direction = 'left';
  }
  print "by turning $direction $turn degrees.\n";
}
```

Great. The new subroutine works nicely in the current navigation program. However, because he had previously cut and pasted it into a half-dozen other navigation programs, those other programs will still annoy the Skipper with extraneous turning messages.

The Skipper needs a way to write the code in one place and then share it among many programs. And, like most things in Perl, there's more than one way to do it.

Inserting Code with eval

The Skipper can save disk space (and brain space) by bringing the definition for turn_toward_heading out into a separate file. For example, suppose the Skipper figures out a half-dozen common subroutines related to navigating the *Minnow* that he seems to use in most or all of the programs he's writing for the task. He can put them in a separate file called navigation.pm, which consists only of the needed subroutines.

But now, how can we tell Perl to pull in that program snippet from another file? We could do it the hard way, using the string form of eval that we discussed in Chapter 2.

```perl
sub load_common_subroutines {
  open MORE_CODE, 'navigation.pm' or die "navigation.pm: $!";
```

```
    undef $/; # enable slurp mode
    my $more_code = <MORE_CODE>;
    close MORE_CODE;
    eval $more_code;
    die $@ if $@;
}
```

Perl reads the code from navigation.pm into the $more_code variable. We then use eval to process that text as Perl code. Any lexical variables in $more_code remain local to the evaluated code.[*] If there's a syntax error, Perl sets the $@ variable and causes the subroutine to die with the appropriate error message.

Now, instead of a few dozen lines of common subroutines to place in each file, we simply have one subroutine to insert in each file.

But that's not very nice, especially if we need to keep doing this kind of task repeatedly. Luckily, Perl has several ways to help us out.

Using do

The Skipper placed a few common navigation subroutines into navigation.pm. If the Skipper merely inserts:

```
do 'navigation.pm';
die $@ if $@;
```

into his typical navigation program, it's almost the same as if the eval code were executed right at that point in the program.[†]

That is, the do operator acts as if the code from navigation.pm were incorporated into the current program, although in its own scope block, so that lexicals (my variables) and most directives (such as use strict) from the included file don't leak into the main program.

Now the Skipper can safely update and maintain one copy of the common subroutines without having to copy and recopy all the fixes and extensions into the many separate navigation programs he creates and uses. Figure 10-1 illustrates how the Skipper can use his common library.

Of course, this requires a bit of discipline, because breaking the expected interface of a given subroutine now breaks many programs instead of just one.[‡] The Skipper needs to give special thought to his design for reusable components and modularity

---

[*] Oddly, the variable $more_code is also visible to the evaluated code, not that it is of any use to change that variable during the eval.

[†] Except in regard to @INC, %INC, and missing file handling, which we'll show later.

[‡] In later chapters, we'll show how to set up tests to be used while maintaining reused code.

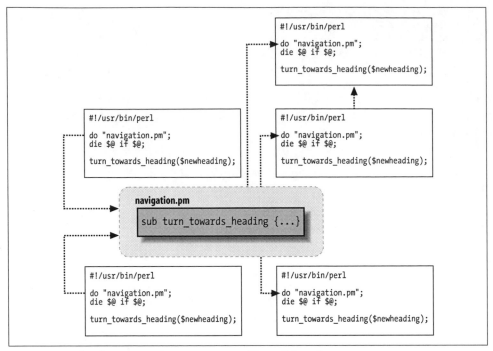

Figure 10-1. The Skipper uses the navigation.pm file in all his other navigation programs

design. We'll presume the Skipper has had some experience at that, but we'll show some more on that in later chapters.

By placing some of the code into a separate file, other programmers can reuse the Skipper's routines, and vice versa. If Gilligan writes a routine to drop_anchor( ) and places it in the file drop_anchor.pm, then the Skipper can use Gilligan's code by including his library:

```
do 'drop_anchor.pm';
die $@ if $@;
...
drop_anchor( ) if at_dock( ) or in_port( );
```

Thus, the code that we bring in from separate files permits easy maintenance and interprogrammer cooperation.

While the code we brought in from a .pm file can have direct executable statements, it's much more common to simply define subroutines that we can load using do.

Going back to that drop_anchor.pm library for a second, what if the Skipper wrote a program that needed to "drop anchor" as well as navigate?

```
do 'drop_anchor.pm';
die $@ if $@;
do 'navigation.pm';
die $@ if $@;
```

```
...
turn_toward_heading(90);
...
drop_anchor( ) if at_dock( );
```

That works fine and dandy. The subroutines defined in both libraries are available to this program.

Using require

Suppose navigation.pm itself also pulls in drop_anchor.pm for some common navigation task. Perl reads the file once directly and then again while processing the navigation package. This needlessly redefines drop_anchor( ). Worse than that, if we have warnings enabled,* we'll get a warning from Perl that we've redefined the subroutine, even if it's the same definition.

We need a mechanism that tracks which files we've brought in and then brings them in only once. Perl has such an operation, called require. Change the previous code to simply:

```
require 'drop_anchor.pm';
require 'navigation.pm';
```

The require operator keeps track of the files Perl has read.† Once Perl has processed a file successfully, it simply ignores any further require operations on that same file. This means that even if navigation.pm contains require "drop_anchor.pm", Perl imports the drop_anchor.pm file exactly once, and we'll get no annoying error messages about duplicate subroutine definitions (see Figure 10-2). Most importantly, we'll also save time by not processing the file more than once.

The require operator also has two additional features:

- Any syntax error in the required file causes the program to die; thus, the many die $@ if $@ statements are unnecessary.
- The last expression evaluated in the file must return a true value.

Because of the second point, most files evaluated for require have a cryptic 1; as their last line of code. This ensures that the last evaluated expression is, in fact, true. Try to carry on this tradition as well.

Originally, the mandatory true value was intended as a way for an included file to signal to the invoker that the code was processed successfully and that no error condition existed. However, nearly everyone has adopted the die if ... strategy instead, deeming the "last expression evaluated is false" strategy a mere historic annoyance.

---

* You *are* using warnings, right? You can enable them with either -w or use warnings;.

† In the %INC hash, as described in the entry for require in the *perlfunc* documentation.

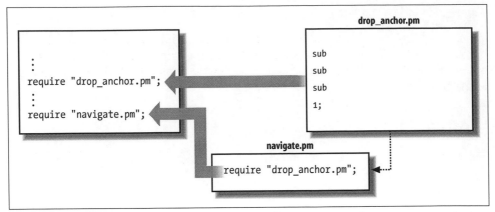

Figure 10-2. Once Perl brings in the drop_anchor.pm file, it ignores another attempt to require it

require and @INC

So far, the examples have glossed over how we've set up the directory structure of where the main code and the included files are located. That's because it "just works" for the simplest case where we have a program and its libraries in the same directory and we run the program from that directory.

Things get a bit more complicated when the libraries aren't in the current directory. In fact, Perl searches for libraries along a library search path, similar to what the shell does with the PATH environment variable. The current directory (represented in Unix by a single dot) is an element of the search path. So, as long as our libraries are in our current working directory, everything is fine.

The search path is a list of elements in the special @INC array, as we briefly discussed in Chapter 3. By default, the array contains the current directory and a half-dozen or so directories specified by the person who compiled Perl. Typing perl -V on the command line shows what these directories are, in the last dozen lines of the output. Also, the following command displays just the @INC directories:[*]

```
perl -le 'print for @INC'
```

Except for . in that list, we probably won't be able to write to any of the other directories unless we're the person responsible for maintaining Perl on our machine, in which case, we should be able to write to all of them. The remaining directories are where Perl searches for system-wide libraries and modules, as we'll see later.

---

[*] On a Windows machine, use double quotes instead of single quotes on the command line.

Extending @INC

We may run into some cases where we can't install modules in the pre-configured directories in @INC. We can change @INC itself before the require, so Perl searches our directories too. The @INC array is an ordinary array, so have the Skipper add a directory below his home directory to the mix:

```
unshift @INC, '/home/skipper/perl-lib';
```

Now, in addition to searching the standard directories and the current directory, Perl searches the Skipper's personal Perl library. In fact, Perl searches in that directory first, since it is the first one in @INC. By using unshift rather than push, Perl resolves any conflict in names between the Skipper's private files and the system-installed files, with the Skipper's file-taking precedence.

Normally we want to ensure that this happens before anything else, so we can wrap it in a BEGIN block. Perl executes the code in the BEGIN block during the compile phase before the require executes at runtime. Otherwise, Perl executes statements in the order that it finds them, and we have to ensure that our unshift shows up before our require.

```
BEGIN {
  unshift @INC, '/home/skipper/perl-lib';
};
```

This is such a common operation, though, that Perl has a pragma for it. The pragma makes everything happen before runtime, so we'll get what we expect. It puts the directories we specify at the beginning of @INC, just like we did before.

```
use lib qw(/home/skipper/perl-lib);
```

We don't always have to know the path ahead of time, either. In the previous examples, we've hardcoded the paths. If we don't know what those will be because we're passing code around to several machines, the FindBin module, which comes with Perl, can help. It finds the full path to the script directory so we can use it to build paths.

```
use FindBin qw($Bin);
```

Now, in $Bin is the path to the directory that holds our script. If we have our libraries in the same directory, our next line can be:

```
use lib $Bin;
```

If we have the libraries in a directory close to the script directory, we put the right path components together to make it work.

```
use lib "$Bin/lib";    # in a subdirectory

use lib "$Bin/../lib"; # up one, then down into lib
```

So, if we know the relative path from the script directory, we don't have to hardcode the whole path. This makes the script more portable.

Extending @INC with PERL5LIB

The Skipper must edit each program that uses his private libraries to include those lines from the previous section. If that seems like too much editing, he can instead set the PERL5LIB environment variable to the directory name. For example, in the C shell, he'd use the line:

```
setenv PERL5LIB /home/skipper/perl-lib
```

In Bourne-style shells, he'd use something like:

```
PERL5LIB=/home/skipper/perl-lib; export PERL5LIB
```

The Skipper can set PERL5LIB once and forget about it. However, unless Gilligan has the same PERL5LIB environment variable, his program will fail! While PERL5LIB is useful for personal use, we can't rely on it for programs we intend to share with others. (And we can't make our entire team of programmers add a common PERL5LIB variable. Believe us, we've tried.)

The PERL5LIB variable can include multiple directories separated by colons. Perl inserts all specified directories at the beginning of @INC.

While a system administrator might add a setting of PERL5LIB to a system-wide startup script, most people frown on that. The purpose of PERL5LIB is to enable non-administrators to extend Perl to recognize additional directories. If a system administrator wants additional directories, he merely needs to recompile and reinstall Perl.

Extending @INC with -I

If Gilligan recognizes that one of the Skipper's programs is missing the proper directive, Gilligan can either add the proper PERL5LIB variable or invoke Perl directly with one or more -I options. For example, to invoke the Skipper's get_us_home program, the command line might be something like:

```
perl -I/home/skipper/perl-lib /home/skipper/bin/get_us_home
```

Obviously, it's easier for Gilligan if the program itself defines the extra libraries. But sometimes just adding a -I fixes things right up.* This works even if Gilligan can't edit the Skipper's program. He still has to be able to read it, of course, but Gilligan can use this technique to try a new version of his library with the Skipper's program, for example.

---

* Extending @INC with either PERL5LIB or—I also automatically adds the version—and architecture-specific subdirectories of the specified directories. Adding these directories automatically simplifies the task of installing Perl modules that include architecture- or version-sensitive components, such as compiled C code.

The Problem of Namespace Collisions

Sometimes the Skipper runs a ship into an island, but sometimes the collision involved is just a couple of names in a Perl program. Suppose that the Skipper has added all his cool and useful routines to navigation.pm and that Gilligan has incorporated the library into his own navigation package, head_toward_island:

```
#!/usr/bin/perl

require 'navigation.pm';

sub turn_toward_port {
  turn_toward_heading(compute_heading_to_island(  ));
}

sub compute_heading_to_island {
  .. code here ..
}

.. more program here ..
```

Gilligan then has his program debugged (perhaps with the aid of a smart person whom we'll call "the Professor"), and everything works well.

However, now the Skipper decides to modify his navigation.pm library, adding a routine called turn_toward_port that makes a 45-degree turn toward the left (known as "port" in nautical jargon).

Gilligan's program will fail in a catastrophic way as soon as he tries to head to port: he'll start steering the ship in circles! The problem is that the Perl compiler first compiles turn_toward_port from Gilligan's main program, then when Perl evaluates the require at runtime, it redefines turn_toward_port as the Skipper's definition. Sure, if Gilligan has warnings enabled, he'll notice something is wrong, but why should he have to count on that?

The problem is that Gilligan defined turn_toward_port as meaning "turn toward the port on the island," while the Skipper defined it as "turn toward the left." How do we resolve this?

One way is to require that the Skipper put an explicit prefix in front of every name defined in the library, say, navigation_. Thus, Gilligan's program ends up looking like:

```
#!/usr/bin/perl

require 'navigation.pm';

sub turn_toward_port {
  navigation_turn_toward_heading(compute_heading_to_island(  ));
}

sub compute_heading_to_island {
  .. code here ..
}
```

```
.. more program here ..
```

Clearly, the `navigation_turn_toward_heading` comes from the `navigation.pm` file. This is great for Gilligan but awkward for the Skipper, as his file now has longer subroutine names:

```
sub navigation_turn_toward_heading {
  .. code here ..
}

sub navigation_turn_toward_port {
  .. code here ..
}

1;
```

Yes, every scalar, array, hash, filehandle, or subroutine now has to have a `navigation_` prefix in front of it to guarantee that the names won't collide with any potential users of the library. Obviously, for that old sailor, this ain't gonna float his boat. What do we do instead?

Packages as Namespace Separators

If the name prefix of the last example didn't have to be spelled out on every use, things would work much better. We can improve the situation by using a package:

```
package Navigation;

sub turn_toward_heading {
  .. code here ..
}

sub turn_toward_port {
  .. code here ..
}

1;
```

The package declaration at the beginning of this file tells Perl to virtually insert `Navigation::` in front of most names within the file. Thus, the code above practically says:

```
sub Navigation::turn_toward_heading {
  .. code here ..
}

sub Navigation::turn_toward_port {
  .. code here ..
}

1;
```

Now when Gilligan uses this file, he simply adds Navigation:: to the subroutines defined in the library and leaves the Navigation:: prefix off for subroutines he defines on his own:

```
#!/usr/bin/perl

require 'navigation.pm';

sub turn_toward_port {
  Navigation::turn_toward_heading(compute_heading_to_island(  ));
}

sub compute_heading_to_island {
  .. code here ..
}

.. more program here ..
```

Package names are like variable names: they consist of alphanumerics and underscores but can't begin with a digit. Also, for reasons explained in the perlmodlib documentation, a package name should begin with a capital letter and not overlap an existing CPAN or core module name. Package names can also have multiple names separated by double colons, such as Minnow::Navigation and Minnow::Food::Storage.

Nearly every scalar, array, hash, subroutine, and filehandle name* is actually prefixed by the current package, unless the name already contains one or more double-colon markers.

So, in navigation.pm, we can use variables such as:†

```
package Navigation;
@homeport = (21.283, -157.842);

sub turn_toward_port {
  .. code ..
}
```

We can refer to the @homeport variable in the main code with its full package specification:

```
@destination = @Navigation::homeport;
```

If every name has a package name inserted in front of it, what about names in the main program? Yes, they are also in a package, called main. It's as if package main; were at the beginning of each file. Thus, to keep Gilligan from having to say Navigation::turn_toward_heading, the navigation.pm file can say:

```
sub main::turn_toward_heading {
  .. code here ..
}
```

* Except lexicals, as we'll show in a moment.

† Trivia note: 21.283 degrees north, 157.842 degrees west is the location of the real-life marina where the opening shot of a famous television series was filmed. Check it out on Google Maps if you don't believe us.

Now the subroutine is defined in the main package, not the Navigation package. This isn't an optimal solution (we'll show better solutions in Chapter 15 when we talk about Exporter), but at least there's nothing sacred or terribly unique about main compared to any other package.

This is what the modules in Chapter 3 were doing when they imported symbols into our scripts, but we didn't tell you the whole story then. Those modules imported the subroutines and variables into the current package (again, that's main in our scripts, usually). That is, those symbols are only available in that package unless we use the full package specification. We'll get more into how this works later.

Scope of a Package Directive

All files start as if we had said package main;.* Any package directive remains in effect until the next package directive, unless that package directive is inside a curly-braced scope. In that case, Perl remembers the prior package and restores it when that scope ends. Here's an example:

```
package Navigation;

{  # start scope block
  package main;  # now in package main

  sub turn_toward_heading {  # main::turn_toward_heading
    .. code here ..
  }

}  # end scope block

# back to package Navigation

sub turn_toward_port { # Navigation::turn_toward_port
  .. code here ..
}
```

The current package is lexically scoped, similar to the scope of my variables, narrowed to the innermost-enclosing brace pair or file in which we introduced the package.

Most libraries have only one package declaration at the top of the file. Most programs leave the package as the default main package. However it's nice to know that we can temporarily have a different current package.†

---

* Perl doesn't make us create an explicit main( ) loop like C. Perl knows that every script needs one, so it gives it to us for free.

† Some names are always in package main regardless of the current package: ARGV, ARGVOUT, ENV, INC, SIG, STDERR, STDIN, and STDOUT. We can always refer to @INC and be assured of getting @main::INC. The punctuation mark variables, such as $_, $2, and $!, are either all lexicals or forced into package main, so when we write $., we never get $Navigation::. by mistake.

Packages and Lexicals

A lexical variable (a variable introduced with my) isn't prefixed by the current package because package variables are always *global*: we can always reference a package variable if we know its full name. A lexical variable is usually temporary and accessible for only a portion of the program. If we declare a lexical variable, then using that name without a package prefix gets the lexical variable. A package prefix ensures that we are accessing a package variable and never a lexical variable.

For example, suppose a subroutine within navigation.pm declares a lexical @homeport variable. Any mention of @homeport will then be the newly introduced lexical variable, but a fully qualified mention of @Navigation::homeport accesses the package variable instead.

```
package Navigation;
@homeport = (21.283, -157.842);

sub get_me_home {
  my @homeport;

  .. @homeport ..  # refers to the lexical variable
  .. @Navigation::homeport ..  # refers to the package variable

}

  .. @homeport ..  # refers to the package variable
```

Obviously, this can lead to confusing code, so we shouldn't introduce such duplication needlessly. The results are completely predictable, though.

Exercises

You can find the answers to these exercises in "Answers for Chapter 10" in the Appendix.

Exercise 1 [25 min]

The Oogaboogoo natives on the island have unusual names for the days and months. Here is some simple but not very well-written code from Gilligan. Fix it up, add a conversion function for the month names, and make the whole thing into a library. For extra credit, add suitable error checking and consider what should be in the documentation.

```
@day = qw(ark dip wap sen pop sep kir);
sub number_to_day_name { my $num = shift @_; $day[$num]; }
@month = qw(diz pod bod rod sip wax lin sen kun fiz nap dep);
```

Exercise 2 [15 min]

Make a program that uses your library and the following code to print out a message, such as Today is dip, sen 15, 2011, meaning that today is a Monday in August. (Hint: the year and month numbers returned by localtime may not be what you'd expect, so you need to check the documentation.)

```
my($sec, $min, $hour, $mday, $mon, $year, $wday) = localtime;
```

## CHAPTER 11

Introduction to Objects

Object-oriented programming (OOP) helps programmers run code sooner and maintain it easier by organizing the code into things that we can name. We need a little more infrastructure to get going with objects, but in the long run, it's worth it.

The benefits of OOP become worthwhile when our program (including all external libraries and modules) exceeds about N lines of code. Unfortunately, nobody can agree on what the value of N is, but for Perl programs, it's arguably around 1,000 lines of code. If our whole program is only a couple hundred lines of code, using objects is probably overkill.

Like references, Perl's object architecture was grafted on after a substantial amount of existing pre-Perl 5 code was already in use, so we had to ensure that it wouldn't break existing syntax. Amazingly, the only additional syntax to achieve object nirvana is the *method call*, introduced shortly. But the meaning of that syntax requires a bit of study, so let's proceed.

The Perl object architecture relies heavily on packages, subroutines, and references, so if you're skipping around in this book, please go back to the beginning. Ready? Here we go.

If We Could Talk to the Animals...

Obviously, the castaways can't survive on coconuts and pineapples alone. Luckily for them, a barge carrying random farm animals crashed on the island not long after they arrived, and the castaways began farming and raising animals.

Let's listen to those animals for a moment:

```
sub Cow::speak {
  print "a Cow goes moooo!\n";
}
sub Horse::speak {
  print "a Horse goes neigh!\n";
}
```

```
sub Sheep::speak {
  print "a Sheep goes baaaah!\n";
}

Cow::speak;
Horse::speak;
Sheep::speak;
```

This results in:

```
a Cow goes moooo!
a Horse goes neigh!
a Sheep goes baaaah!
```

Nothing spectacular here: simple subroutines, albeit from separate packages, and called using the full package name. Let's create an entire pasture:

```
sub Cow::speak {
  print "a Cow goes moooo!\n";
}
sub Horse::speak {
  print "a Horse goes neigh!\n";
}
sub Sheep::speak {
  print "a Sheep goes baaaah!\n";
}

my @pasture = qw(Cow Cow Horse Sheep Sheep);
foreach my $beast (@pasture) {
  &{$beast."::speak"};                    # Symbolic coderef
}
```

This results in:

```
a Cow goes moooo!
a Cow goes moooo!
a Horse goes neigh!
a Sheep goes baaaah!
a Sheep goes baaaah!
```

Wow. That symbolic coderef dereferencing there in the body of the loop is pretty nasty. We're counting on no strict 'refs' mode, certainly not recommended for larger programs.* And why was that necessary? Because the name of the package seems inseparable from the name of the subroutine we want to invoke within that package.

Or is it?

---

* Although all examples in this book should be valid Perl code, some examples in this chapter will break the rules enforced by use strict to make them easier to understand. By the end of the chapter, though, we'll show how to make strict-compliant code again.

Introducing the Method Invocation Arrow

A *class* is a group of things with similar behaviors and traits. For now, let's say that Class->method invokes subroutine method in package Class. A method is the object-oriented version of the subroutine, so we'll say "method" from now on.* That's not completely accurate, but we'll go on one step at a time. Let's use it like so:

```
sub Cow::speak {
  print "a Cow goes moooo!\n";
}
sub Horse::speak {
  print "a Horse goes neigh!\n";
}
sub Sheep::speak {
  print "a Sheep goes baaaah!\n";
}

Cow->speak;
Horse->speak;
Sheep->speak;
```

And once again, this results in:

```
a Cow goes moooo!
a Horse goes neigh!
a Sheep goes baaaah!
```

That's not fun yet. We've got the same number of characters, all constant, no variables. However, the parts are separable now:

```
my $beast = 'Cow';
$beast->speak;                  # invokes Cow->speak
```

Ahh! Now that the package name is separated from the subroutine name, we can use a variable package name. This time, we've got something that works even when we enable use strict 'refs'.

Take the arrow invocation and put it back in the barnyard example:

```
sub Cow::speak {
  print "a Cow goes moooo!\n";
}
sub Horse::speak {
  print "a Horse goes neigh!\n";
}
sub Sheep::speak {
  print "a Sheep goes baaaah!\n";
}

my @pasture = qw(Cow Cow Horse Sheep Sheep);
```

---

* In Perl, there really isn't a difference between a subroutine and a method. They both get an argument list in @_, and we have to make sure we do the right thing.

```
foreach my $beast (@pasture) {
  $beast->speak;
}
```

There! Now all the animals are talking, and safely at that, without the use of symbolic coderefs.

But look at all that common code. Each speak method has a similar structure: a print operator and a string that contains common text, except for two words. One of OOP's core principles is to minimize common code: if we write it only once, we'll save time. If we test and debug it only once, we'll save more time.

Now that we know more about what the method invocation arrow actually does, we've got an easier way to do the same thing.

The Extra Parameter of Method Invocation

The invocation of:

```
Class->method(@args)
```

attempts to invoke the subroutine Class::method as:

```
Class::method('Class', @args);
```

(If it can't find the method, inheritance kicks in, but we'll show that later.) This means that we get the class name as the first parameter, or the only parameter, if no arguments are given. We can rewrite the Sheep speaking method as:

```
sub Sheep::speak {
  my $class = shift;
  print "a $class goes baaaah!\n";
}
```

The other two animals come out similarly:

```
sub Cow::speak {
  my $class = shift;
  print "a $class goes moooo!\n";
}
sub Horse::speak {
  my $class = shift;
  print "a $class goes neigh!\n";
}
```

In each case, $class gets the value appropriate for that method. But once again, we have a lot of similar structure. Can we factor out that commonality even further? Yes—by calling another method in the same class.

Calling a Second Method to Simplify Things

We can call out from speak to a helper method called sound. This method provides the constant text for the sound itself:

```
{ package Cow;
  sub sound { 'moooo' }
  sub speak {
    my $class = shift;
    print "a $class goes ", $class->sound, "!\n";
  }
}
```

Now, when we call Cow->speak, we get a $class of Cow in speak. This, in turn, selects the Cow->sound method, which returns moooo. How different would this be for the Horse?

```
{ package Horse;
  sub sound { 'neigh' }
  sub speak {
    my $class = shift;
    print "a $class goes ", $class->sound, "!\n";
  }
}
```

Only the name of the package and the specific sound change. So can we share the definition for speak between the cow and the horse? Yes, with inheritance!

Now let's define a common method package called Animal with the definition for speak:

```
{ package Animal;
  sub speak {
    my $class = shift;
    print "a $class goes ", $class->sound, "!\n";
  }
}
```

Then, for each animal, we can say it inherits from Animal, along with the animal-specific sound:

```
{ package Cow;
  @ISA = qw(Animal);
  sub sound { "moooo" }
}
```

Note the added @ISA array. We'll get to that in a minute.

What happens when we invoke Cow->speak now?

First, Perl constructs the argument list. In this case, it's just Cow. Then Perl looks for Cow::speak. That's not there, so Perl checks for the inheritance array @Cow::ISA. It's there and contains the single name Animal.

Perl next checks for speak inside Animal instead, as in Animal::speak. That found, Perl invokes that method with the already frozen argument list, as if we had said:

```
Animal::speak('Cow');
```

Inside the Animal::speak method, $class becomes Cow as the first argument is shifted off. When we get to the step of invoking $class->sound while performing the print, it looks for Cow->sound:

```
print "a $class goes ", $class->sound, "!\n";
# but $class is Cow, so...
print 'a Cow goes ', Cow->sound, "!\n";
# which invokes Cow->sound, returning 'moooo', so
print 'a Cow goes ', 'moooo', "!\n";
```

and we get our desired output.

A Few Notes About @ISA

This magical @ISA variable (pronounced "is a" not "ice-uh") declares that Cow "is a" Animal.* Note that it's an array, not a simple single value, because on rare occasions it makes sense to have more than one parent class searched for the missing methods. We'll show more about that later.

If Animal also had an @ISA, Perl would check there too.† Typically, each @ISA has only one element (multiple elements means multiple inheritance and multiple head-aches), so we get a nice tree of inheritance.‡

When we turn on use strict, we'll get complaints on @ISA because it's not a variable containing an explicit package name, nor is it a lexical (my) variable. We can't make it a lexical variable, though: it has to belong to the package to be found by the inheritance mechanism.

There are a couple of straightforward ways to handle the declaration and setting of @ISA. The easiest is to just spell out the package name:

```
@Cow::ISA = qw(Animal);
```

We can also allow it as an implicitly named package variable:

```
package Cow;
use vars qw(@ISA);
@ISA = qw(Animal);
```

If you're on a recent-enough Perl (5.6 or later), you can use the our declaration to shorten it to:

---

* ISA is actually a linguistic term. Once again, Larry Wall's background as a linguist has come back to influence Perl.

† The search is recursive, depth-first, and left to right in each @ISA.

‡ There is also inheritance through UNIVERSAL and AUTOLOAD; see the perlobj manpage for the whole story.

```
package Cow;
our @ISA = qw(Animal);
```

However, if you think your code might be used by people stuck with Perl 5.005 or earlier, it's best to avoid our.

If we're bringing in the class from outside, via an object-oriented module, we can change:

```
package Cow;
use Animal;
use vars qw(@ISA);
@ISA = qw(Animal);
```

to just:

```
package Cow;
use base qw(Animal);
```

That's pretty darn compact. Furthermore, use base has the advantage that it's performed at compile time, eliminating a few potential errors from setting @ISA at runtime, like some of the other solutions.

Overriding the Methods

Let's add a mouse that can barely be heard:

```
{ package Animal;
  sub speak {
    my $class = shift;
    print "a $class goes ", $class->sound, "!\n";
  }
}
{ package Mouse;
  @ISA = qw(Animal);
  sub sound { 'squeak' }
  sub speak {
    my $class = shift;
    print "a $class goes ", $class->sound, "!\n";
    print "[but you can barely hear it!]\n";
  }
}

Mouse->speak;
```

which results in:

```
a Mouse goes squeak!
[but you can barely hear it!]
```

Here, Mouse has its own speaking routine, so Mouse->speak doesn't immediately invoke Animal->speak. This is known as *overriding*. We use overriding to shadow the method in the derived class (Mouse) because we have a specialized version of the routine, instead of calling the more general base class's method (in Animal). In fact, we didn't even need to initialize @Mouse::ISA to say that a Mouse was an Animal, because all the methods needed for speak are defined completely with Mouse.

We've now duplicated some of the code from Animal->speak; this can be a maintenance headache. For example, suppose someone decides that the word goes in the output of the Animal class is a bug. Now the maintainer of that class changes goes to says. Our mice will still say goes, which means the code still has the bug. The problem is that we invoked cut and paste to duplicate code, and in OOP, that's a sin. We should reuse code through inheritance, not by cut and paste.

How can we avoid that? Can we say somehow that a Mouse does everything any other Animal does, but add in the extra comment? Sure!

As our first attempt, let's invoke the Animal::speak method directly:

```
{ package Animal;
  sub speak {
    my $class = shift;
    print "a $class goes ", $class->sound, "!\n";
  }
}
{ package Mouse;
  @ISA = qw(Animal);
  sub sound { 'squeak' }
  sub speak {
    my $class = shift;
    Animal::speak($class);
    print "[but you can barely hear it!]\n";
  }
}
```

Note that because we've stopped using the method arrow, we have to include the $class parameter (almost surely the value Mouse) as the first parameter to Animal::speak.

Why did we stop using the arrow? Well, if we invoke Animal->speak there, the first parameter to the method is "Animal" not "Mouse" and when the time comes for it to call for the sound, it won't have the right class to select the proper methods for this object.

Invoking Animal::speak directly is a mess, however. What if Animal::speak didn't exist before, and it inherited from a class mentioned in @Animal::ISA? For example, suppose the code was:

```
{ package LivingCreature;
  sub speak { ... }
  ...
}
{ package Animal;
  @ISA = qw(LivingCreature);
  # no definition for speak(  )
  ...
}
{ package Mouse;
```

```
    @ISA = qw(Animal);
    sub speak {
      ...
      Animal::speak(  ... );
    }
    ...
}
```

Because we no longer use the method arrow, we get one and only one chance to hit the right method because we're treating it like a regular subroutine with no inheritance magic. We'll look for it in Animal and not find it, and the program aborts.

The Animal class name is now hardwired into the method selection. This is a mess if someone maintains the code, changing @ISA for Mouse, and doesn't notice Animal there in speak. Thus, this is probably not the right way to go.

Starting the Search from a Different Place

A better solution is to tell Perl to search from a different place in the inheritance chain:

```
{ package Animal;
  sub speak {
    my $class = shift;
    print "a $class goes ", $class->sound, "!\n";
  }
}
{ package Mouse;
  @ISA = qw(Animal);
  sub sound { 'squeak' }
  sub speak {
    my $class = shift;
    $class->Animal::speak(@_);
    print "[but you can barely hear it!]\n";
  }
}
```

Ahh. As ugly as this is, it works. Using this syntax, start with Animal to find speak and use all of Animal's inheritance chain if not found immediately. The first parameter is $class (because we're using an arrow again), so the found speak method gets Mouse as its first entry and eventually works its way back to Mouse::sound for the details.

This isn't the best solution, however. We still have to keep the @ISA and the initial search package in sync (changes in one must be considered for changes in the other). Worse, if Mouse had multiple entries in @ISA, we wouldn't necessarily know which one had actually defined speak.

So, is there an even better way?

The SUPER Way of Doing Things

By changing the `Animal` class to the `SUPER` class in that invocation, we get a search of all our superclasses (classes listed in `@ISA`) automatically:

```
{ package Animal;
  sub speak {
    my $class = shift;
    print "a $class goes ", $class->sound, "!\n";
  }
}
{ package Mouse;
  @ISA = qw(Animal);
  sub sound { 'squeak' }
  sub speak {
    my $class = shift;
    $class->SUPER::speak;
    print "[but you can barely hear it!]\n";
  }
}
```

Thus, `SUPER::speak` means to look in the current package's `@ISA` for speak, invoking the first one found if there's more than one. In this case, we look in the one and only base class, `Animal`, find `Animal::speak`, and pass it `Mouse` as its only parameter.

What to Do with @_

In that last example, had there been any additional parameters to the speak method (like how many times, or in what pitch for singing, for example), the parameters would be ignored by the `Mouse::speak` method. If we want them to be passed uninterpreted to the parent class, we can add it as a parameter:

```
$class->SUPER::speak(@_);
```

This invokes the speak method of the parent class, including all the parameters that we've not yet shifted off of our parameter list.

Which one is correct? It depends. If we are writing a class that simply adds to the parent class behavior, it's best to simply pass along arguments we haven't dealt with. However, if we want precise control over the parent class's behavior, we should determine the argument list explicitly and pass it.

Where We Are So Far...

So far, we've used the method arrow syntax:

```
Class->method(@args);
```

or the equivalent:

```
my $beast = 'Class';
$beast->method(@args);
```

which constructs an argument list of:

```
('Class', @args)
```

and attempts to invoke:

```
Class::method('Class', @args);
```

However, if Perl doesn't find `Class::method`, it examines `@Class::ISA` (recursively) to locate a package that does indeed contain `method` and then invokes that version instead.

Chapter 12 shows how to distinguish the individual animals by giving them associated properties, called *instance variables*.

Exercises

You can find the answers to these exercises in "Answers for Chapter 11" in the Appendix.

Exercise 1 [20 min]

Type in the `Animal`, `Cow`, `Horse`, `Sheep`, and `Mouse` class definitions. Make it work with `use strict`. Use `our` if you're using a recent enough version of Perl. Your program should ask the user to enter the names of one or more barnyard animals. Create a barnyard with those animals, and have each animal speak once.

Exercise 2 [40 min]

Add a `Person` class at the same level as `Animal`, and have both of them inherit from a new class called `LivingCreature`. Also make the `speak` method take a parameter of what to say, falling back to the sound (humming for a `Person`) if no parameter is given. Since this isn't Dr. Dolittle, make sure the animals can't talk. (That is, don't let `speak` have any parameters for an animal.) Try not to duplicate any code, but be sure to catch likely errors of usage, such as forgetting to define a `sound` for an animal.

Demonstrate the `Person` class by invoking a person with nothing to say, and then demonstrate it a second time by invoking a person with something to say.

CHAPTER 12
Objects with Data

Using the simple syntax introduced in Chapter 11, we have class methods, (multiple) inheritance, overriding, and extending. We've been able to factor out common code and provide a way to reuse implementations with variations. This is at the core of what objects provide, but objects also provide *instance data*, which we haven't even begun to cover.

A Horse Is a Horse, of Course of Course—or Is It?

Let's look at the code used in Chapter 11 for the Animal classes and Horse classes:

```
{ package Animal;
  sub speak {
    my $class = shift;
    print "a $class goes ", $class->sound, "!\n"
  }
}
{ package Horse;
  @ISA = qw(Animal);
  sub sound { 'neigh' }
}
```

This lets us invoke Horse->speak to ripple upward to Animal::speak, calling back to Horse::sound to get the specific sound, and the output of:

```
a Horse goes neigh!
```

But all Horse objects would have to be absolutely identical. If we add a method, all horses automatically share it. That's great for making horses identical, but how do we capture the properties of an individual horse? For example, suppose we want to give our horse a name. There's got to be a way to keep its name separate from those of other horses.

We can do so by establishing an instance. An *instance* is generally created by a class, much like a car is created by a car factory. An instance will have associated properties, called *instance variables* (or member variables, if you come from a C++ or Java background). An instance has a unique identity (like the serial number of a registered horse), shared properties (the color and talents of the horse), and common behavior (e.g., pulling the reins back tells the horse to stop).

In Perl, an instance must be a reference to one of the built-in types. Start with the simplest reference that can hold a horse's name, a scalar reference:[*]

```
my $name = 'Mr. Ed';
my $tv_horse = \$name;
```

Now $tv_horse is a reference to what will be the instance-specific data (the name). The final step in turning this into a real instance involves a special operator called bless:

```
bless $tv_horse, 'Horse';
```

The bless operator follows the reference to find what variable it points to—in this case, the scalar $name. Then it "blesses" that variable, turning $tv_horse into an object—a Horse object, in fact. (Imagine that a little sticky-note that says Horse is now attached to $name.)

At this point, $tv_horse is an instance of Horse.[†] That is, it's a specific horse. The reference is otherwise unchanged and can still be used with traditional dereferencing operators.[‡]

Invoking an Instance Method

The method arrow can be used on instances, as well as names of packages (classes). Let's get the sound that $tv_horse makes:

```
my $noise = $tv_horse->sound;
```

To invoke sound, Perl first notes that $tv_horse is a blessed reference, and thus an instance. Perl then constructs an argument list, similar to the way an argument list was constructed when we used the method arrow with a class name. In this case, it'll be just ($tv_horse). (Later we'll show that arguments will take their place following the instance variable, just as with classes.)

Now for the fun part: Perl takes the class in which the instance was blessed, in this case, Horse, and uses it to locate and invoke the method, as if we had said Horse->sound instead of $tv_horse->sound. The purpose of the original blessing is to associate a class with that reference to allow Perl to find the proper method.

---

[*] It's the simplest, but rarely used in real code for reasons we'll show shortly.

[†] Actually, $tv_horse points to the object, but, in common terms, we nearly always deal with objects by references to those objects. Hence, it's simpler to say that $tv_horse is the horse, not "the thing that $tv_horse references."

[‡] Although doing so outside the class is a bad idea, as we'll show later.

In this case, Perl finds Horse::sound directly (without using inheritance), yielding the final subroutine invocation:

```
Horse::sound($tv_horse)
```

Note that the first parameter here is still the instance, not the name of the class as before. neigh is the return value, which ends up as the earlier $noise variable.

If Perl did not find Horse::sound, it would walk up the @Horse::ISA list to try to find the method in one of the superclasses, just as for a class method. The only difference between a class method and an instance method is whether the first parameter is an instance (a blessed reference) or a class name (a string).*

Accessing the Instance Data

Because we get the instance as the first parameter, we can now access the instance-specific data. In this case, let's add a way to get at the name:

```
{ package Horse;
  @ISA = qw(Animal);
  sub sound { 'neigh' }
  sub name {
    my $self = shift;
    $$self;
  }
}
```

Now we call for the name:

```
print $tv_horse->name, " says ", $tv_horse->sound, "\n";
```

Inside Horse::name, the @_ array contains just $tv_horse, which the shift stores into $self. It's traditional to shift the first parameter into a variable named $self for instance methods, so stay with that unless you have strong reasons to do otherwise (Perl places no significance on the name $self, however).† Then we dereference $self as a scalar reference, yielding Mr. Ed. The result is:

```
Mr. Ed says neigh.
```

How to Build a Horse

If we constructed all our horses by hand, we'd most likely make mistakes from time to time. Making the "inside guts" of a Horse visible also violates one of the principles

---

* This is perhaps different from other OOP languages with which you may be familiar.

† If you come from another OO language background, you might choose $this or $me for the variable name, but you'll probably confuse most other Perl OO hackers.

of OOP. That's good if we're a veterinarian but not if we just like to own horses. We let the Horse class build a new horse:

```perl
{ package Horse;
  @ISA = qw(Animal);
  sub sound { 'neigh' }
  sub name {
    my $self = shift;
    $$self;
  }
  sub named {
    my $class = shift;
    my $name = shift;
    bless \$name, $class;
  }
}
```

Now, with the new named method, we build a Horse:

```perl
my $tv_horse = Horse->named('Mr. Ed');
```

We're back to a class method, so the two arguments to Horse::named are "Horse" and "Mr. Ed". The bless operator not only blesses $name, it also returns the reference to $name, so that's fine as a return value. And that's how we build a horse.

We called the constructor named here so it quickly denotes the constructor's argument as the name for this particular Horse. We can use different constructors with different names for different ways of "giving birth" to the object (such as recording its pedigree or date of birth). However, we'll find that most people use a single constructor named new, with various ways of interpreting the arguments to new. Either style is fine, as long as we document our particular way of giving birth to an object. Most core and CPAN modules use new, with notable exceptions, such as DBI's DBI->connect( ). It's really up to the author.

Inheriting the Constructor

Was there anything specific to Horse in that method? No. Therefore, it's also the same recipe for building anything else inherited from Animal, so let's put it there:

```perl
{ package Animal;
  sub speak {
    my $class = shift;
    print "a $class goes ", $class->sound, "!\n"
  }
  sub name {
    my $self = shift;
    $$self;
  }
  sub named {
    my $class = shift;
    my $name = shift;
    bless \$name, $class;
```

```
    }
  }
  { package Horse;
    @ISA = qw(Animal);
    sub sound { 'neigh' }
  }
```

Ahh, but what happens if we invoke speak on an instance?

```
  my $tv_horse = Horse->named('Mr. Ed');
  $tv_horse->speak;
```

We get a debugging value:

```
  a Horse=SCALAR(0xaca42ac) goes neigh!
```

Why? Because the Animal::speak method expects a class name as its first parameter, not an instance. When we pass in the instance, we'll use a blessed scalar reference as a string, which shows up as we showed it just now—similar to a stringified reference, but with the class name in front.

Making a Method Work with Either Classes or Instances

All we need to fix this is a way to detect whether the method is called on a class or an instance. The most straightforward way to find out is with the ref operator. This operator returns a string (the class name) when used on a blessed reference, and undef when used on a string (like a class name). We modify the name method first to notice the change:

```
  sub name {
    my $either = shift;
    ref $either
      ? $$either              # it's an instance, return name
      : "an unnamed $either"; # it's a class, return generic
  }
```

Here the ?: operator selects either the dereference or a derived string. Now we can use it with either an instance or a class. Note that we changed the first parameter holder to $either to show that it is intentional:

```
  print Horse->name, "\n";      # prints "an unnamed Horse\n"

  my $tv_horse = Horse->named('Mr. Ed');
  print $tv_horse->name, "\n";  # prints "Mr. Ed.\n"
```

and now we'll fix speak to use this:

```
  sub speak {
    my $either = shift;
    print $either->name, ' goes ', $either->sound, "\n";
  }
```

Since sound already worked with either a class or an instance, we're done!

Adding Parameters to a Method

Let's train our animals to eat:

```perl
{ package Animal;
  sub named {
    my $class = shift;
    my $name = shift;
    bless \$name, $class;
  }
  sub name {
    my $either = shift;
    ref $either
      ? $$either # it's an instance, return name
      : "an unnamed $either"; # it's a class, return generic
  }
  sub speak {
    my $either = shift;
    print $either->name, ' goes ', $either->sound, "\n";
  }
  sub eat {
    my $either = shift;
    my $food = shift;
    print $either->name, " eats $food.\n";
  }
}
{ package Horse;
  @ISA = qw(Animal);
  sub sound { 'neigh' }
}
{ package Sheep;
  @ISA = qw(Animal);
  sub sound { 'baaaah' }
}
```

Now try it out:

```perl
my $tv_horse = Horse->named('Mr. Ed');
$tv_horse->eat('hay');
Sheep->eat('grass');
```

It prints:

```
Mr. Ed eats hay.
an unnamed Sheep eats grass.
```

An instance method with parameters gets invoked with the instance, and then the list of parameters. That first invocation is like:

```perl
Animal::eat($tv_horse, 'hay');
```

The instance methods form the *Application Programming Interface* (API) for an object. Most of the effort involved in designing a good object class goes into the API design, because the API defines how reusable and maintainable the object and its subclasses will be. Don't rush to freeze an API design before you've considered how you (or others) will use the object.

More Interesting Instances

What if an instance needs more data? Most interesting instances are made of many items, each of which can, in turn, be a reference or another object. The easiest way to store these items is often in a hash. The keys of the hash serve as the names of parts of the object (also called instance or member variables), and the corresponding values are, well, the values.

How do we turn the horse into a hash?* Recall that an object is any blessed reference. We can just as easily make it a blessed hash reference as a blessed scalar reference, as long as everything that looks at the reference is changed accordingly.

Let's make a sheep that has a name and a color:

```
my $lost = bless { Name => 'Bo', Color => 'white' }, Sheep;
```

$lost->{Name} has Bo, and $lost->{Color} has white. But we want to make $lost-> name access the name, and that's now messed up because it's expecting a scalar reference. Not to worry, because it's pretty easy to fix:

```
## in Animal
sub name {
  my $either = shift;
  ref $either
    ? $either->{Name}
    : "an unnamed $either";
}
```

named still builds a scalar sheep, so let's fix that as well:

```
## in Animal
sub named {
  my $class = shift;
  my $name = shift;
  my $self = { Name => $name, Color => $class->default_color };
  bless $self, $class;
}
```

What's this default_color? If named has only the name, we still need to set a color, so we'll have a class-specific initial color. For a sheep, we might define it as white:

```
## in Sheep
sub default_color { 'white' }
```

---

* Other than calling on a butcher, that is.

Then, to keep from having to define one for each additional class, define a backstop method, which serves as the "default default," directly in Animal:

```
## in Animal
sub default_color { 'brown' }
```

Thus, all animals are brown (muddy, perhaps), unless a specific animal class gives a specific override to this method.

Now, because name and named were the only methods that referenced the structure of the object, the remaining methods can stay the same, so speak still works as before. This supports another basic rule of OOP: if only the object accesses its internal data, there's less code to change when it's time to modify that structure.

A Horse of a Different Color

Having all horses be brown would be boring. Let's add a method or two to get and set the color:

```
## in Animal
sub color {
  my $self = shift;
  $self->{Color};
}
sub set_color {
  my $self = shift;
  $self->{Color} = shift;
}
```

Now we can fix that color for Mr. Ed:

```
my $tv_horse = Horse->named('Mr. Ed');
$tv_horse->set_color('black-and-white');
print $tv_horse->name, ' is colored ', $tv_horse->color, "\n";
```

which results in:

```
Mr. Ed is colored black-and-white
```

Getting Our Deposit Back

Because of the way the code is written, the setter also returns the updated value. Think about this (and document it) when we write a setter. What does the setter return? Here are some common variations:

- The updated parameter (same as what was passed in)
- The previous value (similar to the way umask or the single-argument form of select works)
- The object itself
- A success/fail code

Each has advantages and disadvantages. For example, if we return the updated parameter, we can use it again for another object:

```
$tv_horse->set_color( $eating->set_color( color_from_user( ) ));
```

The implementation given earlier returns the newly updated value. Frequently, this is the easiest code to write, and often the fastest to execute.

If we return the previous parameter, we can easily create "set this value temporarily to that" functions:

```
{
  my $old_color = $tv_horse->set_color('orange');
  ... do things with $tv_horse ...
  $tv_horse->set_color($old_color);
}
```

This is implemented as:

```
sub set_color {
  my $self = shift;
  my $old = $self->{Color};
  $self->{Color} = shift;
  $old;
}
```

For more efficiency, we can avoid stashing the previous value when in a void context using the wantarray function:

```
sub set_color {
  my $self = shift;
  if (defined wantarray) {
    # this method call is not in void context, so
    # the return value matters
    my $old = $self->{Color};
    $self->{Color} = shift;
    $old;
  } else {
    # this method call is in void context
    $self->{Color} = shift;
  }
}
```

If we return the object itself, we can chain settings:

```
my $tv_horse =
  Horse->named('Mr. Ed')
        ->set_color('grey')
        ->set_age(4)
        ->set_height('17 hands');
```

This works because the output of each setter is the original object, becoming the object for the next method call. Implementing this is, again, relatively easy:

```
sub set_color {
  my $self = shift;
```

```
    $self->{Color} = shift;
    $self;
}
```

The void context trick can be used here too, although with questionable value because we've already established $self.

Finally, returning a success status is useful if it's fairly common for an update to fail, rather than an exceptional event. The other variations would have to indicate failure by throwing an exception with die.

In summary: use what you want, be consistent if you can, but document it nonetheless (and don't change it after you've already released one version).

Don't Look Inside the Box

We might have obtained or set the color outside the class simply by following the hash reference: $tv_horse->{Color}. However, this violates the *encapsulation* of the object by exposing its internal structure. The object is supposed to be a black box, but we've pried off the hinges and looked inside.

One purpose of OOP is to enable the maintainer of Animal or Horse to make reasonably independent changes to the implementation of the methods and still have the exported interface work properly. To see why accessing the hash directly violates this, let's say that Animal no longer uses a simple color name for the color, but instead changes to use a computed RGB triple to store the color (holding it as an arrayref). In this example, we use a fictional (at the time of this writing) Color::Conversions module to change the format of the color data behind the scenes:

```
use Color::Conversions qw(color_name_to_rgb rgb_to_color_name);
...
sub set_color {
  my $self = shift;
  my $new_color = shift;
  $self->{Color} = color_name_to_rgb($new_color);  # arrayref
}
sub color {
  my $self = shift;
  rgb_to_color_name($self->{Color});                # takes arrayref
}
```

We can still maintain the old interface if we use a setter and getter, because they can perform the translations without the user knowing about it. We can also add new interfaces now to enable the direct setting and getting of the RGB triple:

```
sub set_color_rgb {
  my $self = shift;
  $self->{Color} = [@_];                    # set colors to remaining parameters
}
sub get_color_rgb {
```

```
    my $self = shift;
    @{ $self->{Color} };                   # return RGB list
}
```

If we use code outside the class that looks at $tv_horse->{Color} directly, this change is no longer possible. It won't work to store a string ('blue') where an arrayref is needed ([0,0,255]) or to use an arrayref as a string. This is why OO programming encourages you to call getters and setters, even if they take some time.

Faster Getters and Setters

Because we're going to play nice and always call the getters and setters instead of reaching into the data structure, getters and setters are called frequently. To save a teeny-tiny bit of time, we might see these getters and setters written as:

```
## in Animal
sub color     { $_[0]->{Color} }
sub set_color { $_[0]->{Color} = $_[1] }
```

We save a bit of typing when we do this, and the code is slightly faster, although probably not enough for us to notice it with everything else that's going on in our program. The $_[0] is just the single element access to the @_ array. Instead of using shift to put the argument into another variable, we can simply use it directly.

Getters That Double as Setters

Another alternative to the pattern of creating two different methods for getting and setting a parameter is to create one method that notes whether or not it gets any additional arguments. If the arguments are absent, it's a get operation; if the arguments are present, it's a set operation. A simple version looks like:

```
sub color {
  my $self = shift;
  if (@_) {                  # are there any more parameters?
    # yes, it's a setter:
    $self->{Color} = shift;
  } else {
    # no, it's a getter:
    $self->{Color};
  }
}
```

Now we can say:

```
my $tv_horse = Horse->named('Mr. Ed');
$tv_horse->color('black-and-white');
print $tv_horse->name, ' is colored ', $tv_horse->color, "\n";
```

The presence of the parameter in the second line denotes that we are setting the color, while its absence in the third line indicates a getter.

This strategy is attractive because of its simplicity, but it also has disadvantages. It complicates the actions of the getter, which is called frequently. It also makes it difficult to search through our code to find the setters of a particular parameter, which are often more important than the getters. We've been burned in the past when a setter became a getter because another function returned more parameters than expected after an upgrade.

Restricting a Method to Class-Only or Instance-Only

Setting the name of an unnameable generic Horse is probably not a good idea; neither is calling named on an instance. Nothing in the Perl method definition says "this is a class method" or "this is an instance method." Fortunately, the ref operator lets us throw an exception when called incorrectly. As an example of instance- or class-only methods, consider the following, where we check the argument to see what to do:

```
use Carp qw(croak);

sub instance_only {
  ref(my $self = shift) or croak "instance variable needed";
  ... use $self as the instance ...
}

sub class_only {
  ref(my $class = shift) and croak "class name needed";
  ... use $class as the class ...
}
```

The ref function returns true for an instance, which is just a blessed reference, or false for a class, which is just a string. If it returns an undesired value, we use the croak function from the Carp module (which comes in the standard distribution). The croak function places the blame on the caller by making the error message look like it came from the spot where we called the method instead of the spot where we issued the error. The caller will get an error message like this, giving the line number in their code where the wrong method was called:

```
instance variable needed at their_code line 1234
```

Just as croak is provided as the alternate form of die, Carp also provides carp as a replacement for warn. Each tells the user which line of code called the code that caused the problem. Instead of using die or warn in your modules, use the Carp functions instead. Your users will thank you for it.

Exercise

You can find the answer to this exercise in "Answer for Chapter 12" in the Appendix.

Exercise [45 min]

Give the Animal class the ability to get and set the name and color. Be sure that your result works under use strict. Also make sure your get methods work with both a generic animal and a specific animal instance. Test your work with:

```
my $tv_horse = Horse->named('Mr. Ed');
$tv_horse->set_name('Mister Ed');
$tv_horse->set_color('grey');
print $tv_horse->name, ' is ', $tv_horse->color, "\n";
print Sheep->name, ' colored ', Sheep->color, ' goes ', Sheep->sound, "\n";
```

What should you do if you're asked to set the name or color of a generic animal?

## CHAPTER 13

Object Destruction

In the previous two chapters, we looked at basic object creation and manipulation. In this chapter, we'll look at an equally important topic: what happens when objects go away.

As we showed in Chapter 4, when the last reference to a Perl data structure goes away, Perl automatically reclaims the memory of that data structure, including destroying any links to other data. Of course, that in turn may cause Perl to destroy other ("contained") structures as well.

By default, objects work in this manner because objects use the same reference structure to make more complex objects. An object built of a hash reference is destroyed when the last reference to that hash goes away. If the values of the hash elements are also references, they're similarly removed, possibly causing further destruction.

Cleaning Up After Yourself

Suppose our object uses a temporary file to hold data that won't fit entirely in memory. The object can include the filehandle for this temporary file in its instance data. While the normal object destruction sequence will properly close the handle, we still have the temporary file on disk unless we take further action.

To perform the proper cleanup operations when an object is destroyed, we need to know when that happens. Thankfully, Perl provides such notification upon request. We can request this notification by giving the object a DESTROY method.

When the last reference to an object—say, $bessie—disappears, Perl invokes that object's DESTROY method automatically, as if we had called it ourselves.

```
$bessie->DESTROY
```

This method call is like most other method calls: Perl starts at the class of the object and works its way up the inheritance hierarchy until it finds a suitable method. However, unlike other method calls, there's no error if Perl doesn't find a suitable method.*

For example, going back to the Animal class defined in Chapter 11, we can add a DESTROY method to know when objects go away, purely for debugging purposes:

```
## in Animal
sub DESTROY {
  my $self = shift;
  print '[', $self->name, " has died.]\n";
}
```

Now when we create any Animals in the program, we get notification as they leave. For example:

```
## include animal classes from previous chapter...

sub feed_a_cow_named {
  my $name = shift;
  my $cow = Cow->named($name);
  $cow->eat('grass');
  print "Returning from the subroutine.\n";    # $cow is destroyed here
}
print "Start of program.\n";
my $outer_cow = Cow->named('Bessie');
print "Now have a cow named ", $outer_cow->name, ".\n";
feed_a_cow_named('Gwen');
print "Returned from subroutine.\n";
```

This prints:

```
Start of program.
Now have a cow named Bessie.
Gwen eats grass.
Returning from the subroutine.
[Gwen has died.]
Returned from subroutine.
[Bessie has died.]
```

Note that Gwen is active inside the subroutine. However, as the subroutine exits, Perl notices there are no references to Gwen; it automatically invokes Gwen's DESTROY method, printing the Gwen has died message.

What happens at the end of the program? Since objects don't live beyond the end of the program, Perl makes one final pass over all remaining data and destroys it. This is true whether the data is held in lexical variables or package global variables.

---

* Normally, our own method calls will cause an error if Perl doesn't find them. If we want to prevent that, we just put a do-nothing method into the base class.

Because Bessie is still alive at the end of the program, she needs to be recycled, and so we get the message for Bessie after all other steps in the program are complete.*

Nested Object Destruction

If an object holds another object (say, as an element of an array or the value of a hash element), Perl DESTROYs the containing object before any of the contained objects begin their discarding process. This is reasonable because the containing object may need to reference its contents in order to disappear gracefully. To illustrate this, let's build a "barn" and tear it down. And, just to be interesting, we'll make the barn a blessed array reference, not a hash reference.

```
{ package Barn;
  sub new { bless [   ], shift }
  sub add { push @{+shift}, shift }
  sub contents { @{+shift} }
  sub DESTROY {
    my $self = shift;
    print "$self is being destroyed...\n";
    for ($self->contents) {
      print '   ', $_->name, " goes homeless.\n";
    }
  }
}
```

Here, we're really being minimalistic in the object definition. To create a new barn, we simply bless an empty array reference into the class name passed as the first parameter. Adding an animal just pushes it to the back of the barn. Asking for the barn's contents merely dereferences the object array reference to return the contents.† The fun part is the destructor. Let's take the reference to ourselves, display a debugging message about the particular barn being destroyed, and then ask for the name of each inhabitant in turn. In action, this would be:

```
my $barn = Barn->new;
$barn->add(Cow->named('Bessie'));
$barn->add(Cow->named('Gwen'));
print "Burn the barn:\n";
$barn = undef;
print "End of program.\n";
```

---

* This is just after the END blocks are executed and follows the same rules as END blocks: there must be a nice exit of the program rather than an abrupt end. If Perl runs out of memory, all bets are off.

† Did you wonder why there's a plus sign (+) before shift in two of those subroutines? That's due to one of the quirks in Perl's syntax. If the code were simply @{shift}, because the curly braces contain nothing but a bareword, it would be interpreted as a soft reference: @{"shift"}. In Perl, the unary plus (a plus sign at the beginning of a term) is defined to do nothing (not even turning what follows into a number), just so it can distinguish cases such as this.

This prints:

```
Burn the barn:
Barn=ARRAY(0x541c) is being destroyed...
  Bessie goes homeless.
  Gwen goes homeless.
[Gwen has died.]
[Bessie has died.]
End of program.
```

Note that Perl first destroys the barn, letting us get the name of the inhabitants cleanly. However, once the barn is gone, the inhabitants have no additional references, so they also go away, and thus Perl invokes their destructors too. Compare that with the cows having a life outside the barn:

```
my $barn = Barn->new;
my @cows = (Cow->named('Bessie'), Cow->named('Gwen'));
$barn->add($_) for @cows;
print "Burn the barn:\n";
$barn = undef;
print "Lose the cows:\n";
@cows = ( );
print "End of program.\n";
```

This produces:

```
Burn the barn:
Barn=ARRAY(0x541c) is being destroyed...
  Bessie goes homeless.
  Gwen goes homeless.
Lose the cows:
[Gwen has died.]
[Bessie has died.]
End of program.
```

The cows will now continue to live until the only other reference to the cows (from the @cows array) goes away.

The references to the cows disappear only when the barn destructor is completely finished. In some cases, we may wish instead to shoo the cows out of the barn as we notice them. In this case, it's as simple as destructively altering the barn array, rather than iterating over it.* Let's alter the Barn to Barn2 to illustrate this:

```
{ package Barn2;
  sub new { bless [  ], shift }
  sub add { push @{+shift}, shift }
  sub contents { @{+shift} }
  sub DESTROY {
    my $self = shift;
    print "$self is being destroyed...\n";
    while (@$self) {
```

---

* If we're using a hash instead, we can use delete on the elements we wish to process immediately.

```
        my $homeless = shift @$self;
        print ' ', $homeless->name, " goes homeless.\n";
      }
    }
  }
```

Now use it in the previous scenarios:

```
my $barn = Barn2->new;
$barn->add(Cow->named('Bessie'));
$barn->add(Cow->named('Gwen'));
print "Burn the barn:\n";
$barn = undef;
print "End of program.\n";
```

This produces:

```
Burn the barn:
Barn2=ARRAY(0x541c) is being destroyed...
  Bessie goes homeless.
[Bessie has died.]
  Gwen goes homeless.
[Gwen has died.]
End of program.
```

As we can see, Bessie had no home by being booted out of the barn immediately, so she also died. (Poor Gwen suffers the same fate.) There were no references to her at that moment, even before the destructor for the barn was complete.

Thus, back to the temporary file problem. We modify our Animal class to use a temporary file by using the File::Temp module, which is part of the standard distribution. Its tempfile routine knows how to make temporary files, including where to put them and so on, so we don't have to. The tempfile function returns a file-handle and a filename, and we store both of those because we need both of them in the destructor.

```
## in Animal
use File::Temp qw(tempfile);

sub named {
  my $class = shift;
  my $name = shift;
  my $self = { Name => $name, Color => $class->default_color };
  ## new code here...
  my ($fh, $filename) = tempfile( );
  $self->{temp_fh} = $fh;
  $self->{temp_filename} = $filename;
  ## .. to here
  bless $self, $class;
}
```

We now have a filehandle and its filename stored as instance variables of the Animal class (or any class derived from Animal). In the destructor, we close it down and delete the file:*

```
sub DESTROY {
  my $self = shift;
  my $fh = $self->{temp_fh};
  close $fh;
  unlink $self->{temp_filename};
  print '[', $self->name, " has died.]\n";
}
```

When Perl destroys the last reference to the Animal-ish object (even if it's at the end of the program), it also automatically removes the temporary file to avoid a mess.

Beating a Dead Horse

Because the destructor method is inherited, we can also override and extend super-class methods. For example, we'll decide the dead horses need a further use. In our Horse class, we override the DESTROY method we inherited from Animal so we can do extra processing. However, since the Animal class might be doing things we aren't supposed to know about, we call its version of DESTROY using the SUPER:: pseudo-class we saw in Chapter 11.

```
## in Horse
sub DESTROY {
  my $self = shift;
  $self->SUPER::DESTROY;
  print "[", $self->name, " has gone off to the glue factory.]\n";
}

my @tv_horses = map Horse->named($_), ('Trigger', 'Mr. Ed');
$_->eat('an apple') for @tv_horses;     # their last meal
print "End of program.\n";
```

This prints:

```
Trigger eats an apple.
Mr. Ed eats an apple.
End of program.
[Mr. Ed has died.]
[Mr. Ed has gone off to the glue factory.]
[Trigger has died.]
[Trigger has gone off to the glue factory.]
```

We'll feed each horse a last meal; at the end of the program, each horse's destructor is called.

---

* As it turns out, we can tell File::Temp to do this automatically, but then we wouldn't be able to illustrate doing it manually. Doing it manually allows us to do extra processing, such as storing a summary of the information from the temporary file into a database.

The first step of this destructor is to call the parent destructor. Why is this important? Without calling the parent destructor, the steps taken by superclasses of this class will not properly execute. That's not much if it's simply a debugging statement, as we've shown, but if it was the "delete the temporary file" cleanup method, you wouldn't have deleted that file!

So, the rule is:

Always include a call to `$self->SUPER::DESTROY` *in our destructors (even if we don't yet have any base/parent classes).*

Whether we call it at the beginning or the end of our own destructor is a matter of hotly contested debate. If our derived class needs some superclass instance variables, we should probably call the superclass destructor after we complete our operations, because the superclass destructor will likely alter them in annoying ways. On the other hand, in the example, we called the superclass destructor before the added behavior, because we wanted the superclass behavior first.

Indirect Object Notation

The arrow syntax used to invoke a method is sometimes called the *direct object* syntax because there's also the *indirect object* syntax, also known as the "only works sometimes" syntax, for reasons we explain in a moment. We can generally replace what we'd write with the arrow notation:

```
Class->class_method(@args);
$instance->instance_method(@other);
```

with the method name preceding the class name and the arguments at the end.

```
classmethod Class @args;
instancemethod $instance @other;
```

This idiom was much more prevalent in the earlier days of Perl 5, and we're still trying to eradicate it from the world. We wish that we didn't have to cover it here (if you don't know about it, you can't use it), but it sticks around in otherwise good code, so you need to know what is going on. You'll typically see this with the new method where module authors replace the arrow syntax:

```
my $obj = Some::Class->new(@constructor_params);
```

with something that reads more like English:

```
my $obj = new Some::Class @constructor_params;
```

which makes the C++ people feel right at home. Of course, in Perl, there's nothing special about the name new, but at least the syntax is hauntingly familiar.

Why the "generally" caveat on when you can replace the arrow syntax with indirect object syntax? Well, if the instance is something more complicated than a simple scalar variable:

```
$somehash->{$somekey}->[42]->instance_method(@parms);
```

then we can't just swap it around to the indirect notation:

```
instance_method $somehash->{$somekey}->[42] @parms;
```

The only things acceptable to indirect object syntax are a bareword (e.g., a class name), a simple scalar variable, or braces denoting a block returning either a blessed reference or a classname.* This means we have to write it like so:

```
instance_method { $somehash->{$somekey}->[42] } @parms;
```

And that goes from simple to ugly in one step. There's another downside: ambiguous parsing. When we developed the classroom materials concerning indirect object references, we wrote:

```
my $cow = Cow->named('Bessie');
print name $cow, " eats.\n";
```

because we were thinking about the indirect object equivalents for:

```
my $cow = Cow->named('Bessie');
print $cow->name, " eats.\n";
```

However, the latter works; the former doesn't. We were getting no output. Finally, we enabled warnings (via -w on the command line)† and got this interesting series of messages:

```
Unquoted string "name" may clash with future reserved word at ./foo line 92.
Name "main::name" used only once: possible typo at ./foo line 92.
print( ) on unopened filehandle name at ./foo line 92.
```

Ahh, so that line was being parsed as:

```
print name ($cow, " eats.\n");
```

In other words, print the list of items to the filehandle named name. That's clearly not what we wanted, so we had to add additional syntax to disambiguate the call.‡

This leads us to our next strong suggestion: *Use direct object syntax at all times.*

We realize, though, that people write new Class ... rather than Class->new(...) and that most of us are fine with that. Older modules preferred that notation in their

---

* Astute readers will note that these are the same rules as for an indirect filehandle syntax, which indirect object syntax directly mirrors, as well as the rules for specifying a reference to be dereferenced.

† Using -w should be the first step when Perl does something we don't understand. Or maybe it should be the zeroth, because we should normally have -w in effect whenever we're developing code.

‡ The ambiguity shows up because print( ) itself is a method called on the filehandle. You're probably used to thinking of it as a function, but remember that missing comma after the filehandle. It looks just like our indirect object calling syntax, because it is.

examples, and once you write it that way, you tend to keep doing it that way. However, there are circumstances in which even that can lead to ambiguity (e.g., when a subroutine named new has been seen, and the class name itself has not been seen as a package). When in doubt, ignore indirect object syntax. Your maintenance programmer will thank you.

Additional Instance Variables in Subclasses

One of the nice things about using a hash for a data structure is that derived classes can add additional instance variables without the superclass needing to know of their addition. For example, let's derive a RaceHorse class that is everything a Horse is but also tracks its win/place/show/lose standings. The first part of this is trivial:

```
{ package RaceHorse;
  our @ISA = qw(Horse);
  ...
}
```

We'll also want to initialize "no wins of no races" when we create the RaceHorse. We do this by extending the named subroutine and adding four additional fields (wins, places, shows, losses, for first-, second-, and third-place finishes, and none of the above):

```
{ package RaceHorse;
  our @ISA = qw(Horse);
  ## extend parent constructor:
  sub named {
    my $self = shift->SUPER::named(@_);
    $self->{$_} = 0 for qw(wins places shows losses);
    $self;
  }
}
```

Here, we pass all parameters to the superclass, which should return a fully formed Horse. However, because we pass RaceHorse as the class, it is blessed into the RaceHorse class.* Next, we add the four instance variables that go beyond those defined in the superclass, setting their initial values to 0. Finally, return the modified RaceHorse to the caller.

It's important to note here that we've actually "opened the box" a bit while writing this derived class. We know that the superclass uses a hash reference and that the superclass hierarchy doesn't use the four names chosen for a derived class. This is because RaceHorse will be a "friend" class (in C++ or Java terminology), accessing the instance variables directly. If the maintainer of Horse or Animal ever changes representation or names of variables, there could be a collision, which might go undetected until that important day when we're showing off our code to the investors. Things get even more interesting if the hashref is changed to an arrayref as well.

---

* Similar to the way the Animal constructor creates a Horse, not an Animal, when passed Horse as the class.

One way to decouple this dependency is to use composition rather than inheritance as a way to create a derived class. In this example, we need to make a Horse object an instance variable of a RaceHorse and put the rest of the data in separate instance variables. You also need to pass any inherited method calls on the RaceHorse down to the Horse instance, through delegation. However, even though Perl can certainly support the needed operations, that approach is usually slower and more cumbersome. Enough on that for this discussion, however.

Next, let's provide some access methods:

```perl
{ package RaceHorse;
  our @ISA = qw(Horse);
  ## extend parent constructor:
  sub named {
    my $self = shift->SUPER::named(@_);
    $self->{$_} = 0 for qw(wins places shows losses);
    $self;
  }
  sub won { shift->{wins}++; }
  sub placed { shift->{places}++; }
  sub showed { shift->{shows}++; }
  sub lost { shift->{losses}++; }
  sub standings {
    my $self = shift;
    join ', ', map "$self->{$_} $_", qw(wins places shows losses);
  }
}

my $racer = RaceHorse->named('Billy Boy');
# record the outcomes: 3 wins, 1 show, 1 loss
$racer->won;
$racer->won;
$racer->won;
$racer->showed;
$racer->lost;
print $racer->name, ' has standings of: ', $racer->standings, ".\n";
```

This prints:

```
Billy Boy has standings of: 3 wins, 0 places, 1 shows, 1 losses.
[Billy Boy has died.]
[Billy Boy has gone off to the glue factory.]
```

Note that we're still getting the Animal and Horse destructor. The superclasses are unaware that we've added four additional elements to the hash, so they still function as they always have.

Using Class Variables

What if we want to iterate over all the animals we've made so far? Animals may exist all over the program namespace but are lost once they're handed back from the named constructor method.[*]

However, we can record the created animal in a hash and iterate over that hash. The key to the hash can be the stringified form of the animal reference,[†] while the value can be the actual reference, allowing us to access its name or class.

For example, let's extend named as follows:

```perl
## in Animal
our %REGISTRY;
sub named {
  my $class = shift;
  my $name = shift;
  my $self = { Name => $name, Color => $class->default_color };
  bless $self, $class;
  $REGISTRY{$self} = $self;  # also returns $self
}
```

The uppercase name for %REGISTRY is a reminder that this variable is more global than most variables. In this case, it's a meta-variable that contains information about many instances.

When we use $self as a key, Perl *stringifies* it, which means it turns into a string unique to the object.

We also need to add a new method:

```perl
sub registered {
  return map { 'a '.ref($_)." named ".$_->name } values %REGISTRY;
}
```

Now we can see all the animals we've made:

```perl
my @cows = map Cow->named($_), qw(Bessie Gwen);
my @horses = map Horse->named($_), ('Trigger', 'Mr. Ed');
my @racehorses = RaceHorse->named('Billy Boy');
print "We've seen:\n", map("  $_\n", Animal->registered);
print "End of program.\n";
```

This prints:

```
We've seen:
  a RaceHorse named Billy Boy
  a Horse named Mr. Ed
  a Horse named Trigger
  a Cow named Gwen
```

---

[*] Well, not really lost. Perl knows where they are, but we don't.

[†] Or any other convenient and unique string.

```
    a Cow named Bessie
End of program.
[Billy Boy has died.]
[Billy Boy has gone off to the glue factory.]
[Bessie has died.]
[Gwen has died.]
[Trigger has died.]
[Trigger has gone off to the glue factory.]
[Mr. Ed has died.]
[Mr. Ed has gone off to the glue factory.]
```

Note that the animals die at their proper time because the variables holding the animals are all being destroyed at the final step. Or are they?

Weakening the Argument

The %REGISTRY variable also holds a reference to each animal. So even if we toss away the containing variables, for instance by letting them go out of scope:

```
{
  my @cows = map Cow->named($_), qw(Bessie Gwen);
  my @horses = map Horse->named($_), ('Trigger', 'Mr. Ed');
  my @racehorses = RaceHorse->named('Billy Boy');
}
print "We've seen:\n", map("  $_\n", Animal->registered);
print "End of program.\n";
```

we'll still see the same result. The animals aren't destroyed, even though none of the code is holding the animals. At first glance, it looks like we can fix this by altering the destructor:

```
## in Animal
sub DESTROY {
  my $self = shift;
  print '[', $self->name, " has died.]\n";
  delete $REGISTRY{$self};
}
## this code is bad (see text)
```

But this still results in the same output. Why? Because the destructor isn't called until the last reference is gone, but the last reference won't be destroyed until the destructor is called.*

One solution for fairly recent Perl versions† is to use weak references. A *weak* reference doesn't count as far as the reference counting, um, counts. It's best illustrated by example.

---

* We'd make a reference to chickens and eggs, but that would introduce yet another derived class to Animal.
† 5.6 and later.

The weak reference mechanism is built into the core of Perl version 5.8. We need an external interface for the weaken routine, though, which can be imported from the Scalar::Util module. In Perl 5.6, we can emulate the same function using the WeakRef CPAN module. After installing this module (if needed),* we can update the constructor as follows:

```
## in Animal
use Scalar::Util qw(weaken); # in 5.8 and later
use WeakRef qw(weaken);      # in 5.6 after CPAN installation

sub named {
  ref(my $class = shift) and croak 'class only';
  my $name = shift;
  my $self = { Name => $name, Color => $class->default_color };
  bless $self, $class;
  $REGISTRY{$self} = $self;
  weaken($REGISTRY{$self});
  $self;
}
```

When Perl counts the number of active references to a thingy,† it won't count any that have been converted to weak references by weaken. If all ordinary references are gone, Perl deletes the thingy and turns any weak references to undef.

Now we'll get the right behavior for:

```
my @horses = map Horse->named($_), ('Trigger', 'Mr. Ed');
print "alive before block:\n", map(" $_\n", Animal->registered);
{
  my @cows = map Cow->named($_), qw(Bessie Gwen);
  my @racehorses = RaceHorse->named('Billy Boy');
  print "alive inside block:\n", map(" $_\n", Animal->registered);
}
print "alive after block:\n", map(" $_\n", Animal->registered);
print "End of program.\n";
```

This prints:

```
alive before block:
  a Horse named Trigger
  a Horse named Mr. Ed
alive inside block:
  a RaceHorse named Billy Boy
  a Cow named Gwen
  a Horse named Trigger
  a Horse named Mr. Ed
  a Cow named Bessie
[Billy Boy has died.]
[Billy Boy has gone off to the glue factory.]
```

---

* See Chapter 3 for information on installing modules.

† A *thingy*, as defined in Perl's own documentation, is anything a reference points to, such as an object. If you are an especially boring person, you could call it a referent instead.

```
[Gwen has died.]
[Bessie has died.]
alive after block:
   a Horse named Trigger
   a Horse named Mr. Ed
End of program.
[Mr. Ed has died.]
[Mr. Ed has gone off to the glue factory.]
[Trigger has died.]
[Trigger has gone off to the glue factory.]
```

Notice that the racehorses and cows die at the end of the block, but the ordinary horses die at the end of the program. Success!

Weak references can also solve some memory leak issues. For example, suppose an animal wanted to record its pedigree. The parents might want to hold references to all their children, while each child might want to hold references to each parent.

We can weaken one or the other (or even both) of these links. If we weaken the link to the child, Perl can destroy the child when all other references are lost, and the parent's link simply becomes undef (or we can set a destructor to completely remove it). However, a parent won't disappear as long as it still has offspring. Similarly, if the link to the parent is weakened, we'll simply get it as undef when the parent is no longer referenced by other data structures. It's really quite flexible.*

Without weakening, as soon as we create any parent-child relationship, both the parent and the child remain in memory until the final global destruction phase, regardless of the destruction of the other structures holding either the parent or the child.

Be aware though: use weak references carefully and don't just throw them at a problem of circular references. If you destroy data that is held by a weak reference before its time, you may have some very confusing programming problems to solve and debug.

Exercise

You can find the answer to this exercise in "Answer for Chapter 13" in the Appendix.

---

* When using weak references, always ensure you don't dereference a weakened reference that has turned to undef.

Exercise [45 min]

Modify the RaceHorse class to get the previous standings from a DBM hash (keyed by the horse's name) when the horse is created, and update the standings when the horse is destroyed. For example, running this program four times:

```
my $runner = RaceHorse->named('Billy Boy');
$runner->won;
print $runner->name, ' has standings ', $runner->standings, ".\n";
```

should show four additional wins. Make sure that a RaceHorse still does everything a normal Horse does otherwise.

For simplicity, use four space-separated integers for the value in the DBM hash.

CHAPTER 14

Some Advanced Object Topics

You might wonder, "Do all objects inherit from a common class?" "What if a method is missing?" "What about multiple inheritance?" or "How can I tell what sort of object I have?" Well, wonder no more. This chapter covers these subjects and more.

UNIVERSAL Methods

As we define classes, we create inheritance hierarchies through the global @ISA variables in each package. To search for a method, Perl wanders through the @ISA tree until it finds a match or fails.

After the search fails, however, Perl always looks in one special class called UNIVERSAL and invokes a method from there, if found, just as if it had been located in any other class or superclass.

One way to look at this is that UNIVERSAL is the base class from which all objects derive. Any method we place here, such as:

```
sub UNIVERSAL::fandango {
  warn 'object ', shift, " can do the fandango!\n";
}
```

enables all objects of our program to be called as $some_object->fandango.

Generally, we should provide a fandango method for specific classes of interest and then provide a definition in UNIVERSAL::fandango as a backstop, in case Perl can't find a more specific method. A practical example might be a data-dumping routine for debugging or maybe a marshaling strategy to dump all application objects to a file. We simply provide the general method in UNIVERSAL and override it in the specific classes for unusual objects.

Obviously, we should use UNIVERSAL sparingly, because there's only one universe of objects, and our fandango might collide with some other included module's fandango. For this reason, UNIVERSAL is hardly used for anything except methods that must be completely, well, universal, like during debugging or other Perl-internal behavior that ordinary programmers may blissfully ignore.

Testing Our Objects for Good Behavior

Besides providing a place for us to put universally available methods, the UNIVERSAL package comes preloaded with two very useful utility methods: isa and can. Because UNIVERSAL defines these methods, they are available to all objects.

The isa method tests to see whether a given class or instance is a member of a given class or a member of a class that inherits from the given class. For example, continuing on with the Animal family from the previous chapters:

```
if (Horse->isa('Animal')) {    # does Horse inherit from Animal?
  print "A Horse is an Animal.\n";
}

my $tv_horse = Horse->named("Mr. Ed");
if ($tv_horse->isa('Animal')) { # is it an Animal?
  print $tv_horse->name, " is an Animal.\n";
  if ($tv_horse->isa('Horse')) { # is it a Horse?
    print 'In fact, ', $tv_horse->name, " is a Horse.\n";
  } else {
    print "...but it's not a Horse.\n";
  }
}
```

This is handy when we have a heterogeneous mix of objects in a data structure and want to distinguish particular categories of objects:

```
my @horses = grep $_->isa('Horse'), @all_animals;
```

The result will be only the horses (or racehorses) from the array. We compare that with:

```
my @horses_only = grep ref $_ eq 'Horse', @all_animals;
```

which picks out *just* the horses, because a RaceHorse won't return Horse for ref.

In general, we shouldn't use:

```
ref($some_object) eq 'SomeClass'
```

in our programs because it prevents future users from subclassing that class. Use the isa construct as given earlier.

One downside of the isa call here is that it works only on blessed references or scalars that look like class names. If we happen to pass it an unblessed reference, we get a fatal (but trappable) error of:

```
Can't call method "isa" on unblessed reference at ...
```

To call isa more robustly, we could call it as a subroutine:

```
if (UNIVERSAL::isa($unknown_thing, 'Animal')) {
  ... it's an Animal! ...
}
```

This runs without an error, no matter what $unknown_thing contains. But it's subverting the OO mechanism, which has its own set of problems.* This is a job for an exception mechanism, which is eval. If the value in $unknown_thing isn't a reference, then we can't call a method on it. The eval traps that error and returns undef, which is false.

```
if (eval { $unknown_thing->isa('Animal') }) {
    ... it's an Animal ...
}
```

As in the case of isa, we can test for acceptable behaviors with the can method. For example:

```
if ($tv_horse->can('eat')) {
  $tv_horse->eat('hay');
}
```

If the result of can is true, then somewhere in the inheritance hierarchy, a class claims it can handle the eat method. Again, the caveats about $tv_horse being only either a blessed reference or a class name as a scalar still apply, so the robust solution when we might deal with nearly anything looks like:

```
if (eval { $tv_horse->can('eat') } ) { ... }
```

Note that if we defined UNIVERSAL::fandango earlier, then:

```
$object->can('fandango')
```

always returns true, because all objects can do the fandango.

AUTOLOAD as a Last Resort

After Perl searches the inheritance tree and UNIVERSAL for a method, it doesn't just stop there if the search is unsuccessful. Perl repeats the search through the very same hierarchy (including UNIVERSAL), looking for a method named AUTOLOAD.

If an AUTOLOAD exists, the subroutine is called in place of the original method, passing it the normal predetermined argument list: the class name or instance reference, followed by any arguments provided to the method call. The original method name is passed in the package variable called $AUTOLOAD (in the package where the subroutine was compiled) and contains the fully qualified method name, so we should generally strip everything up to the final double colon if we want a simple method name.

The AUTOLOAD subroutine can execute the desired operation itself, install a subroutine and then jump into it, or perhaps just die if asked to perform an unknown method.

One use of AUTOLOAD defers the compilation of a large subroutine until it is actually needed. For example, suppose the eat method for an animal is complex but unused in nearly every invocation of the program. We can defer its compilation as follows:

---

* Particularly, if Animal has a custom isa method (perhaps it rejects a mutant branch of talking animals in the family tree), calling UNIVERSAL::isa skips past Animal::isa and may give you the wrong answer.

```
## in Animal
sub AUTOLOAD {
  our $AUTOLOAD;
  (my $method = $AUTOLOAD) =~ s/.*:://s; # remove package name
  if ($method eq "eat") {
    ## define eat:
    eval q{
      sub eat {
        ...
        long
        definition
        goes
        here
        ...
      }
    };                      # End of eval's q{ } string
    die $@ if $@;                      # if typo snuck in
    goto &eat;                         # jump into it
  } else {                            # unknown method
    croak "$_[0] does not know how to $method\n";
  }
}
```

If the method name is eat, we'll define eat (which we had previously in a string but had not compiled) and then jump into it with a special construct that replaces the current subroutine invocation of AUTOLOAD with an invocation of eat, just as if we invoked &eat instead of AUTOLOAD.* After the first AUTOLOAD hit, the eat subroutine is now defined, so we won't be coming back here. This is great for compile-as-you-go programs because it minimizes startup overhead.

For a more automated way of creating code to do this, which makes it easy to turn the autoloading off during development and debugging, see the AutoLoader and SelfLoader core module documentation.

Using AUTOLOAD for Accessors

Chapter 12 showed how to create color and set_color to get and set the color of an animal. If we had 20 attributes instead of 1 or 2, the code would be painfully repetitive. However, using an AUTOLOAD method, we can construct the nearly identical accessors as needed, saving both compilation time and wear-and-tear on the developer's keyboard.

We use a code reference as a closure to do the job. First, we set up an AUTOLOAD for the object and define a list of hash keys for which we want trivial accessors:

---

* Although goto is generally (and rightfully) considered evil, this form of goto, which gives a subroutine name as a target, is not really the evil goto; it's the good goto. In particular, this is the "magic goto." Its trick is that AUTOLOAD is completely invisible to the subroutine.

```
sub AUTOLOAD {
  my @elements = qw(color age weight height);
```

Next, we'll see if the method is a getter for one of these keys, and, if so, we install a getter and jump to it:

```
our $AUTOLOAD;
if ($AUTOLOAD =~ /::(\w+)$/ and grep $1 eq $_, @elements) {
  my $field = ucfirst $1;
  {
    no strict 'refs';
    *{$AUTOLOAD} = sub { $_[0]->{$field} };
  }
  goto &{$AUTOLOAD};
}
```

We need to use ucfirst because we named the method color to fetch the hash element called Color. The glob notation here installs a wanted subroutine as defined by the coderef closure, which fetches the corresponding key from the object hash. Consider this part to be magic that we just cut and paste into our program. Finally, the goto construct jumps into the newly defined subroutine.

Otherwise, perhaps it's a setter:

```
if ($AUTOLOAD =~ /::set_(\w+)$/ and grep $1 eq $_, @elements) {
  my $field = ucfirst $1;
  {
    no strict 'refs';
    *{$AUTOLOAD} = sub { $_[0]->{$field} = $_[1] };
  }
  goto &{$AUTOLOAD};
}
```

If it is neither, death awaits:

```
croak "$_[0] does not understand $method\n";
  }
```

Again, we pay the price for the AUTOLOAD only on the first hit of a particular getter or setter. After that, a subroutine is now already defined, and we can just invoke it directly.

Creating Getters and Setters More Easily

If all that coding for creating accessors using AUTOLOAD looks messy, rest assured that we really don't need to tackle it, because there's a CPAN module that does it a bit more directly: Class::MethodMaker.[*]

For example, a simplified version of the Animal class might be defined as follows:

---

[*] Sometimes Class::MethodMaker can be a bit much. We can also check out the lighter Class::Accessor.

```
package Animal;
use Class::MethodMaker
  new_with_init => 'new',
  get_set => [-eiffel => [qw(color height name age)]],
  abstract => [qw(sound)],
;
sub init {
  my $self = shift;
  $self->set_color($self->default_color);
}
sub named {
  my $self = shift->new;
  $self->set_name(shift);
  $self;
}
sub speak {
  my $self = shift;
  print $self->name, ' goes ', $self->sound, "\n";
}
sub eat {
  my $self = shift;
  my $food = shift;
  print $self->name, " cats $food\n";
}
sub default_color {
  'brown';
}
```

The getters and setters for the four instance attributes (name, height, color, and age) are defined automatically, using the method color to get the color and set_color to set the color. (The eiffel flag says "do it the way the Eiffel language does it," which is the way it should be done here.) The messy blessing step is now hidden behind a simple new method. We define the initial color as the default color, as before, because the generated new method calls the init method.

However, we can still call Horse->named('Mr. Ed') because it immediately calls the new routine as well.

Class::MethodMaker generated the sound method as an abstract method. *Abstract* methods are placeholders, meant to be defined in a subclass. If a subclass fails to define the method, the method Class::MethodMaker generates for Animal's sound dies.

We lose the ability to call the getters (such as name) on the class itself, rather than an instance. In turn, this breaks our prior usage of calling speak and eat on generic animals, since they call the accessors. One way around this is to define a more general version of name to handle either a class or instance and then change the other routines to call it:

```
sub generic_name {
  my $either = shift;
  ref $either ? $either->name : "an unnamed $either";
}
```

```
sub speak {
  my $either = shift;
  print $either->generic_name, ' goes ', $either->sound, "\n";
}
sub eat {
  my $either = shift;
  my $food = shift;
  print $either->generic_name, " eats $food\n";
}
```

There. Now it's looking nearly drop-in compatible with the previous definition, except for those friend classes that referenced the attribute names directly in the hash as the initial-cap-keyed versions (such as Color) rather than through the accessors ($self->color).

That brings up the maintenance issue again. The more we can decouple our implementation (hash versus array, names of hash keys, or types of elements) from the interface (method names, parameter lists, or types of return values), the more flexible and maintainable our system becomes.

The flexibility isn't free, however. Since the performance cost of a method call is higher than the cost of a hash lookup, in some circumstances it may make sense to have a friend class peek inside.

Multiple Inheritance

How does Perl wander through the @ISA tree? The answer may be simple or complex. If we don't have multiple inheritance (that is, if no @ISA has more than one element), it is simple: Perl simply goes from one @ISA to the next until it finds the ultimate base class whose @ISA is empty.

Multiple inheritance is more complex. It occurs when a class's @ISA has more than one element. For example, suppose we have a class called Racer, which has the basic abilities for anything that can race, so that it's ready to be the base class for a runner, a fast car, or a racing turtle. With that, we could make the RaceHorse class as simply as this:[*]

```
{
  package RaceHorse;
  our @ISA = qw{ Horse Racer };
}
```

Now a RaceHorse can do anything a Horse can do, and anything a Racer can do as well. When Perl searches for a method that's not provided directly by RaceHorse, it first searches through all the capabilities of the Horse (including all its parent classes,

---

[*] If there is a conflict among the methods of Horse and Racer, or if their implementations aren't able to work together, the situation can become much more difficult. The various classes in @ISA may not play well together and may step on one another's data, for instance.

such as `Animal`). When the `Horse` possibilities are exhausted, Perl turns to see whether `Racer` (or one of its subclasses) supplies the needed method. On the other hand, if we want Perl to search `Racer` and its subclasses before searching `Horse`, we can put them into `@ISA` in that order (see Figure 14-1).

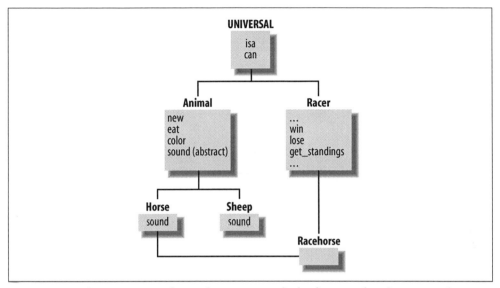

Figure 14-1. A class may not need to implement any methods of its own if it inherits everything it needs from its parent classes through multiple inheritance

Exercises

You can find the answers to these exercises in "Answers for Chapter 14" in the Appendix.

Exercise 1 [20 min]

Write a module named `MyDate` that has an `AUTOLOAD` method that handles the calls to the methods named `day`, `month`, and `year`, returning the appropriate value for each one. For any other method, the `AUTOLOAD` should carp about the unknown method name. Write a script that uses your module and prints the values for the date, month, and year.

Exercise 2 [40 min]

Starting with the script you wrote for the previous exercise, add a `UNIVERSAL::debug` function that prints a timestamp before the message you pass to it. Call the `debug` method on the `MyDate` object. What happens? How does this get around the `AUTOLOAD` mechanism?

CHAPTER 15

Exporter

In Chapter 3, we showed you how to use modules, some of which pulled functions into the current namespace. Now we're going to show you how to get your own modules to do that.

What use Is Doing

So, just what does use do? How does the import list come into action? Perl interprets the use list as a particular form of BEGIN block wrapped around a require and a method call. For example, the following two operations are equivalent:

```
use Island::Plotting::Maps qw( load_map scale_map draw_map );

BEGIN {
  require Island::Plotting::Maps;
  Island::Plotting::Maps->import( qw( load_map scale_map draw_map ) );
}
```

Let's break this code down, piece by piece. First, the require is a package-name require, rather than the string-expression require from Chapter 10. The colons are turned into the native directory separator (such as / for Unix-like systems), and the name is suffixed with .pm (for "Perl module"). For this example on a Unix-like system, we end up with:

```
require "Island/Plotting/Maps.pm";
```

Recalling the operation of require from earlier, this means Perl looks in the current value of @INC, checking through each directory for a subdirectory named Island that contains a further subdirectory named Plotting that contains the file named Maps.pm.* If Perl doesn't find an appropriate file after looking at all of @INC, the program dies.†

---

* The .pm portion is defined by the interface and can't be changed. Thus, all module filenames must end in dot-p-m.

† Trappable with an eval, of course.

Otherwise, the first file found is read and evaluated. As always with require, the last expression evaluated must be true (or the program dies),* and once Perl has read a file, it will not reread if requested again. In the module interface, we expect the require'd file to define subroutines in the same-named package, not the caller's package. So, for example, a portion of the File::Basename file might look something like this, if we took out all the good stuff:

```
package File::Basename;
sub dirname { ... }
sub basename { ... }
sub fileparse { ... }
1;
```

These three subroutines are then defined in the File::Basename package, not the package in which our use occurs. A require'd file must return a true value, and it's traditional to use 1; as the last line of a module's code.

How do these subroutines get from the module's package into the user's package? That's the second step inside the BEGIN block. Perl automatically calls a routine called import in the module's package, passing along the entire import list. Typically, this routine aliases some of the names from the imported namespace to the importing namespace. The module author is responsible for providing an appropriate import routine. It's easier than it sounds, as discussed later in this chapter.

Finally, the whole thing is wrapped in a BEGIN block. This means that the use operation happens at compile time, rather than runtime, and indeed it does. Thus, subroutines are associated with those defined in the module, prototypes are properly defined, and so on.

Importing with Exporter

In Chapter 3, we skipped over that "and now magic happens" part where the import routine (defined by the module author) is supposed to take File::Basename::fileparse and somehow alias it into the caller's package so it's callable as fileparse.

Perl provides a lot of introspection capabilities. Specifically, we can look at the symbol table (where all subroutines and many variables are named), see what is defined, and alter those definitions. You saw a bit of that back in the AUTOLOAD mechanism earlier in Chapter 14. In fact, as the author of File::Basename, if we simply want to force filename, basename, and fileparse from the current package into the main package, we can write import like this:

```
sub import {
  no strict 'refs';
  for (qw(filename basename fileparse)) {
```

---

* Again, trappable with eval.

```
    *{"main::$_"} = \&$_;
    }
  }
}
```

Boy, is that cryptic! And limited. What if the caller didn't want fileparse? What if the caller invoked use in a package other than main?

Thankfully, there's a standard import that's available in the Exporter module. As the module author, all we do is add:

```
use base qw(Exporter);
```

Now the import call to the package will inherit upward to the Exporter class, providing an import routine that knows how to take a list of subroutines* and export them to the caller's package.

@EXPORT and @EXPORT_OK

The import provided by Exporter examines the @EXPORT variable in the module's package to determine which variables it exports by default. For example, File::Basename might do something like:

```
package File::Basename;
our @EXPORT = qw( basename dirname fileparse );
use base qw(Exporter);
```

The @EXPORT list both defines a list of available subroutines for export (the public interface) and provides a default list for Perl to use when we don't specify an import list. For example, these two calls are equivalent:

```
use File::Basename;

BEGIN { require File::Basename; File::Basename->import }
```

We pass no list to import. In that case, the Exporter->import routine looks at @EXPORT and provides everything in the list.†

What if we had subroutines we didn't want as part of the default import but that would still be available if we asked for them? We can add those subroutines to the @EXPORT_OK list in the module's package. For example, suppose that Gilligan's module provides the guess_direction_toward routine by default but could also provide the ask_the_skipper_about and get_north_from_professor routines, if requested. We can start it like this:

```
package Navigate::SeatOfPants;
our @EXPORT = qw(guess_direction_toward);
our @EXPORT_OK = qw(ask_the_skipper_about get_north_from_professor);
use base qw(Exporter);
```

---

* And variables, although far less common, and arguably the wrong thing to do.

† Remember, having no list is not the same as having an empty list. If the list is empty, the module's import method is simply not called at all.

The following invocations would then be valid:

```
use Navigate::SeatOfPants;  # gets guess_direction_toward

use Navigate::SeatOfPants qw(guess_direction_toward); # same

use Navigate::SeatOfPants
  qw(guess_direction_toward ask_the_skipper_about);

use Navigate::SeatOfPants
  qw(ask_the_skipper_about get_north_from_professor);
  ## does NOT import guess_direction_toward!
```

If we specify any names, they must be in either @EXPORT or @EXPORT_OK, so this request is rejected by Exporter->import:

```
use Navigate::SeatOfPants qw(according_to_GPS);
```

because according_to_GPS is in neither @EXPORT nor @EXPORT_OK.* Thus, with those two arrays, we have control over our public interface. This does not stop someone from saying Navigate::SeatOfPants::according_to_GPS (if it existed), but at least now it's obvious that they're using something we didn't intend to offer them.

%EXPORT_TAGS

We don't have to list every function or variable that we want to import, either. We can create shortcuts, or tags, to group them under a single name. In the import list, we precede the tag name with a colon. For example, the core Fcntl module makes the flock constants available as a group with the :flock tag:

```
use Fcntl qw( :flock );       # import all flock constants
```

As described in the Exporter documentation, a few shortcuts are available automatically. The DEFAULT tag pulls in the same things as if we had provided no import list:

```
use Navigate::SeatOfPants qw(:DEFAULT);
```

That isn't very useful on its own, but if we want to pull in the default symbols and more, we don't have to type everything out simply because we supply an import list:

```
use Navigate::SeatOfPants qw(:DEFAULT get_north_from_professor);
```

These are rarely seen in practice. Why? The purpose of explicitly providing an import list is generally to control the subroutine names we use in our program. Those last examples do not insulate us from future changes to the module, which may import additional subroutines that could collide with our code.† In a few cases,

---

* This check also catches misspellings and mistaken subroutine names, keeping you from wondering why the get_direction_from_professor routine isn't working.

† For this reason, it is generally considered a bad idea for an update to a released module to introduce new default imports. If you know that your first release is still missing a function, though, there's no reason why you can't put in a placeholder: sub according_to_GPS { die "not implemented yet" }.

a module may supply dozens or hundreds of possible symbols. These modules can use advanced techniques (described in the Exporter documentation) to make it easy to import batches of related symbols.

In our modules, we use the %EXPORT_TAGS hash to define these tags. The hash key is the name of the tag (without the colon), and the value is an anonymous array of symbols.

```
package Navigate::SeatOfPants;
use base qw(Exporter);

our @EXPORT    = qw(guess_direction_toward);
our @EXPORT_OK = qw(
                get_north_from_professor
                according_to_GPS
                ask_the_skipper_about
                );

our %EXPORT_TAGS = (
        all       => [ @EXPORT, @EXPORT_OK ],
        gps       => [ qw( according_to_GPS ) ],
        direction => [ qw(
                get_north_from_professor
                according_to_GPS
                guess_direction_toward
                ask_the_skipper_about
                ) ],
        );
```

Our first tag, all, includes all of the exportable symbols (everything in both @EXPORT and @EXPORT_OK). The gps tag comprises only the functions that deal with GPS, and the direction tag includes all the functions that deal with direction. The tags can contain overlaps too, and you'll notice that according_to_GPS shows up in each one of them. No matter how we define our tags, everything they include has to be either in @EXPORT or @EXPORT_OK.

Once we define our export tags, our users can use them in their import lists:

```
use Navigate::SeatOfPants qw(:direction);
```

Exporting in a Primarily OO Module

As seen earlier, the normal means of using an object-oriented module is to call class methods and then methods against instances resulting from constructors of that class. This means that an OO module typically exports nothing, so we'll have:

```
package My::OOModule::Base;
our @EXPORT = ( ); # you may even omit this line
use base qw(Exporter);
```

What if we then derive a class from this base class? The most important thing to remember is that the import method must be defined from the Exporter class, so we add it like so:

```
package My::OOModule::Derived;
use base qw(Exporter My::OOModule::Base);
```

However, wouldn't the call to My::OOModule::Derived->import eventually find its way up to Exporter via My::OOModule::Base? Sure it would. So we can leave that out:

```
package My::OOModule::Derived;
use base qw(My::OOModule::Base);
```

Only the base classes at the top of the tree need to specify Exporter, and only when they derive from no other classes.

Please be aware of all the other reserved method names that can't be used by your OO module (as described in the Exporter manpage). At the time of this writing, the list is export_to_level, require_version, and export_fail. Also, we may wish to reserve unimport because Perl will call that routine when we replace use with no. That use is rare for user-written modules, however, although it often shows up with pragmas such as strict and warnings.

Even though an OO module typically exports nothing, we might choose to export a named constructor or management routine. This routine typically acts a bit like a class method, but we want users to call it as a regular subroutine.

One example is the LWP library, available on the CPAN as part of the libwww-perl distribution. The URI::URL module, now deprecated and replaced by the URI module, deals with universal resource identifiers, most commonly seen as URLs such as *http://www.gilligan.crew.hut/maps/island.pdf*. We can construct a URI::URL object as a traditional object constructor with:

```
use URI::URL;
my $u = URI::URL->new('http://www.gilligan.crew.hut/maps/island.pdf');
```

The default import list for URI::URL also imports a url subroutine, which we can use as a constructor as well:

```
use URI::URL;
my $u = url('http://www.gilligan.crew.hut/maps/island.pdf');
```

Because this imported routine isn't a class method, we don't use the arrow method call to invoke it. Also, the routine is unlike anything else in the module: it gets no initial class parameter. Even though normal subroutines and method calls are both defined as subroutines in the package, the caller and the author must agree as to which is which.

The url convenience routine was nice, initially. However, it clashed with the same-name routine that CGI.pm tried to export as well, leading to interesting errors (especially in a mod_perl setting). The module that got there last won. (The modern interface in the URI module doesn't export such a constructor.) Prior to that, in order to prevent a crash, we had to remember to bring it in with an empty import list:

```
use URI::URL ( );        # don't import "url"
my $u = URI::URL->new(...);
```

Custom Import Routines

Let's use CGI.pm as an example of a custom import routine before we show you how to write your own. Not satisfied with the incredible flexibility of the Exporter's import routine, CGI.pm author Lincoln Stein created a special import for the CGI module.* If you've ever gawked at the dizzying array of options that can appear after use CGI and wondered how it all worked, it's all a simple matter of programming. You can just look at the source yourself.

As part of the extension provided by this custom import, you can use the CGI module as an object-oriented module:

```
use CGI;
my $q = CGI->new;        # create a query object
my $f = $q->param('foo'); # get the foo field
```

or a function-oriented module:

```
use CGI qw(param);       # import the param function
my $f = param('foo');    # get the foo field
```

If you don't want to spell out every possible subfunction, bring them all in:

```
use CGI qw(:all);        # define 'param' and 800-gazillion others
my $f = param('foo');
```

And then there's pragmata available. For example, if you want to disable the normal sticky field handling, simply add -nosticky into the import list:

```
use CGI qw(-nosticky :all);
```

If you want to create the start_table and end_table routines, in addition to the others, it's simply:

```
use CGI qw(-nosticky :all *table);
```

Truly a dizzying array of options. How did Lincoln make it all work? You can just look in the CGI.pm code, see for yourself, but we'll show you the basics.

The import method is just a regular method, so we can make it do anything that we want. Earlier we showed a simple (although hypothetical) example for File::Basename. In that case, instead of using the import method from Exporter as the real module does, we wrote our own to force the symbols into the main namespace.

```
sub import {
  no strict 'refs';
  for (qw(filename basename fileparse)) {
    *{"main::$_"} = \&$_;
  }
}
```

---

* Some have dubbed this the "Lincoln Loader" out of a simultaneous deep respect for Lincoln and the sheer terror of having to deal with something that just doesn't work like anything else they've encountered.

This only works for main since that's what we hardcoded into the routine. We can figure out the calling package on the fly, however, by using the built-in caller. In scalar context, caller returns the calling package:

```
sub import {
  no strict 'refs';
  my $package = caller;
  for (qw(filename basename fileparse)) {
    *{$package . "::$_"} = \&$_;
  }
}
```

We can get even more information from caller by using it in list context.

```
sub import {
  no strict 'refs';
  my( $package, $file, $line ) = caller;
  warn "I was called by $package in $file\n";
  for (qw(filename basename fileparse)) {
    *{$package . "::$_"} = \&$_;
  }
}
```

Since import is just a method, any arguments to it (that's the import list, remember) show up in @_. We can inspect the argument list and decide what to do. Let's turn on debugging output only if debug shows up in the import list. We're not going to import a subroutine named debug. We're only going to set $debug to a true value if it's there, then do the same stuff we did before. This time we only print the warning if we've turned on debugging.

```
sub import {
  no strict 'refs';
  my $debug = grep { $_ eq 'debug' } @_;
  my( $package, $file, $line ) = caller;
  warn "I was called by $package in $file\n" if $debug;
  for (qw(filename basename fileparse)) {
    *{$package . "::$_"} = \&$_;
  }
}
```

These are the basic tricks that Lincoln used to work his CGI magic, and it's the same stuff that the Test::More module, which we introduce in Chapter 17, uses in its own import to control how testing works.

Exercises

You can find the answers to these exercises in "Answers for Chapter 15" in the Appendix.

Exercise 1 [15 min]

Take the Oogaboogoo library you created in Chapter 10, Exercise 1 and turn it into a module you can bring in with use. Alter the invoking code so that it uses the imported routines (rather than the full package specification, as you did before), and test it.

Exercise 2 [15 min]

Modify your answer to Exercise 1 to use an export tag named all. When the user uses all, your module should import all of the subroutine names.

```
use Oogaboogoo::date qw(:all);
```

## CHAPTER 16

Writing a Distribution

In Chapter 15, we created a fictional `Island::Plotting::Maps` module and built the right support for `Exporter` so that we could include use `Island::Plotting::Maps` in a program.

While the resulting *.pm* file was useful, it wasn't very practical. We have a lot more work to do before we can share our work, whether that means simply installing it ourselves on another one of our machines or giving it to someone else to use.

Installation location

How does everything get in the right place so Perl can find it? Where is our code going to be stored on the system? Can users make it available to everyone on the system because they have root or administrator privileges, or do they have to install it in their own directories?

Documentation

Where is the documentation for the module? How is the documentation installed so the user can read it?

Archive completeness

Is there anything extra that the users of our software will need? What else do I have to include with my code to make it usable?

Testing

How do we know our software works? Have we verified that it does what we say it does? How do we know it works the same on other operating systems or versions of Perl?

C-language interfaces

If our module contains C or C++ code (not covered here), how can the developer describe how to compile and link the code in the developer's environment or the end user environment?

There's More Than One Way To Do It

A distribution contains the module (or collection of related modules), plus all the support files required to document, test, ship, and install the module. While you could potentially construct all these files by hand, it's much simpler to use something to do it for you.

In the beginning,* we had to create modules by hand. Soon after, the *h2xs* program grew into a module distribution creator, and that worked well for a while. Andy Lester created `Module::Starter` to make a better starter distribution, Jim Keenan created `ExtUtils::ModuleMaker` to make a better *h2xs*, and many other module creation systems popped up.†

No matter which way we create our distribution or which tools we use, the process is the same. We run a Perl script that creates a file that pulls together all the information it needs to prepare and install the code. From there, we can test and install the modules.

If we are using the traditional *Makefile.PL*, we start the installation with:

```
$ perl Makefile.PL
```

After that, we can test and install the module by telling *make* to perform the actions for those targets.‡

```
$ make all test install
```

We may not want to use a *Makefile.PL,* though. It relies on the external program *make,* which, since it started life as a Unix tool, may not be available on all systems.§ Ken Williams created the pure-Perl `Module::Build` system as a *make* replacement. Since we know that we must already have Perl installed and that Perl is portable, we can use it to install modules.

The `Module::Build` process looks the same, except that we start with a `Build.PL` file.

```
$ perl Build.PL
```

From there, we do the same sort of thing we did before.

```
perl Build
perl Build test
perl Build install
```

---

* Well, since Perl 5 at least, when the third party module system came into being.

† brian simply creates a template directory he processes with *ttree* from `Template::Toolkit`. You can read about it in the December 2004 issue of *The Perl Journal* at *http://www.tpj.com/documents/s=9622/tpj0412e/0412e.html*.

‡ We can specify the test and install targets in the same *make* invocation. If *make* encounters an error, it won't go on.

§ There is an *nmake* for Windows that is available from Microsoft.

There are reasons to decide to use one or the other. The *Makefile.PL* method has been around for a long time, and it mostly works, except in odd cases. Its underpinnings depend on ExtUtils::Makemaker, which comes with Perl. Unfortunately, ExtUtils:: Makemaker has become a bear to maintain, since it has to handle all of the special cases for the many, many systems on which Perl works. The Module::Build method is much newer, so it's still maturing and not as many people use it.[*] However, since Module:: Build doesn't require an external program, it's easier for some people to use.

Using h2xs

We'll explain the *Makefile.PL* process using the awkwardly named *h2xs*.[†] We use *h2xs* to create a set of template files that are a starting point for our distribution files. We simply need to say h2xs -XAn, followed by the name of the module—in this case, Island::Plotting::Maps.[‡] Here's what the output looks like:[§]

```
Defaulting to backwards compatibility with perl 5.8.7
If you intend this module to be compatible with earlier perl versions, please
specify a minimum perl version with the -b option.

Writing Island-Plotting-Maps/lib/Island/Plotting/Maps.pm
Writing Island-Plotting-Maps/Makefile.PL
Writing Island-Plotting-Maps/README
Writing Island-Plotting-Maps/t/Island-Plotting-Maps.t
Writing Island-Plotting-Maps/Changes
Writing Island-Plotting-Maps/MANIFEST
```

MANIFEST

The *h2xs* program created a directory and several files. These are mostly the same files that the other module creation tools set up for us, so even if you decide not to use *h2xs,* you still need to understand these files. Let's examine the *MANIFEST* file, which contains the list of files that the distribution will contain. At the start, our *MANIFEST* contains:[**]

```
Changes
Makefile.PL
```

---

[*] Yet. Module::Build will be part of the Perl standard distribution starting with Perl 5.10 and is likely the future for Perl modules.

[†] The name *h2xs* has an interesting pedigree. Back in the early days of Perl 5, Larry invented the XS language to describe the glue code that Perl needs to talk to C-language functions and libraries. Originally, this code was written entirely by hand, but the *h2xs* tool was written to scan simple C-include header files (ending in .*h*) and generate most of the XS directly. Hence, *h* 2 (to) *XS*. Over time, more functions were added, including generating template files for the rest of the distribution. Now here we are, about to describe how to use *h2xs* for things that aren't either *h* or *XS*. Amazing.

[‡] If there's more than one module in the distribution, it should be the name of the most important module. Others can be added later.

[§] The exact behavior and output of *h2xs* may vary depending upon the version of Perl.

[**] Again, there may be slight variations based on tool and Perl versions.

```
MANIFEST
README
t/Island-Plotting-Maps.t
lib/Island/Plotting/Maps.pm
```

The *MANIFEST* file is really a table of contents for our distribution. When we decide to bundle the archive, all of the files in *MANIFEST* go into the archive. When the end user unpacks the distribution, the module installer tool verifies that all of the files in *MANIFEST* are in the archive. In fact, we're ready to make an archive right now. First, we need to run the *Makefile.PL*. After that, we find a new file, *Makefile*, in our directory.

```
$ perl Makefile.PL
$ make tardist
```

If we don't want to make a tar achive, we can create a zip file.

```
$ make zipdist
```

While maintaining a *MANIFEST* sounds like it might be painful, we know that we won't accidentally include our "notes to self" in the distribution just because those files happened to be in the wrong directory. Later, we'll show you how to update *MANIFEST*.

README

The next file is *README*, which is a standard name for the first bit of information you want all users of your module to read. It's customary to include at least a brief description of the module, installation instructions, and licensing details.

```
Island-Plotting-Maps version 0.01
= == == == == == == == == == == == == == == == ==

The README is used to introduce the module and provide instructions on
how to install the module, any machine dependencies it may have (for
example C compilers and installed libraries) and any other information
that should be provided before the module is installed.

A README file is required for CPAN modules since CPAN extracts the
README file from a module distribution so that people browsing the
archive can use it get an idea of the modules uses. It is usually a
good idea to provide version information here so that people can
decide whether fixes for the module are worth downloading.

INSTALLATION

To install this module type the following:

    perl Makefile.PL
    make
    make test
    make install
```

```
DEPENDENCIES

This module requires these other modules and libraries:

  blah blah blah

COPYRIGHT AND LICENSE

Put the correct copyright and license information here.

Copyright (C) 2005 by Ginger Grant

This library is free software; you can redistribute it and/or modify
it under the same terms as Perl itself, either Perl Version 5.8.7 or,
at your option, any later version of Perl 5 you may have available.
```

Obviously, you will want to edit this file to be whatever you want it to be. The phrase "blah blah blah" is often used in the templates to indicate things that must be changed.* If we leave unchanged the blah blah blah and other placeholder notes from *h2xs*, potential users will suspect that bugs in our code have also escaped our scrutiny, so we should proofread this stuff (along with our code) before we distribute our module.

Pay special attention to the copyright and license section. (It should have your name in place of Ginger's name, unless your machine is very confused about who is sitting at the keyboard.) Your employer may require you to change the copyright notice to include your company name rather than your name, for example. Or, if you're including someone else's code in your module, you may need to mention their copyright (or lack thereof) as well.

The *README* file also has a special responsibility: the master CPAN archiving tools pull out the *README* file as a separate entry automatically, permitting the search engines on the various worldwide archives to index them. The CPAN installation tools can download it and display it without downloading the entire distribution. In the CPAN.pm shell, for example, you can say:†

```
$ perl -MCPAN -eshell
cpan> readme Island::Plotting::Maps
```

In CPANPLUS, the successor to CPAN.pm, we do something similar:

```
$ perl -MCPANPLUS -eshell
cpanp> r Island::Plotting::Maps
```

Depending on your version of Perl, you might have the *cpan* or *cpanp* programs:

```
$ cpan
cpan> readme Island::Plotting::Maps
```

---

* When you're bored, you might find it amusing to do a search on CPAN for all places in which blah blah blah occurs.

† Well, you *would* be able to do this, if there were actually a module on CPAN named Island::Plotting::Maps.

Changes

The *Changes* file tracks the evolution of our code. Users typically check this file to see what's new with the module and to decide if they want to upgrade.* In this file, we note any bugs we fixed, features we added, and how important the changes are (i.e., should everyone upgrade right away?).

```
$ cat Changes
Revision history for Perl extension Island::Plotting::Maps.

0.01  Wed Oct 16 15:53:23 2002
          - original version; created by h2xs 1.22 with options
                  -XAn Island::Plotting::Maps
```

We need to maintain this file manually unless our interactive development environment has automated tools for such maintenance. We can also use this file to help us track changes and their effects: if we realize that a certain bug turned up three releases back, we can look here to remind ourselves of new features or bug fixes that we introduced in that release.

META.yml

Recent versions of the module tools create a file named *META.yml* that presents the module information in a human-readable form that is also easy to parse. It uses the YAML format we told you about in Chapter 6.

```
# http://module-build.sourceforge.net/META-spec.html
#XXXXXXX This is a prototype!!!  It will change in the future!!! XXXXX#
name:         HTTP-Size
version:      0.91
version_from: lib/Size.pm
installdirs:  site
requires:
        HTML::SimpleLinkExtor:        0
        HTTP::Request:                0
        URI:                          0

distribution_type: module
generated_by: ExtUtils::MakeMaker version 6.17
```

In this case, ExtUtils::MakeMaker automatically created this file for me. When we create the distribution archive, the *Makefile* creates this file, ensures that it's in *MANIFEST*, and includes it in distribution. Other tools and services, including the ones we cover in Chapter 19, can use this file to discover things about the module without having to run any of the distribution code. There is a lot more to this file, and its format documentation reference is right there in the file.

---

* Why not upgrade? Some people are content, and rightfully so, with something they already know works. Why chance breaking anything if you don't need to?

The Prototype Module Itself

Finally we come to the most important part of the distribution, which is the actual code:

```
package Island::Plotting::Maps;
```

It looks good so far. The module automatically starts with an appropriate package directive. Following that, we get the standard, good-practice pragmas.

```
use 5.008007;
use strict;
use warnings;
```

Now we're declaring that the module is compatible with Perl 5.8.7 or later and that the compiler restrictions and warnings are enabled automatically. We like to encourage good practices. Obviously, we're free to delete or modify anything inappropriate. If we know that our module works with earlier versions of Perl, we can modify the use 5.008007; line (or delete it altogether).

Next comes the mechanism by which we can make our functions and variables show up in the package that called the module. The Exporter function takes care of all of that for us by providing the import method that we talked about in Chapter 15.

```
require Exporter;

our @ISA = qw(Exporter);
```

This is fine for non-object-oriented modules, but object-oriented modules typically don't export anything since they require the user to call methods on an object. We'll replace the Exporter lines with one that declares the class that we inherit from, if any.

```
use base qw(Geo::Maps);
```

We have to include some information for Exporter, and *h2xs* sets that up for us. We have to fill in (or not fill in) three variables:

```
our %EXPORT_TAGS = ( 'all' => [ qw(

) ] );

our @EXPORT_OK = ( @{ $EXPORT_TAGS{'all'} } );

our @EXPORT = qw(

);
```

The @EXPORT array contains the names of all the variables and subroutines that use will automatically import into the caller by default. All of those show up in the calling package unless we tell use otherwise.

```
use Island::Plotting::Maps;  # import everything in @EXPORT
```

We won't get anything imported if we give use an empty import list.

```
use Island::Plotting::Maps ();  # import nothing
```

The @EXPORT_OK array contains the names of all the variables and subroutines that use can import if the user asks for them by name (and @EXPORT_OK implicitly contains @EXPORT). If the variables or subroutines are not in one of these arrays, use won't be able to import them.

```
use Island::Plotting::Maps ();  # import nothing
```

The %EXPORT_TAGS hash lets us give names to sets of variables and functions so we can export groups of symbols without making the user type too much. The keys to %EXPORT_TAGS are the group labels, and the hash values are anonymous arrays of symbols that belong to that tag. In the use statement's import list, we include the tag name preceded by a colon.*

```
use Island::Plotting::Maps qw(:all)
```

After the Exporter setup, we get the version number for our new module.

```
our $VERSION = '0.01';
```

This version number is important for many reasons, and we need to pay special attention to it. Choose the version number carefully, because many other things use it and depend on it:

Unique identification
> The version number identifies a particular release of a particular module as it floats around the Internet.

Filename generation
> The archive of the distribution includes the version number of the primary module by default. PAUSE won't let us upload the same filename twice, either, so if our code changes but our version number doesn't, we'll have some trouble there.

Upgrade indication
> Generally, numbers that increase numerically supersede previous versions. For this test, the number is considered a floating-point number, so 2.10 (which is really 2.1) is less than 2.9 (which must be the same as 2.90, by the same logic). To avoid confusion, if we've have two digits after the decimal point in one release, we should have two digits in the next release.†

Interface stability
> Generally, numbers that begin with 0 are alpha or beta, with external interfaces that may still be in flux. Also, most people use a major version number change (from 1.x to 2.x, etc.) to indicate a potential break in upward compatibility.

---

* Technically, you don't need :all because /^/ (include all symbols that match at least a beginning of string) does the same. Many people are familiar with typing :all, and it's far more self-documenting than /^/ is, so include it if you can.

† *Perl Best Practices* recommends using a three-part version string, such as qv(1.2.3), but their use is not widespread, requires version.pm (a non-core module as of Perl 5.8), does not integrate with common tools yet, and has lexical issues.

Recognition by the various CPAN tools

The CPAN distribution management tools use the version number to track a particular release, and the CPAN installation tools can determine missing or out-of-date distributions.

Perl's own operators

The use operator can be given a version number in addition to (or instead of) the import list, forcing the use operation to fail if the imported module is not equal to or greater than that version:

```
use Island::Plotting::Maps 1.10 qw{ map_debugger };
```

Generally, you can start with the 0.01 given by the template and increase it consistently with each new test release.* Now you're past the header information and down to the core of your module. In the template, it is indicated by a simple comment:

```
# Preloaded methods go here.
```

What? You didn't think the *h2xs* tool would even write the module for you, now did you? Anyway, this is where the code goes, usually as a series of subroutines, possibly preceded by some shared module data (using my declarations) and perhaps a few package variables (using our declarations in recent Perl versions). Following the code, you'll find your necessary true value:

```
1;
```

so the require (inside the use) doesn't abort.

Embedded Documentation

Immediately following the mandatory true value in the file, you'll find the __END__ marker. That's double underscore followed by END followed by another double underscore. It's at the beginning of the line and has a newline immediately following it:

```
__END__
```

This marker tells Perl that there's no Perl code anywhere later in the file and that the Perl parser can stop now.† Following the __END__ marker, you'll find the embedded documentation for the module:

```
# Below is stub documentation for your module. You'd better edit it!

=head1 NAME
```

---

* The *perlmod* page includes an example that extracts the CVS/RCS version number for the module's version number.

† The data immediately following the __END__ marker is available by reading from the DATA filehandle, which is a great way to include a small amount of constant data with your program. However, that's not why we're using it here.

```
Island::Plotting::Maps - Perl extension for blah blah blah

=head1 SYNOPSIS

  use Island::Plotting::Maps;
  blah blah blah

=head1 ABSTRACT

  This should be the abstract for Island::Plotting::Maps.
  The abstract is used when making PPD (Perl Package Description) files.
  If you don't want an ABSTRACT you should also edit Makefile.PL to
  remove the ABSTRACT_FROM option.

=head1 DESCRIPTION

Stub documentation for Island::Plotting::Maps, created by h2xs. It looks like the
author of the extension was negligent enough to leave the stub
unedited.

Blah blah blah.

=head1 EXPORT

None by default.

=head1 SEE ALSO

Mention other useful documentation such as the documentation of
related modules or operating system documentation (such as manpages
in UNIX), or any relevant external documentation such as RFCs or
standards.

If you have a mailing list set up for your module, mention it here.

If you have a web site set up for your module, mention it here.

=head1 AUTHOR

Ginger Grant, <ginger@island.coconet>

=head1 COPYRIGHT AND LICENSE

Copyright 2006 by Ginger Grant

This library is free software; you can redistribute it and/or modify
it under the same terms as Perl itself.

=cut
```

This documentation is in POD format. The *perlpod* manpage describes the POD format in detail. Like Perl itself, POD is said to mean various things, such as Perl Online Documentation or Plain Old Documentation, and so on. To most of us, it's just POD.

As the template describes, you're expected to edit portions of this text to fit your particular module. In particular, leaving the blah blah blah is considered bad form.

The POD information is extracted automatically by the installation process to create the native documentation format, such as Unix manpages or HTML. Also, the *perldoc* command can locate POD in the installed scripts and modules and format it for the screen.

One nice thing about POD is that it can be interspersed with the Perl implementation code it describes. Each POD directive (a line beginning with an equals sign) switches from Perl mode (lines interpreted as Perl code) to POD mode (lines interpreted as documentation), and each line beginning with =cut switches back. For example, you had three subroutines in the Island::Plotting::Maps module. The resulting file with mixed code and documentation looks something like:

```
package Island::Plotting::Maps;
[... stuff down to the $VERSION setting above ...]

=head1 NAME

Island::Plotting::Maps - Plot maps on the island

=head1 SYNOPSIS

  use Island::Plotting::Maps;
  load_map("/usr/share/map/hawaii.map");
  scale_map(20, 20);
  draw_map(*STDOUT);

=head1 DESCRIPTION

This module draws maps. [ more here ]

=over

=item load_map($filename)

This function [ more here ].

=cut

sub load_map {
  my $filename = shift;
  [ rest of subroutine ]
}

=item scale_map($x, $y)

This function [ more here ].

=cut
```

```
sub scale_map {
  my ($x, $y) = (shift, shift);
  [ rest of subroutine ]
}

=item draw_map($filehandle)

This function [ more here ].

=cut

sub draw_map {
  my $filehandle = shift;
  [ rest of subroutine ]
}

=back

=head1 SEE ALSO

"Map Reading for Dummies", "First Mates: why they're not the captain",
and be sure to consult with the Professor.

=head1 AUTHOR

Ginger Grant, <ginger@island.coconet>

=head1 COPYRIGHT AND LICENSE

Copyright 2006 by Ginger Grant

This library is free software; you can redistribute it and/or modify
it under the same terms as Perl itself.

=cut

1;
```

As you can see, the documentation for the subroutines is now very near the subroutine definition, in the hope that as one gets updated, the other will be similarly changed. (Out-of-date documentation is often worse than no documentation at all, because at least with no documentation at all, the user is forced to look at the source code.) Many modules in the CPAN do this. The penalty is a *very* slight increase in compile-time activity because the Perl parser has to skip over the embedded POD directives.

Whether you place your POD at the end of the file (as the template suggests) or intertwined with your code (as presented in the preceding paragraphs), the important thing to remember is always to document your code. Even if it's just for you, a few months later, when your brain has been 42,000 other places before you look at the code again, you'll be glad to have those notes. Documentation is important.

Controlling the Distribution with Makefile.PL

The Perl developers have chosen to rely on the standard Unix *make* utility to build and install Perl itself, and that same mechanism is used for additional modules. If you have a non-Unix system, a *make*-like utility should also be available. On Windows, for example, you may have *dmake* or another program. The command `perl -V:make` will tell you the name of your *make* utility program; if it says `make='nmake'`, simply use *nmake* wherever you use *make*. In any case, you should call the controlling file a *Makefile*, even though its name may vary as well.

However, crafting a *Makefile* is tricky but repetitive. And what better way to accomplish a tricky but repetitive task than with a program? Since you're talking about Perl add-on modules, you know that Perl is available, so how about a Perl program to generate the *Makefile*?

That's exactly what happens. The distribution is required to contain a *Makefile.PL*, which is a Perl program to build a *Makefile*. Then from there, you use *make* (or something like it) to control all of the remaining tasks.

The *h2xs* tool generates a template *Makefile.PL* that you probably won't even need to touch for single-module distributions:

```
$ cat Makefile.PL
use 5.008;
use ExtUtils::MakeMaker;
# See lib/ExtUtils/MakeMaker.pm for details of how to influence
# the contents of the Makefile that is written.
WriteMakefile(
    'NAME'              => 'Island::Plotting::Maps',
    'VERSION_FROM'      => 'Maps.pm', # finds $VERSION
    'PREREQ_PM'              => {  }, # e.g., Module::Name => 1.1
    ($] >= 5.005 ?     ## Add these new keywords supported since 5.005
      (ABSTRACT_FROM => 'Maps.pm', # retrieve abstract from module
       AUTHOR      => 'Ginger Grant <ginger@island.coconet>') : (  )),
);
```

Yes, this is a Perl program. The `WriteMakefile` routine is defined by the `ExtUtils::MakeMaker` module (included with Perl) to generate a *Makefile*. As the developer of the module, use this makefile to build and test your module and prepare a distribution file:

```
$ perl Makefile.PL
Checking if your kit is complete...
Looks good
Writing Makefile for Island::Plotting::Maps
```

The ultimate user of your distribution will execute the identical command at his site. However, the *Makefile* will most likely be different, reflecting the differences in installation locations, local policies, and even the C compiler and linking instructions appropriate for their architecture. It's a nice system that has worked quite well over the years.

The creation of the *Makefile.PL* (and resulting *Makefile*) is quite flexible. For example, you can run code to ask the person installing your module about the locations of other installed libraries or tools, or get options for variations in activity.*

The PREREQ_PM setting is important if your module depends on non-core Perl modules, especially if you plan to upload your code to the CPAN. Proper use of the prerequisites list can make installing your module nearly painless, and your user community will thank you.

Alternate Installation Locations (PREFIX=...)

The *Makefile* built by the default invocation of *Makefile.PL* presumes that the module will be installed in the system-wide Perl directory that all Perl programs can access directly with the built-in @INC path.

However, if you are testing a module, you certainly don't want to install it into the system directories, possibly corrupting a previous version of your module and breaking production programs.

Also, if you're not the system administrator, it's unlikely that you can change those central Perl directories, because that would be a great way to insert a Trojan horse for privileged users to stumble across.†

Luckily, the *Makefile* contains provisions for considering an alternate installation location for scripts, manpages, and libraries. The easiest way to specify an alternate location is with a PREFIX value as a parameter on the command line:

```
$ perl Makefile.PL PREFIX=~/Testing
Checking if your kit is complete...
Looks good
Writing Makefile for Island::Plotting::Maps
```

Although the messages don't indicate anything different, the *Makefile* will now install scripts to $PREFIX/bin, manpages below $PREFIX/man, and libraries below $PREFIX/lib/site_perl. In this case, you've selected a subdirectory of your home directory called *Testing* as the value of $PREFIX.

If you were a project librarian, managing code for a team of developers, you might instead say something like:

```
$ perl Makefile.PL PREFIX=/path/to/shared/area
```

---

* Please keep the number of questions to a minimum, however. Most people are irritated when asked a series of questions, especially when they are just upgrading your module. If possible, store the answers in a configuration module that you install, so that a later invocation of your installer can pull the previous answers as defaults.

† Even if you weren't the system administrator, you'd soon have all the powers of the system administrator.

---

which then builds the files into a shared area. Of course, you'd need write privileges to such a directory, and the rest of the team would have to add the *bin* subdirectory to their PATH, the *man* subdirectory to their MANPATH, and the *lib/site_perl* directory to their @INC path, as you'll see shortly.

Trivial make test

Testing. Testing. Testing. We talk more about testing in depth in Chapters 17 and 18, but here's a brief introduction.

Testing is important. First, you should at least ensure that the code you've written even compiles before you install it and start playing with it. That test is free. You can invoke it directly from the newly created *Makefile* by simply typing make test, as in:

```
$ make test
cp Maps.pm blib/lib/Island/Plotting/Maps.pm
PERL_DL_NONLAZY=1 /usr/local/bin/perl "-MExtUtils::Command::MM" "-e" "test_harness(0,
'blib/lib', 'blib/arch')" t/*.t
t/1....ok
All tests successful.
Files=1, Tests=1,  1 wallclock secs ( 0.08 cusr + 0.04 csys =  0.12 CPU)
```

But what happened there?

First, the *.pm* file was copied to the testing staging area: the area headed by *blib* (build library) below the current directory.* Next, the *perl* that invoked the *Makefile. PL* is called upon to run the *test harness*—a program that manages all test invocations and reports the results at the end.†

The test harness runs all files in the *t* subdirectory that end in *.t* in their natural order. You have only one file (created by *h2xs*), which looks like this:

```
$ cat t/1.t
# Before 'make install' is performed this script should be runnable with
# 'make test'. After 'make install' it should work as 'perl 1.t'

#########################

# change 'tests => 1' to 'tests => last_test_to_print';

use Test::More tests => 1;
BEGIN { use_ok('Island::Plotting::Maps') };

#########################
```

---

* Had there been XS files or other more complex build steps, these also would have happened here.

† The *perl* that invoked the *Makefile.PL* is used for all configuration decisions. If you have more than one version of Perl installed on your system, be sure to execute the *Makefile.PL* with the correct one. From there, full paths are always used, so there's no chance of mixing anything else up.

```
# Insert your test code below, the Test::More module is use( )ed here so read
# its manpage ( perldoc Test::More ) for help writing this test script.
```

It's a simple test program. The test pulls in the Test::More module, described further in Chapter 17. The import list for the module is treated specially; you're declaring that this test file consists of only one "test."

The test is given in the following line and attempts to use the module. If this succeeds, you get an "OK" sign, and the overall test file succeeds. This would fail if the module had a syntax error, or if you forgot to have that true value at the end of the file.

In this example, the test succeeds, so you get a message for it and a summary of the CPU time used for the test.

Trivial make install

Since you know the module can at least compile, let's be daring and install it. Of course, you're installing it only into the path specified by the PREFIX in the earlier step, but that's enough to show how it would have worked for the user's installation.* The installation is triggered with make install:

```
$ make install
Manifying blib/man3/Island::Plotting::Maps.3
Installing /home/ginger/Testing/lib/site_perl/5.8.7/Island/Plotting/Maps.pm
Installing /home/ginger/Testing/man/man3/Island::Plotting::Maps.3
Writing /home/ginger/Testing/lib/site_perl/5.8.7/darwin/auto/Island/Plotting/Maps/.
packlist
Appending installation info to /home/ginger/Testing/lib/site_perl/5.8.7/darwin/
perllocal.pod
```

Note that you're installing the module below the $PREFIX/lib/site_lib directory (presuming a PREFIX of *home/ginger/Testing* from earlier) and a manpage below $PREFIX/man (on Unix machines, in the Section 3 area for subroutines, for example). The manpage comes automatically when you extract the module's POD data and convert it to troff -man code, making it compatible with the Unix *man* command.†

Trivial make dist

After some testing, you may decide it's time to share your work with friends and associates. To do this, make a single distribution file. Many mechanisms are available to do this, but the most common one on most modern Unix platforms is the GNU *gzip* compressed *tar* archive, commonly named with a *.tar.gz* or *.tgz* extension.

---

* If you're playing along at home, be sure *not* to install this pretend module anywhere but in a temporary, testing directory. Although removing an installed module is generally difficult, you'll be able to simply delete the testing directory, along with its contents.

† On a non-Unix system, or even a few odd Unix systems, you'll see different behavior but roughly the same overall result.

Again, with a simple *make* invocation (make dist), you end up with the required file:

```
$ make dist
rm -rf Island-Plotting-Maps-0.01
/usr/local/bin/perl "-MExtUtils::Manifest=manicopy,maniread" \
        -e "manicopy(maniread(  ),'Island-Plotting-Maps-0.01', 'best');"
mkdir Island-Plotting-Maps-0.01
mkdir Island-Plotting-Maps-0.01/t
tar cvf Island-Plotting-Maps-0.01.tar Island-Plotting-Maps-0.01
Island-Plotting-Maps-0.01/
Island-Plotting-Maps-0.01/Changes
Island-Plotting-Maps-0.01/Makefile.PL
Island-Plotting-Maps-0.01/MANIFEST
Island-Plotting-Maps-0.01/Maps.pm
Island-Plotting-Maps-0.01/README
Island-Plotting-Maps-0.01/t/
Island-Plotting-Maps-0.01/t/1.t
rm -rf Island-Plotting-Maps-0.01
gzip --best Island-Plotting-Maps-0.01.tar
```

Now there's a file named *Island-Plotting-Maps-0.01.tar.gz* in the directory. The version number in the name comes from the module's $VERSION variable.*

Using the Alternate Library Location

The libraries are installed relative to the PREFIX specified earlier. If Ginger used a PREFIX of */home/ginger/Testing*, you need to add the appropriate directory below it to the search path. The use lib directive of:

```
use lib '/home/ginger/Testing/lib/site_perl';
```

does the right thing to find the version-specific directory below it, as well as the architecture-specific directory below it, if needed (usually for architecture-specific files, such as compiled binaries).

You can also specify the include directory on the command line with a -M option:

```
$ perl -Mlib=/home/ginger/Testing/lib/site_perl myproggy
```

or a -I option:

```
$ perl -I /home/ginger/Testing/lib/site_perl myproggy
```

or even by setting the PERL5LIB environment variable (using sh-like syntax here):

```
$ PERL5LIB=/home/ginger/Testing/lib/site_perl; export PERL5LIB
$ ./myproggy
```

However, the downside of any of these methods (other than the use lib method) is that they require you to do something more than just execute the file. If someone (or something) else (such as a coworker or a web server) executes your program, it's

---

* If there's more than one module, you need to designate the primary module in the *Makefile.PL*.

unlikely that the proper environment variable or command-line option will be present. Your program will fail because it can't find your locally installed module.

Use use lib when you can. The other ways are useful mainly for trying out a new version of an old module before replacing the old module (and possibly breaking the programs that use it).

Exercise

You can find the answer to this exercise in "Answer for Chapter 16" in the Appendix.

Exercise [30 min]

Package up the Animal and Horse classes from Chapter 12 as a distribution. Be sure to add the proper POD documentation for the subroutine. Test the module, install it locally, and then build a distribution file. If you have time, unpack the distribution into a different directory, pick a new prefix, and install it again to verify that the distribution archive contains everything necessary.

## CHAPTER 17

Essential Testing

As we briefly described in Chapter 16, a distribution contains a testing facility that we can invoke from make test. This allows us to write and run tests during development and maintenance, and it also lets our end user verify that the module works in her environment.

Although we cover testing briefly here, you should check out *Perl Testing: A Developer's Notebook* (O'Reilly), which covers the subject in depth.

More Tests Mean Better Code

Why should we test during development? The short answer is that we find out about problems sooner and tests force us to program in much smaller chunks (since they are easier to test), which is generally good programming practice. Although we may think we have extra work to do, that's only short-term overhead. We win down the line when we spend less time debugging, both because we've fixed most of the problems before they were problems and because the tests usually point us right at the problem we need to fix.

Along with that, we'll find that it's psychologically easier to modify code because the tests will tell us if we broke something. When we talk to our boss or coworkers, we'll also have the confidence in our code to answer their queries and questions. The tests tell us how healthy our code is.

Different people have different ideas about testing. One school of thought, known as Test-Driven Development, says that we should write the tests before we write the code that is being tested. On the first go-around, the test fails. What good is the test if it doesn't fail when it should? Once we know it fails, we write the code to make it work. When that works, we write a test for another feature, repeat the process, and keep doing that until we're done. Along the way, we've verified the functionality and features.

We're never really done, though. Even when the module ships, we shouldn't abandon the test suite! Unless we code the mythical "bug-free module," our users will send us bug reports. We can turn each report into a test case.* While fixing the bug, the remaining tests prevent our code from regressing to a less functional version of the code—hence the name *regression testing*.

Then there are always the future releases to think about. When we want to add new features, we start by adding tests.† Because the existing tests ensure our upward compatibility, we can be confident that our new release does everything the old release did, and then some.

A Simple Test Script

Before we go on, let's write some Perl code. We just told you about creating the tests before you write the code, so maybe we should follow our own advice. We'll get to the details later, but for now we start with the Test::More module,‡ which comes with the standard Perl distribution.

To start our testing, we write a simple Perl script. All of our tests are going to be scripts, so we can use the stuff you already know about Perl. We load Test::More and tell it how many tests we want to run. After that, we use the convenience functions from Test::More, which we'll go through later. In short, most of them compare their first argument, which is the result we got, to the second argument, which is what we expected.

```
#!/usr/bin/perl

use Test::More tests => 4;

ok( 1, '1 is true' );

is( 2 + 2, 4, 'The sum is 4' );

is( 2 * 3, 5, 'The product is 5' );

isnt( 2 ** 3, 6, "The result isn't 6" );

like( 'Alpaca Book', qr/alpaca/i, 'I found an alpaca!' );
```

When we run this simple script, we get this output. When the received and expected values are the same, Test::More outputs a line starting with ok. When those values

---

* If we're reporting a bug in someone else's code, we can generally assume that they'll appreciate us sending them a test for the bug. They'll appreciate a patch even more!

† And writing the documentation at the same time, made easier by Test::Inline, as we'll see later.

‡ There is also a Test::Simple module, but most people use its successor, Test::More, so we'll stick to that.

---

don't match, it outputs a line starting with not ok. It also outputs some diagnostic information that tells us what the test expected and what we actually gave it.

```
1..4
ok 1 - 1 is true
ok 2 - The sum is 4
not ok 3 - The product is 5
#   Failed test 'The product is 5'
#   in /Users/brian/Desktop/test at line 9.
#          got: '6'
#     expected: '5'
# Looks like you planned 4 tests but ran 1 extra.
# Looks like you failed 1 test of 5 run.
ok 4 - The result isn't 6
ok 5 - I found an alpaca!
```

Later on, we'll see how Perl takes all of this output to create a nice report for us. We won't have to look at a lot of output to find the important bits once Test::Harness goes through it for us.

The Art of Testing

Good tests also give small examples of what we meant in our documentation. It's another way to express the same thing, and some people may like one way over the other.* Good tests also give confidence to the user that your code (and all its dependencies) is portable enough to work on her system.

Testing is an art. People have written and read dozens of how-to-test books (and then ignore them, it seems). Mostly, it's important to remember everything we have ever done wrong while programming (or heard other people do), and then test that we didn't do it again for this project.

When you create tests, think like a person using a module, not like one writing a module. You know how you should use your module, because you invented it and had a specific need for it. Other people will probably have different uses for it and they'll try to use it in all sorts of different ways. You probably already know that given the chance, users will find every other way to use your code. You need to think like that when you test.

Test things that should break as well as things that should work. Test the edges and the middle. Test one more or one less than the edge. Test things one at a time. Test many things at once. If something should throw an exception, make sure it doesn't also have bad side effects. Pass extra parameters. Pass insufficient parameters. Mess

---

* A few of the modules we've used from CPAN are easier to learn from test examples than by the actual POD. Of course, any really good example should be repeated in your module's POD documentation.

up the capitalization on named parameters. Throw far too much or too little data at it. Test what happens for unexpected values such as undef.

Since we can't look at your module, let's suppose that we want to test Perl's sqrt function, which calculates square roots. It's obvious that we need to make sure it returns the right values when its parameter is 0, 1, 49, or 100. It's nearly as obvious to see that sqrt(0.25) should come out to be 0.5. We should also ensure that multiplying the value for sqrt(7) by itself gives something between 6.99999 and 7.00001.[*]

Let's express that as code. We use the same stuff that we used for our first example. This script tests things that should work.

```perl
#!/usr/bin/perl

use Test::More tests => 6;

is( sqrt(  0),  0, 'The square root of 0   is  0' );
is( sqrt(  1),  1, 'The square root of 1   is  1' );
is( sqrt( 49),  7, 'The square root of 49  is  7' );
is( sqrt(100), 10, 'The square root of 100 is 10' );

is( sqrt(0.25), 0.5, 'The square root of 0.25 is 0.5' );

my $product = sqrt(7) * sqrt(7);

ok( $product > 6.999 && $product < 7.001,
        "The product [$product] is around 7" );
```

We should make sure that sqrt(-1) yields a fatal error and that sqrt(-100) does too. What happens when we request sqrt(&test_sub( )), and &test_sub returns a string of "10000"? What does sqrt(undef) do? How about sqrt( ) or sqrt(1,1)? Maybe we want to give our function a googol: sqrt(10**100). Because this function is documented to work on $_ by default, we should ensure that it does so. Even a simple function such as sqrt should get a couple dozen tests; if our code does more complex tasks than sqrt does, expect it to need more tests, too. There are never too many tests.

In this simple script, we tested a lot of odd conditions.[†]

```perl
#!/usr/bin/perl

use Test::More tests => 9;

sub test_sub { '10000' }

is( $@, '', '$@ is not set at start' );
```

[*] Remember, floating-point numbers aren't always exact; there's usually a little roundoff. The Test::Number::Delta module can handle those situations.

[†] And in writing this, we discovered that we can't write sqrt(-1) because eval doesn't trap that. Apparently, Perl catches it at compile time.

```perl
{
$n = -1;
eval { sqrt($n) };
ok( $@, '$@ is set after sqrt(-1)' );
}

eval { sqrt(1) };
is( $@, '', '$@ is not set after sqrt(1)' );

{
my $n = -100;
eval { sqrt($n) };
ok( $@, '$@ is set after sqrt(-100)' );
}

is( sqrt( test_sub() ), 100, 'String value works in sqrt()' );

eval { sqrt(undef) };
is( $@, '', '$@ is not set after sqrt(undef)' );

is( sqrt, 0, 'sqrt() works on $_ (undefined) by default' );

$_ = 100;
is( sqrt, 10, 'sqrt() works on $_ by default' );

is( sqrt( 10**100 ), 10**50, 'sqrt() can handle a googol' );
```

If you write the code and not just the tests, think about how to get every line of your code exercised at least once for full code coverage. (Are you testing the else clause? Are you testing every elsif case?) If you aren't writing the code or aren't sure, use the code coverage facilities.*

Check out other test suites, too. There are literally tens of thousands of test files on CPAN, and some of them contain hundreds of tests. The Perl distribution itself comes with thousands of tests, designed to verify that Perl compiles correctly on our machine in every possible way. That should be enough examples for anyone. Michael Schwern earned the title of "Perl Test Master" for getting the Perl core completely tested and still constantly beats the drum for "test! test! test!" in the community.

The Test Harness

We usually invoke tests, either as the developer or the user, by using make test. The Makefile uses the Test::Harness module to run the tests, watch the output, and report the results.

---

* Basic code coverage tools such as Devel::Cover are available in CPAN.

Tests live in files in the t directory at the top level of the distribution, and each test file ends in .t. The test harness invokes each file separately, so an exit or die terminates only the testing in that file, not the whole testing process.*

The test file communicates with the test harness through simple messages on standard output.† The three most important messages are the test count, a success message, and a failure message.

An individual test file comprises one or more tests. These tests are numbered as counting numbers, starting with one. The first thing a test file must announce to the test harness (on STDOUT) is the expected number of tests, as a string that looks like a Perl range, 1..N. For example, if there are 17 tests, the first line of output should be:

```
1..17
```

followed by a newline. The test harness uses the upper number to verify that the test file hasn't just terminated early. If the test file is testing optional things and has no testing to do for this particular invocation, the string 1..0 suffices.

We don't have to worry about printing that ourselves, though, because Test::More does it for us. When we load the module, we tell it the number of tests that we want to run, and the module outputs the test range for us. To get that 1..17, we tell Test::More we're running 17 tests.

```
use Test::More tests => 17;
```

After we print the test range, we send to standard output one line per test. That line starts with ok if the test passed, or not ok if the test failed. If we wrote that by hand, a test to check that 1 plus 2 is 3 might look like this:

```
print +(1 + 2 == 3 ? '', 'not '), "ok 1\n";
```

We could also print the not only if the test failed, with the ok as a separate step. But on some platforms, this may fail unnecessarily, due to some I/O-related oddity. For maximum portability, print the entire string of ok N or not ok N in one print step. Don't forget the space after not!

```
print 'not ' unless 2 * 4 == 8;
print "ok 2\n";
```

We don't have to do that much work, though, and we don't have to count the tests ourselves. What if we wanted to add a test between the two previous tests? We'd have to give that new test the test number 2 and change the last test to test number 3. Not only that, we haven't output anything useful if the test fails, so we won't know

---

* If we decide that we need to stop all testing, we can "bail out" of the process by printing "bail out" to standard output. This can be handy if we encounter an error that is going to cause a cascade of errors that we don't want to wait to encounter or sift through.

† The exact details are documented in the perldoc Test::Harness::TAP, if you're curious. Actually, they're there, even if you're not curious.

what went wrong. We could do all that, but it's too much work! Luckily, we can use the convenience functions from Test::More.

Writing Tests with Test::More

The Test::More* module comes with the standard Perl distribution starting with Perl 5.8, and it's available on CPAN if we need to install it on earlier Perl versions. It works all the way back to perl5.6, at least. We rewrite the tests from the previous section (and throw in a couple more) in this test script, which uses the ok() function from Test::More.

```
use Test::More tests => 4;

ok(1 + 2 == 3, '1 + 2 == 3');
ok(2 * 4 == 8, '2 * 4 == 8');
my $divide = 5 / 3;
ok(abs($divide - 1.666667) < 0.001, '5 / 3 == (approx) 1.666667');
my $subtract = -3 + 3;
ok(($subtract eq '0' or $subtract eq '-0'), '-3 + 3 == 0');
```

The ok() function prints "ok" if its first argument is true, and "not ok" otherwise. The optional second argument lets us name the test. After the initial output to indicate success, ok() adds a hyphen and then the name of the test. When we find a test that does not work, we can find it by the name that we gave it.

```
1..4
ok 1 - 1 + 2 == 3
ok 2 - 2 * 4 == 8
ok 3 - 5 / 3 == (approx) 1.666667
ok 4 - -3 + 3 == 0
```

Now Test::More does all of the hard work. We don't have to think about the output or the test numbering. But what about that nasty little 4 constant in the first line? That's fine once we're shipping the code, but while we're testing, retesting (retesting some more), and adding more tests, we don't want to keep updating that number to keep the test harness from complaining about too many or too few tests. We change that to no_plan so Test::More can figure it out later.

```
use Test::More "no_plan";       # during development

ok(1 + 2 == 3, '1 + 2 == 3');
ok(2 * 4 == 8, '2 * 4 == 8');
my $divide = 5 / 3;
ok(abs($divide - 1.666667) < 0.001, '5 / 3 == (approx) 1.666667');
my $subtract = -3 + 3;
ok(($subtract eq '0' or $subtract eq '-0'), '-3 + 3 == 0');
```

* The name plays off Test::Simple, which did some of the same stuff but with far fewer convenience functions.

The output from `Test::More` is a bit different, and the test range moves to the end. That's just the number of tests that we actually ran, which might not be the number we intended to run:

```
ok 1 - 1 + 2 == 3
ok 2 - 2 * 4 == 8
ok 3 - 5 / 3 == (approx) 1.666667
ok 4 - -3 + 3 == 0
1..4
```

The test harness knows that if it doesn't see a header, it's expecting a footer. If the number of tests disagree or there's no footer (and no header), it's a broken result. We can use this during development, but we have to remember to put the final number of tests in the script before we ship it as real code.

But wait: there's more (to `Test::More`). Instead of a simple yes/no, we can ask if two values are the same. The `is()` function, as we showed earlier, compares its first argument, which is the result we got, with the second argument, which is what we expected. The optional third argument is the name we give the test, just as we did with the ok function earlier.

```
use Test::More 'no_plan';

is(1 + 2, 3, '1 + 2 is 3');
is(2 * 4, 8, '2 * 4 is 8');
```

Note that we've gotten rid of numeric equality and instead asked if "this is that." On a successful test, this doesn't give much advantage, but on a failed test, we get much more interesting output.

```
use Test::More 'no_plan';

is(1 + 2, 3, '1 + 2 is 3');
is(2 * 4, 6, '2 * 4 is 6');
```

This script yields much more useful output that tells us what `is()` was expecting and what it actually got.

```
ok 1 - 1 + 2 is 3
not ok 2 - 2 * 4 is 6
#     Failed test (1.t at line 4)
#          got: '8'
#     expected: '6'
1..2
# Looks like you failed 1 tests of 2.
```

Of course, this is an error in the test, but note that the output told us what happened: we got an 8 when we were expecting a 6.* This is far better than just "something went

---

* More precisely: we got an '8' but were expecting a '6'. Did you notice that these are strings? The is() test checks for string equality. If we don't want that, we just build an ok() test instead, or try cmp_ok, coming up in a moment.

wrong" as before. There's also a corresponding isnt( ) when we want to compare for inequality rather than equality.

What about that third test, where we allowed the value to vary within some tolerance? Well, we can just use the cmp_ok routine instead.[*] The first and third arguments are the operands,[†] and the intervening, second argument is the comparison operator (as a string!).

```
use Test::More 'no_plan';

my $divide = 5 / 3;
cmp_ok(abs($divide - 1.666667), '<' , 0.001,
       '5 / 3 should be (approx) 1.666667');
```

If the test we give in the second argument fails between the first and third arguments, then we get a descriptive error message with both of the values and the comparison, rather than a simple pass or fail value as before.

How about that last test? We wanted to see if the result was a 0 or minus 0 (on the rare systems that give back a minus 0). We can do that with the like( ) function:

```
use Test::More 'no_plan';

my $subtract = -3 + 3;
like($subtract, qr/^-?0$/, '-3 + 3 == 0');
```

Here, we take the string form of the first argument and attempt to match it against the second argument. The second argument is typically a regular expression object (created here with qr), but we can also use a simple string, which like( ) will convert to a regular expression object. We can even write the string form as if it were (almost) a regular expression:

```
like($subtract, qr/^-?0$/, '-3 + 3 == 0');
```

The string form is portable back to older Perls.[‡] If the match succeeds, it's a good test. If not, the original string and the regex are reported along with the test failure. We can change like to unlike if we expect the match to fail instead.

Testing Object-Oriented Features

For object-oriented modules, we want to ensure that we get back an object when we call the constructor. For this, isa_ok( ) and can_ok( ) are good interface tests:

```
use Test::More 'no_plan';

use Horse;
```

---

[*] Although Test::Number::Delta can handle this for us.

[†] There's no joy for RPN fans.

[‡] The qr// form wasn't introduced until Perl 5.005.

```
my $trigger = Horse->named('Trigger');
isa_ok($trigger, 'Horse');
isa_ok($trigger, 'Animal');
can_ok($trigger, $_) for qw(eat color);
```

These tests have default test names, so our test output looks like this:

```
ok 1 - The object isa Horse
ok 2 - The object isa Animal
ok 3 - Horse->can('eat')
ok 4 - Horse->can('color')
1..4
```

Here we're testing that it's a horse, but also that it's an animal, and that it can both eat and return a color.* We could further test to ensure that each horse has a unique name:

```
use Test::More 'no_plan';

use Horse;

my $trigger = Horse->named('Trigger');
isa_ok($trigger, 'Horse');

my $tv_horse = Horse->named('Mr. Ed');
isa_ok($tv_horse, 'Horse');

# Did making a second horse affect the name of the first horse?
is($trigger->name, 'Trigger', 'Trigger's name is correct');
is($tv_horse->name, 'Mr. Ed', 'Mr. Ed's name is correct');
is(Horse->name, 'a generic Horse');
```

The output of this shows us that the unnamed Horse is not quite what we thought it was.

```
ok 1 - The object isa Horse
ok 2 - The object isa Horse
ok 3 - Trigger's name is correct
ok 4 - Mr. Ed's name is correct
not ok 5
#       Failed test (1.t at line 13)
#            got: 'an unnamed Horse'
#       expected: 'a generic Horse'
1..5
# Looks like you failed 1 tests of 5.
```

Oops! Look at that. We wrote a generic Horse, but the string really is an unnamed Horse. That's an error in our test, not in the module, so we should correct that test error and retry. Unless, of course, the module's specification actually called for 'a generic Horse.'† You shouldn't be afraid to just write the tests and test the module. If you get either one wrong, the other will generally catch it.

---

* Well, we're testing to see that it can('eat') and can('color'). We haven't checked whether it really can use those method calls to do what we want!

† And, we'll find that the tests not only check the code, but they create the specification in code form.

You can even test the use with Test::More when you want to ensure that the module loads correctly:

```
use Test::More 'no_plan';

BEGIN{ use_ok('Horse') }

my $trigger = Horse->named('Trigger');
isa_ok($trigger, 'Horse');
# .. other tests as before ..
```

The difference between doing this as a test and doing it as a simple use is that the test won't completely abort if the use fails, although many other tests are likely to fail as well. It's also counted as one of the tests, so we get an "ok" for free even if all it does is compile properly to help pad our success numbers for the weekly status report.

We put the use_ok inside a BEGIN block so any exported subroutines from the module are properly declared for the rest of the program, as recommended by the documentation. For most object-oriented modules, this won't matter because they don't export subroutines.

A Testing To-Do List

When we write tests before we write the code, the tests will initially fail. We might even add new features that temporarily fail while we are developing. There are several situations where we realize a test is going to fail, but we don't want to pay attention to its failure. The Test::More module realizes this and allows us to mark a test as TODO, meaning that we expect it to fail and we'll get to it later.

In this example, we know that we want to add the talk() method to our Horses class, but we haven't actually done it. We wrote the test already, since it was part of our specification. We know the test is going to fail, and that's okay. Test::More won't really count it as a failure.

```
use Test::More 'no_plan';

use_ok('Horse');
my $tv_horse = Horse->named('Mr. Ed');

TODO: {
  local $TODO = 'haven\'t taught Horses to talk yet';

  can_ok($tv_horse, 'talk');  # he can talk!
}

is($tv_horse->name, 'Mr. Ed', 'I am Mr. Ed!');
```

The naked block of code we labeled with TODO to mark the section of the tests that we expect to fail. Inside the block, we create a local version of $TODO, which holds as its value the reason we think the tests will fail. Test::More marks the test as a TODO test in the output, and the test harness* notices it and doesn't penalize us for the failure.†

```
ok 1 - use Horse;
not ok 2 - Horse->can('talk') # TODO haven't taught Horses to talk yet
#     Failed (TODO) test (1.t at line 7)
#     Horse->can('talk') failed
ok 3 - I am Mr. Ed!
1..3
```

Skipping Tests

In some cases, we want to skip tests. For instance, some of our features may only work for a particular version of Perl, a particular operating system, or only when optional modules are available. To skip tests, we do much the same thing we did for the TODO tests, but Test::More does something much different.

In this example, we again use a naked block to create a section of code to skip, and we label it with SKIP. While testing, Test::More will not execute these tests, unlike the TODO block where it ran them anyway. At the start of the block, we call the skip() function to tell it why we want to skip the tests and how many tests we want to skip.

In this example, we check if the Mac::Speech module is installed before we try to test the say_it_aloud() method. If it isn't, the eval() block returns false and we execute the skip() function.

```
SKIP: {
        skip 'Mac::Speech is not available', 1
                unless eval { require 'Mac::Speech' };

        ok( $tv_horse->say_it_aloud( 'I am Mr. Ed' ) );
}
```

When Test::More skips tests, it outputs special ok messages to keep the test numbering right and to tell the test harness what happened. Later, the test harness can report how many tests we skipped.

Don't skip tests because they aren't working right. Use the TODO block for that. We use SKIP when we want to make tests optional in certain circumstances.

---

* TODO tests require Test::Harness Version 2.0 or later, which comes with Perl 5.8, but in earlier releases, they have to be installed from CPAN.

† Although, if the test passes when we said it should fail, it warns us that the test unexpectedly passed. That might mean that the test doesn't fail when it should.

More Complex Tests (Multiple Test Scripts)

Initially, the *h2xs* program* gave us a single testing file, t/1.t.† We can stick all our tests into this file, but it generally makes more sense to break the tests into logical groups in separate files.

The easiest way for us to add additional tests is to create t/2.t. That's it—just bump the 1 to a 2. We don't need to change anything in the *Makefile.PL* or in the test harness: the file is noticed and executed automatically.

We can keep adding files until we get to 9.t, but once we add 10.t, we might notice that it gets executed between 1.t and 2.t. Why? Because the tests are always executed in sorted order. This is a good thing because it lets us ensure that the most fundamental tests are executed before the more exotic tests simply by controlling the names.

Many people choose to rename the files to reflect a specific ordering and purpose by using names like 01-core.t, 02-basic.t, 03-advanced.t, 04-saving.t, and so on. The first two digits control the testing order, while the rest of the name gives a hint about the general area of testing.

As we saw earlier in Chapter 16, different module creation tools do different things and create one or more default tests. By default, Test::Harness runs those tests in the same order we just described.

Besides that, brian wrote Test::Manifest to get around this sort of naming scheme. Instead of letting the filenames dictate the order of tests, the file t/test_manifest does. Only the tests in that file run, and they run in the order we have them in the file. We name our test files after what they do rather than what order they should run. Later, when we want to insert new test files anywhere in the testing order, we just change the order in t/test_manifest.

Exercise

You can find the answer to this exercise in "Answer for Chapter 17" in the Appendix.

---

* If you're using one of the other module creation tools from Chapter 16, you probably got other test files, and ones that are more complex.

† As of Perl 5.8, that is. Earlier versions create a test.pl file, which is still run from a test harness during make test, but the output isn't captured in the same way.

Exercise [60 min]

Write a module distribution, starting from the tests first.

Your goal is to create a module My::List::Util that exports two routines on request: sum( ) and shuffle( ). The sum( ) routine takes a list of values and returns the numeric sum. The shuffle( ) routine takes a list of values and randomly shuffles the ordering, returning the list.

Start with sum( ). Write the tests, and then add the code. You'll know you're done when the tests pass. Now include tests for shuffle, and then add the implementation for shuffle. You might peek in the perlfaq to find a shuffle( ) implementation.

Be sure to update the documentation and MANIFEST file as you go along.

If you can pair up with someone on this exercise, even better. One person writes the test for sum( ) and the implementation code for shuffle( ), and the other does the opposite. Swap the t/* files, and see if you can locate any errors!

## CHAPTER 18

Advanced Testing

The Test::More module provides some simple and general functions, but other Test::* modules provide more specific tests for particular problem domains so that we don't have to write much code to do what we need. If we use it once, we'll probably use it again, anyway.

In this chapter, we give you a taste of some of the more popular test modules. Unless we say otherwise, these modules are not part of the Perl standard distribution (unlike Test::More) and you'll need to install them yourself. You might feel a bit cheated by this chapter since we're going to say "See the module documentation" quite a bit, but we're gently nudging you out into the Perl world. For much more detail, you can also check out *Perl Testing: A Developer's Notebook,* which covers the subject further.

Testing Large Strings

We showed in Chapter 17 that when a test fails, Test::More can show us what we expected and what we actually got.

```
#!/usr/bin/perl
use Test::More 'no_plan';
is( "Hello Perl", "Hello perl" );
```

When I run this program, Test::More shows me what went wrong.

```
$ perl test.pl
not ok 1
#     Failed test (test.pl at line 5)
#          got: 'Hello Perl'
#     expected: 'Hello perl'
1..1
# Looks like you failed 1 test of 1.
```

What if that string is really long? We don't want to see the whole string, which might be hundreds or thousands of characters long. We just want to see where they start to be different.

```perl
#!/usr/bin/perl

use Test::More 'no_plan';
use Test::LongString;

is_string(
        "The quick brown fox jumped over the lazy dog\n" x 10,

        "The quick brown fox jumped over the lazy dog\n" x 9 .
        "The quick brown fox jumped over the lazy camel",
        );
```

The error output doesn't have to show us the whole string to tell us where things went wrong. It shows us the relevant parts along with the string lengths. Although our example is a bit contrived, imagine doing this with a web page, configuration file, or some other huge chunk of data that we don't want cluttering our testing output.

```
not ok 1
#    Failed test in long_string.pl at line 6.
#          got: ..." the lazy dog\x{0a}"...
#       length: 450
#     expected: ..." the lazy camel"...
#       length: 451
#      strings begin to differ at char 447
1..1
# Looks like you failed 1 test of 1.
```

Testing Files

The code to test things like file existence and file size is simple, but the more code we write, and the more parts each code statement has, the more likely we are not only to mess up, but to miscommunicate our intent to the maintenance programmer.

We could test for file existence very easily. We use the -e file test operator in the ok( ) function from Test::More. That works just fine.

```perl
use Test::More 'no_plan';

ok( -e 'minnow.db' );
```

Well, it works just fine if that's what we meant to test, but nothing in that code tells anyone what we meant to do. What if we wanted to ensure the file did not exist before we started testing? The code for that is a difference of one character.

```perl
use Test::More 'no_plan';

ok( ! -e 'minnow.db' );
```

We could add a code comment, but as you probably already know, most code comments seem to assume that you already know what's supposed to happen. Does this comment let you know which of the two situations we want? Should we pass the test if the file is there?

```
use Test::More 'no_plan';

# test if the file is there
ok( ! -e 'minnow.db' );
```

The Test::File module, written by brian, encapsulates intent in the name of the function. If we want the test to pass when the file is there, we use file_exists_ok.

```
use Test::More 'no_plan';
use Test::File;

file_exists_ok( 'minnow.db' );
```

If we want the test to pass when the file is not there, we use file_not_exists_ok.

```
use Test::More 'no_plan';
use Test::File;

file_not_exists_ok( 'minnow.db' );
```

That's a simple example, but the module has many other functions that follow the same naming scheme: the first part of the name tells you what the function checks (file_exists) and the last part tells you what happens if that's true (_ok). It's a lot harder to miscommunicate the intent when we have to type it out.

```
use Test::More 'no_plan';
use Test::File;

my $file = 'minnow.db';

file_exists_ok(    $file );
file_not_empty_ok( $file );
file_readable_ok(  $file );
file_min_size_ok(  $file, 500  );
file_mode_is(      $file, 0775 );
```

So, not only do the explicit function names communicate intent, but they also contribute to parallel structure in the code.

Testing STDOUT or STDERR

One advantage to using the ok( ) functions (and friends) is that they don't write to STDOUT directly, but to a filehandle secretly duplicated from STDOUT when our test script begins. If we don't change STDOUT in our program, of course, this is a moot point. But let's say we wanted to test a routine that writes something to STDOUT, such as making sure a horse eats properly:

```
use Test::More 'no_plan';
use_ok 'Horse';
isa_ok(my $trigger = Horse->named('Trigger'), 'Horse');

open STDOUT, ">test.out" or die "Could not redirect STDOUT! $!";
$trigger->eat("hay");
```

```
close STDOUT;

open T, "test.out" or die "Could not read from test.out! $!";
my @contents = <T>;
close T;
is(join("", @contents), "Trigger eats hay.\n", "Trigger ate properly");

END { unlink "test.out" }  # clean up after the horses
```

Note that just before we start testing the eat method, we (re)open STDOUT to our temporary output file. The output from this method ends up in the test.out file. We bring the contents of that file in and give it to the is( ) function. Even though we've closed STDOUT, the is( ) function can still access the original STDOUT, and thus the test harness sees the proper ok or not ok messages.

If you create temporary files like this, please note that your current directory is the same as the test script (even if you're running make test from the parent directory). Also, pick fairly safe cross-platform names if you want people to be able to use and test your module portably.

There is a better way to do this, though. The Test::Output module can handle this for us. This module gives us several functions that automatically take care of all of the details.

```
#!/usr/bin/perl
use strict;

use Test::More "noplan";
use Test::Output;

sub print_hello { print STDOUT "Welcome Aboard!\n" }
sub print_error { print STDERR "There's a hole in the ship!\n" }

stdout_is( \&print_hello, "Welcome Aboard\n" );

stderr_like( \&print_error, qr/ship/ );
```

All of the functions take a code reference as their first argument, but that's not a problem because we told you all about those in Chapter 7. If we don't have a subroutine to test, we wrap the code we want to test in a subroutine and use that.

```
sub test_this {
...
        }

stdout_is( \&test_this, ... );
```

If our code is short enough, we might want to skip the step where we define a named subroutine and use an anonymous one.

```
stdout_is( sub { print "Welcome Aboard" }, "Welcome Aboard" );
```

We can even use an inline block of code, like we did with grep and map. As with those two list operators, notice that we don't have a comma after the inline code block.

```
stdout_is { print "Welcome Aboard" } "Welcome Aboard";
```

Besides Test::Output, we can do something similar with Test::Warn, which specifically tests warning output. Its interface uses the inline block form exclusively.

```
#!/usr/bin/perl

use Test::More "noplan";
use Test::Warn;

sub add_letters { "Skipper" + "Gilligan" }

warning_like { add_letters() }, qr/non-numeric/;
```

We all strive to make our code warning-free, and we can test for that too. Perl warnings can change from version to version, and we want to know when the new warnings pop up, or if Perl will emit warnings on one of our customer's computers. The Test::NoWarnings module is a bit different from the ones we've already shown. It automatically adds a test just by loading the module, and we just have to ensure we add the hidden test to the count we give to Test::More.

```
#!/usr/bin/perl
use warnings;

use Test::More tests => 1;
use Test::NoWarnings;

my( $n, $m );
# let's use an uninitialized value
my $sum = $n + $m;
```

When we try to compute the sum, we use two variables to which we haven't given values. That triggers the annoying "use of uninitialized value" warning (ensure you have warnings turned on!). We don't want those sorts of things filling up our logfiles, now, do we? Test::NoWarnings tells us when that happens so we can fix it.

```
1..1
not ok 1 - no warnings
#   Failed test 'no warnings'
#   in /usr/local/lib/perl5/5.8.7/Test/NoWarnings.pm at line 45.
# There were 2 warning(s)
#       Previous test 0 ''
#       Use of uninitialized value in addition (+) at nowarnings.pl line 6.
#
# ----------
#       Previous test 0 ''
#       Use of uninitialized value in addition (+) at nowarnings.pl line 6.
#
# Looks like you failed 1 test of 1 run.
```

Using Mock Objects

Sometimes we don't want to ramp up the entire system to test only parts of it. We can be fairly certain, or at least assume, that other parts of the system work. We don't need to open expensive database connections or instantiate objects with large memory footprints to test every part of the code.

The Test::MockObject module creates "pretend" objects. We give it information about the part of the object's interface we want to use, and it pretends to be that part of the interface. Basically, the pretend method has to return the right thing when we call it, and it doesn't have to do any processing.

Instead of creating a real Minnow object, which would mean turning on all sorts of things on the boat, we can create a mock object for it. Once we create the mock object and store it in $Minnow, we tell it how to respond to the methods we need to call. In this case, we tell the mock object to return true for engines_on and to return false for moored_to_dock. We're not really testing the object for the ship, but we want to test our quartermaster object, which takes a ship as an argument. Rather than test the quartermaster with a real ship, we use our mock one.

```
#!/usr/bin/perl

use Test::More 'no_plan';
use Test::MockObject;

# my $Minnow = Real::Object::Class->new( ... );
my $Minnow = Test::MockObject->new();

$Minnow->set_true( 'engines_on' );
$Minnow->set_true( 'has_maps' );
$Minnow->set_false( 'moored_to_dock' );

ok( $Minnow->engines_on, "Engines are on" );
ok( ! $Minnow->moored_to_dock, "Not moored to the dock" );

my $Quartermaster = Island::Plotting->new(
        ship => $Minnow,
        # ...
        )

ok( $Quartermaster->has_maps, "We can find the maps" );
```

We can create more complex methods that do anything we like. Suppose, instead of methods that return true or false, we need one that returns a list. Perhaps we need to pretend to connect to a database and retrieve some records. As we're developing, we might try this several times and we'd rather not connect and disconnect from the real database every time we try to track down a bug.

In this example, we mock the database method list_names, which we know will return us three names. Since we already know this, and we're actually testing

---

something else (which we don't show you in this contrived example), it doesn't bother us to create the mock method that stands in place of the real database.

```perl
#!/usr/bin/perl

use Test::More 'no_plan';
use Test::MockObject;

my $db = Test::MockObject->new( );

# $db = DBI->connect( ... );
$db->mock(
        list_names => sub { qw( Gilligan Skipper Professor ) }
        );

my @names = $db->list_names;

is( scalar @names, 3, 'Got the right number of results' );
is( $names[0], 'Gilligan', 'The first result is Gilligan' );

print "The names are @names\n";
```

Testing POD

We can even test things that aren't code. Documentation is just as important as code, since other people can't use our perfect, lovely code unless they know what to do with it. As we mentioned in Chapter 16, the Perl way to document code is by embedding POD formatted text in the code. Tools such as *perldoc* can extract the POD and display it in a variety of formats.

What if we mess up the POD format so that formatters can't parse it as we intended? To solve this problem, brian wrote Test::Pod to go through his modules looking for POD errors.[*] For most things, we can take the entire test code from the Test::Pod documentation.

```perl
use Test::More;
eval "use Test::Pod 1.00";
plan skip_all => "Test::Pod 1.00 required for testing POD" if $@;
all_pod_files_ok( );
```

We don't want to require everyone to install the module though, so the suggested test code first checks if we can load the module by using the string form of eval that we told you about in Chapter 2. If that fails, eval sets the error variable $@, and once that is set, we tell Test::More to skip the rest of the tests.

---

[*] It's now maintained by Andy Lester and is so popular that it's become part of Module::Starter and the CPAN Testers Service's (CPANTS) Kwalitee rating.

If we've installed the module, however, we'll get past the `skip_all` check and run `all_pod_files_ok`. The module takes care of finding all the POD files, which it then checks for format. If we want to change which files it checks, we can do that too. Without arguments, `all_pod_files_ok` tries to find files in the usual places. With arguments, it only tests the files we tell it to test.

```
use Test::More;
eval "use Test::Pod 1.00";
plan skip_all => "Test::Pod 1.00 required for testing POD" if $@;
all_pod_files_ok( 'lib/Maps.pm' );
```

Testing the POD format isn't all we can do, though. What if we want to ensure that we documented all of our methods? It's Test::Pod::Coverage to the rescue. It goes through our embedded documentation and tells us which subroutine names don't have corresponding entries in the documentation. The example use looks almost the same as that for Test::Pod.*

```
use Test::More;
eval "use Test::Pod::Coverage";
plan skip_all =>
        "Test::Pod::Coverage required for testing pod coverage" if $@;
plan tests => 1;
pod_coverage_ok( "Island::Plotting::Maps");
```

Both of these modules can do more than what we've shown you, so check their documentation to get the full story. If you use Module::Starter that we talked about in Chapter 16, you'll probably already have these tests in your distribution.

Coverage Testing

We can also test our testing. In a perfect world, we'd test our program with every possible input and environment so that our program follows every particular path. That's certainly what the Professor would do. In reality, we tend to be more like Gilligan, though.

We won't go too deeply into the theory and practice of coverage tests, but there are many things that we can test. Statement coverage tells us how many of the statements in our code we execute during a run. Branch coverage tells us how many of the decision paths we actually follow. Path coverage, expression coverage, and other sorts of coverage exist too. The best starting point is the Devel::Coverage::Tutorial documentation.

The module comes with a program named *cover*, which handles most of the things that we need to do. For any particular program we want to measure, we simply load the Devel::Cover module when we run it.

---

* That's because Andy Lester wrote both examples.

```
$ perl -MDevel::Cover yourprog args
$ cover
```

After we finish running the program, Devel::Cover leaves behind a file with all of the information it collected. Running the *cover* command turns that information into a set of HTML pages. When we look at the coverage.html page, we see a summary of our project along with its coverage statistics. The links on that page drill down into the individual files to see their coverage statistics too.

If we want to test a distribution, we just do this at the same time that we run our test suite. First, we get rid of any previous coverage results by passing *cover* the -delete option. After that, we have to run our make test and get Devel::Cover to do its magic at the same time. We can set the testing harness switches with the HARNESS_PERL_ SWITCHES environment variable, in which we put the -MDevel::Cover we used on the command line previously. Now every time the test harness wants to invoke Perl (which is for every test file), it also loads Devel::Cover. As that script runs, it adds to the coverage database (which is why we deleted the database before we started). Finally, once we've finished going through the tests, we call *cover* again to turn the results into something we can read.

```
$ cover -delete
$ HARNESS_PERL_SWITCHES=-MDevel::Cover make test
$ cover
```

Everything shows up in a directory named *cover_db* in the current working directory. The coverage database shows up in *cover_db,* and the top-level page shows up in *cover_db/coverage.html.*

Writing Your Own Test::* Modules

You don't have to wait for other people to write cool test modules. If you have a particular testing situation that you'd like to wrap up in a test function, you can write your own Test::* module using the Test::Builder module, which handles all of the tricky integration with Test::Harness and Test::More. If you look behind the scenes of many of the Test::* modules, you'll find Test::Builder.

Again, the advantage to test functions is that they wrap reusable code in a function name. To test something, you use the function name rather than typing out a bunch of separate statements. It's easy for people to understand what you meant to test based on a single function name, but that gets harder as you write out several statements to do the same thing.

In Chapter 4, we wrote some code to check that the castaways had all of their required items. Let's turn that into a Test::* module. Here's the check_required_ items subroutine as we left it:

```
sub check_required_items {
  my $who   = shift;
  my $items = shift;
```

```
  my @required = qw(preserver sunscreen water_bottle jacket);
  my @missing = ( );

  for my $item (@required) {
    unless (grep $item eq $_, @$items) { # not found in list?
      print "$who is missing $item.\n";
      push @missing, $item;
    }
  }

  if (@missing) {
    print "Adding @missing to @$items for $who.\n";
    push @$items, @missing;
  }
}
```

We need to turn this into a Test::* module that simply checks the items (so it
doesn't add the missing ones) and then outputs the right thing. The basics for any
new testing module are the same. We call our new module Test::Minnow::
RequiredItems and start with this stub:

```
package Test::Minnow::RequiredItems;
use strict;

use base qw(Exporter);
use vars qw(@EXPORT $VERSION);

use Test::Builder;

my $Test = Test::Builder->new( );

$VERSION = '0.10';
@EXPORT  = qw(check_required_items_ok);

sub check_required_items_ok {
        # ....
        }

1;
```

We start by declaring the package, then turning on strictures because we want to be
good programmers (even if this three-hour tour is ultimately doomed, it won't be
from one of our software errors). We pull in the Exporter module and add required_
items_ok to @EXPORT, since we want that function to show in the calling namespace,
just as we discussed in Chapter 15. We set $VERSION just like we discussed in
Chapter 16. The only stuff we haven't shown you is Test::Builder. At the beginning
of our test module, we create a new Test::Builder object that we assign to the lexical variable $Test, which is scoped to the entire file.*

---

* It's almost like a global variable, except it doesn't live in a package and can't be seen outside its file.

The $Test object is going to handle all of the testing details for us. We remove all of the output parts from check_required_items, and we take out the parts to modify the input list. Once we go through the other logic, the only thing we need to do at the end is tell the test harness if the test is ok or not_ok.

```
sub check_required_items {
  my $who   = shift;
  my $items = shift;

  my @required = qw(preserver sunscreen water_bottle jacket);
  my @missing = (  );

  for my $item (@required) {
    unless (grep $item eq $_, @$items) { # not found in list?
      push @missing, $item;
    }
  }

  if (@missing) {
  ...
  }
  else {
  ...
  }
}
```

Now we have to add the parts to turn our function into a testing one. We call methods on $Test to tell the test harness what happened. In each case, the last evaluated expression should be a call to $Test->ok( ), so that becomes the return value of the entire function.* If we discovered missing items, we want the test to fail, so we pass a false value to $Test->ok( ), but before we do that we use $Test->diag( ) with a message to tell us what went wrong.

```
sub check_required_items_ok {
  my $who   = shift;
  my $items = shift;

  my @required = qw(preserver sunscreen water_bottle jacket);
  my @missing = (  );

  for my $item (@required) {
    unless (grep $item eq $_, @$items) { # not found in list?
      push @missing, $item;
    }
  }

  if (@missing) {
    $Test->diag( "$who needs @missing.\n" );
```

---

* We often don't use the return value since most people call most test functions in a void context, but we might as well return something that makes sense.

```
      $Test->ok(0);
    }
    else {
      $Test->ok(1);
      }
  }
```

That's it. Although there are more things that we can do, there isn't more that we have to do. Once we save our Test::Minnow::RequiredItems, we can use it immediately in a test script. We still use Test::More to set the plan.*

```
use Test::More 'no_plan';
use Test::Minnow::RequiredItems;

my @gilligan = (
        Gilligan => [ qw(red_shirt hat lucky_socks water_bottle) ]
        );

check_required_items_ok( @gilligan );
```

Since Gilligan doesn't have all of his required items, the test fails. It prints the not_ok along with the diagnostic message.

```
not ok 1
1..1
# Gilligan needs preserver sunscreen jacket.
#     Failed test (/Users/Ginger/Desktop/package_test.pl at line 49)
# Looks like you failed 1 test of 1.
```

And, now that we've created the Test::Minnow::RequiredItems module, how we do we test the test? We can use the Test::Builder::Tester module. You'll have to investigate that one yourself, though.

Exercises

You can find the answers to these exercises in "Answers for Chapter 18" in the Appendix.

Exercise 1 [20 min]

Document the My::List::Util module you created in the exercise for Chapter 17. Add a test for the POD documentation using Test::Pod.

---

* We could do that from our module, but most likely the test script will use other modules too. Only one of them can set the plan, so we let Test::More handle that.

Exercise 2 [20 min]

Write your own test module, Test::My::List::Util, that has a single test function, sum_ok, which takes two arguments: the actual sum and the expected sum. Print a diagnostic message if the two do not match.

```
my $sum = sum( 2, 2 );
sum_ok( $sum, 4 );
```

CHAPTER 19

Contributing to CPAN

Besides allowing others in your organization to receive the benefits of these wonderful modules and distributions you've created, you can contribute to the Perl community at large. The mechanism for sharing your work is called the Comprehensive Perl Archive Network (CPAN), which is 10 years old as we write this and has about 9,000 different modules.

The Comprehensive Perl Archive Network

We covered the basic CPAN history in Chapter 3, but that was from a user's perspective. Now we want to contribute to CPAN, so we have to look at it from an author's perspective.

It's no accident that CPAN is so useful. The ethos of the project has been that anyone should be able to contribute and that it should be easy for people to share their work. Because of that, it has more than 9,000 modules (as we write this) and is the model that other languages wish they could adopt.*

Remember that CPAN is just a big storage device. That's its magic. Everything else that revolves around it, such as CPAN Search (*http://search.cpan.org*), CPAN.pm, and CPANPLUS.pm, merely use what's already there, not create what it is.

Getting Prepared

Since CPAN is just a big file-storage site, you just need to upload your code. To contribute to CPAN, you need two things:

- Something to contribute, ideally already in the shape of a module
- A Perl Authors Upload Server (PAUSE) ID

---

* However, whenever the discussion comes up in other languages, the first thing they do is try to set restrictions, which CPAN purposedly avoided.

The PAUSE ID is your passport to contributing to CPAN. You get a PAUSE ID by simply asking. The details are described at *http://www.cpan.org/modules/04pause.html*. You fill out a web form (linked from there) with a few basic details, such as your name, home web page, email address, and your preferred PAUSE ID. At the moment, PAUSE IDs must be between four and nine characters. (Some legacy PAUSE IDs are only three characters long.)[*] Once you have your PAUSE ID, you need to think globally about your contribution. Because your module will probably be used in programs along with other modules from other authors, you need to ensure that the package names for modules don't collide with existing modules or confuse the people who browse CPAN. Luckily for you, there is a loose collection of volunteers on the Perl Modules list (*modules@perl.org*) who've been working with CPAN and modules for quite a while and can help you sort through most problems.

Before you send your first email to the PAUSE admins, it's probably a good idea to do a few things first:

- Look at the current module list. Get an idea for how things are named. Better yet, are you reinventing a subset of something that already exists, or can you contribute your work as a patch to another module?

- Visit the list archives (pointers can be found at *http://lists.perl.org*) to see what the typical conversations look like. That might help you to avoid shock at your response or better phrase your initial request.

- Above all, get it in your head that this whole process is run by volunteers who aren't perfect and are doing this in their spare time for the good of the Perl community. Have patience. Have tolerance.

Preparing Your Distribution

Once you've gotten your module name settled and you've tested your module with its new name (if needed), you should ensure your distribution is ready for prime time. While this is similar to releasing a distribution in-house, as described in Chapter 16, you might want to ensure a few additional things about your distribution:

- Create a *README* file. This file is automatically extracted to a separate file on the CPAN archives and lets someone view or download just the key facts about your distribution before fetching or unpacking the rest.

- Make and test your *Makefile.PL* or *Build.PL*. Modules without a *Makefile.PL* are accepted via PAUSE to go into the CPAN but usually get a grimace from those of us who download your stuff, because we might have to figure out how to build and install your distribution.

---

[*] Originally, the PAUSE IDs had to be five characters or less, until Randal wanted his MERLYN ID, and the appropriate accommodation was made.

- Bring your *MANIFEST* up to date. If you add files that should be part of the distribution, they also need to be in the *MANIFEST*. One quick trick is to clean things up as you would want them in the distribution, and then invoke make manifest, which updates the *MANIFEST* file to be exactly what you are holding at the moment.*

- Have a logical distribution version number. The *Makefile.PL* file should specify either a VERSION value or a VERSION_FROM value. If you have a single module (such as a *.pm* file) in your distribution, it's usually best to grab the version number from there with VERSION_FROM. If you have multiple files, either designate one of them as the one you'll always update just before a new release or use the VERSION within the *Makefile.PL* instead. Also keep in mind that your version number must always increase *numerically* for newer versions of your distribution. (After Version 1.9, the next release can't be Version 1.10, because even if you're calling it "version one point ten," it's still merely 1.1 to the tools that compare version numbers.)

- Have tests! Reread Chapter 17 if you must. There's nothing that builds more confidence in an installed distribution than at least a few dozen tests that are run during the installation phase. If you're not adding a test for each bug that you find, how do you know the bug is fixed?

- Invoke make disttest, which builds a distribution archive of everything in *MANIFEST*, unpacks the archive into a separate directory, and then runs the tests on your distribution. If that doesn't work for you, you can't expect it to work for anyone else who downloads your distribution from the CPAN.

Uploading Your Distribution

Once you have your distribution ready to share, visit the PAUSE upload page at *https://pause.perl.org/pause/authenquery?ACTION=add_uri*. You'll have to log in using your PAUSE ID and PAUSE password, and then you'll be given several options to upload your distribution.

On that page, you can upload your file directly through the HTTP file upload or tell PAUSE where else on the Web it can fetch the distribution. Besides that, you can FTP the distribution to *ftp://pause.perl.org*.

No matter which way you upload the file, it should appear in the list of uploaded files at the bottom of that page. You might have to wait a bit for PAUSE to fetch remote files, but they usually show up pretty quickly. If you don't see your PAUSE ID next to the distribution name, you can claim it.

---

* If make manifest adds too many files, you can create a *MANIFEST.SKIP* file that has a set of Perl regular expressions that tells make manifest which files to ignore. Once you have that file, make manifest will remove from *MANIFEST* files that match those patterns.

Once PAUSE has the file and knows who it belongs to, it indexes it. You should get email from the PAUSE indexer telling you what happened. After that, your distribution is on its way to CPAN proper. Remember that the N in CPAN is "Network," so your distribution may take hours or days to reach all of the CPAN mirrors. It shouldn't take longer than a couple of days, though.

If you have a problem or think something didn't happen the way it should have, you can ask the PAUSE administrators about it by sending mail to *modules@perl.org*.

Announcing the Module

How will users learn about your module? Your module gets noticed automatically in many places, including:

- The "Recent modules" page of *http://search.cpan.org*
- The "new modules" section of *http://use.perl.org*
- A daily announcement in the "Perl news" mailing list
- An IRC bot on a few of the Perl-related IRC channels announces uploads as soon as they become available
- An update or an uninstalled module in one of the CPAN shells, CPAN.pm, or CPANPLUS.pm

For greater visibility, you can also prepare a short notice to be posted to the Usenet *comp.lang.perl.announce* newsgroup. Just post the notice, and within a day or two, your news posting will be whisking around to news servers all over the globe.

Testing on Multiple Platforms

The CPAN Testers (*http://testers.cpan.org*) automatically test almost all modules uploaded to CPAN. Volunteers around the world automatically download and test each distribution on whatever setup they have. Among them, they test your module on just about every platform, operating system, and Perl version that matters (and many that you probably don't pay attention to). They send email to the module authors telling them what happened, and they automatically update the Testers database. You can look at the results for any module through the Testers web site or on CPAN Search (*http://search.cpan.org*).

Often, testers can help you figure out problems for platforms to which you do not have access.

Consider Writing an Article or Giving a Talk

Many of the short talks at Perl conferences involve the author of a distribution talking about his own work. After all, who is better qualified to help others use your module than you? The more interested other people are in your module, the better it gets as they send in their bug reports, feature requests, and patches.

If the idea of proposing a conference talk intimidates you a bit, or you don't want to wait that long, look to your local Perl user group. They're generally looking for speakers (usually for the meeting coming up in the next week or two), and the group size is usually small enough to be a nice casual setting. You can generally find a Perl user group near you by looking on the Perl Mongers web site at *http://www.pm.org*. If you can't find one, start one!

Exercise

You can find the answer to this exercise in "Answer for Chapter 19" in the Appendix.

Exercise [Infinite min]

Write a module to solve the halting problem with respect to Perl source code.[*] Your module should export a function, will_halt, which takes a string and returns true if the string is the source code for a no-input Perl program that does not infinitely loop, and false otherwise.

[*] *http://en.wikipedia.org/wiki/Halting_problem*

Answers to Exercises

This appendix contains the answers to the exercises presented throughout the book.

Answers for Chapter 2

Exercise 1

Here's one way to do it. The command-line arguments show up in the special array @ARGV, so we use that for our input list. The file test operator -s works on $_ by default, and that's just the current element that grep tests. All of the files with a byte -size smaller than 1,000 bytes end up in @smaller_than_1000. That array becomes the input for the map, which takes each element and returns it with spaces tacked on the front and a newline on the end.

```
#!/usr/bin/perl

my @smaller_than_1000 = grep { -s $_ < 1000 } @ARGV;

print map { "    $_\n" } @smaller_than_1000;
```

Typically we'll do that without the intermediate array, though.

```
print map { "    $_\n" } grep { -s < 1000 } @ARGV;
```

Exercise 2

We chose to use our home directory as the hardcoded directory. When we call chdir without an argument, it goes to our home directory (so this is one of the few places where Perl doesn't use $_ as the default).

After that, an infinite while loop keeps our code running, at least until we can't satisfy the condition to last that breaks us out of the loop. Look at the condition carefully: we don't just test for truth. What would happen if we wanted to find all the files with a 0 in them? We look for defined values with a nonzero length, so undef (end of input) and the empty string (simply hitting enter) stop the loop.

Once we have our regular expression, we do that same thing we did in the previous answer. This time we use the result of glob as the input list and a pattern match inside the grep. We wrap an eval { } around the pattern match in case the pattern doesn't compile (for instance, it has an unmatched parenthesis or square bracket).

```perl
#!/usr/bin/perl

chdir; # go to our home directory

while( 1 )
        {
        print "Please enter a regular expression> ";
        chomp( my $regex = <STDIN> );
        last unless( defined $regex && length $regex );

        print map { "     $_\n" } grep { eval{ /$regex/ } }
                glob( ".* *" );
        }
```

Answers for Chapter 3

Exercise 1

The trick in this exercise is to let the modules do all of the hard work. It's a good thing we've shown you how to use modules! The Cwd module (cwd is an acronym for "current working directory") automatically imports the getcwd function. We don't have to worry about how it does its magic, but we can be confident that it does it correctly for most major platforms.

Once we have the current path in $cwd, we can use that as the first argument to the catfile method from the File::Spec function. The second argument comes from the input list to our map and shows up in $_.

```perl
#!/usr/bin/perl

use Cwd;
use File::Spec;

my $cwd = getcwd;

print map { "     " . File::Spec->catfile( $cwd, $_ ) . "\n" }
                glob( ".* *" );
```

Exercise 2

We can't give you much help installing the module, although if you run into problems, you might want to ask brian about them since he wrote the module, as well as the *cpan* program you can use to install it.

Once we have the module, we just have to follow the example in the documentation. Our program takes the ISBN from the command line and creates the new ISBN object, which we store in $isbn. Once we have the object, we simply follow the examples in the documentation.

```perl
#!/usr/bin/perl

use Business::ISBN;

my $isbn = Business::ISBN->new( $ARGV[0] );

print "ISBN is " . $isbn->as_string . "\n";
print "Country code:   " . $isbn->country_code . "\n";
print "Publisher code: " . $isbn->publisher_code . "\n";
```

Answers for Chapter 4

Exercise 1

They're all referring to the same thing, except for the second one, ${$ginger[2]}[1]. That one is the same as $ginger[2][1], whose base is the array @ginger, rather than the scalar $ginger.

Exercise 2

First, we construct the hash structure:

```perl
my @gilligan = qw(red_shirt hat lucky_socks water_bottle);
my @professor = qw(sunscreen water_bottle slide_rule batteries radio);
my @skipper = qw(blue_shirt hat jacket preserver sunscreen);
my %all = (
  "Gilligan" => \@gilligan,
  "Skipper" => \@skipper,
  "Professor" => \@professor,
);
```

Then we pass it to the first subroutine:

```perl
check_items_for_all(\%all);
```

In the subroutine, the first parameter is a hashref, so we dereference it to get the keys and the corresponding values:

```perl
sub check_items_for_all {
  my $all = shift;
```

```
    for my $person (sort keys %$all) {
      check_required_items($person, $all->{$person});
    }
  }
```

From there, we call the original subroutine:

```
sub check_required_items {
  my $who = shift;
  my $items = shift;
  my @required = qw(preserver sunscreen water_bottle jacket);
  my @missing = ( );
  for my $item (@required) {
    unless (grep $item eq $_, @$items) { # not found in list?
      print "$who is missing $item.\n";
      push @missing, $item;
    }
  }
  if (@missing) {
    print "Adding @missing to @$items for $who.\n";
    push @$items, @missing;
  }
}
```

Answers for Chapter 5

Exercise 1

The curly braces of the anonymous hash constructor make a reference to a hash.
That's a scalar (as are all references), so it's not suitable to use alone as the value of a
hash. Perhaps this code's author intended to assign to scalar variables (like
$passenger_1 and $passenger_2) instead of hashes. But you can fix the problem simply by changing the two pairs of curly braces to parentheses.

If you tried running this, Perl may have given you a helpful diagnostic message as a
warning. If you didn't get the warning, perhaps you didn't have warnings turned on,
either with the -w switch or with the use warnings pragma. Even if you don't usually
use Perl's warnings, you should enable them during debugging. (How long would it
take you to debug this without Perl's warnings to help you? How long would it take
to enable Perl's warnings? 'Nuff said.)

What if you got the warning message but couldn't tell what it meant? That's what
the *perldiag* manpage is for. Warning texts need to be concise because they're compiled into the *perl* binary (the program that runs your Perl code). But *perldiag* should
list all the messages you should ever get from Perl, along with a longer explanation of
what each one means, why it's a problem, and how to fix it.

If you want to be ultimately lazy, you can add use diagnostics; at the beginning of
your program, and any error message will look itself up in the documentation and

display the entire detailed message. Don't leave this in production code, however, unless you like burning a lot of CPU cycles every time your program starts, whether or not an error occurs.

Exercise 2

You will be keeping count of how much data has been sent to all machines, so at the start, set the variable $all to a name that will stand in for all of them. It should be a name that will never be used for any real machine, of course. Storing it in a variable is convenient for writing the program and makes it easy to change later.

```
my $all = "**all machines**";
```

The input loop is nearly the same as given in the chapter, but it skips comment lines. Also, it keeps a second running total, filed under $all.

```
my %total_bytes;
while (<>) {
  next if /^#/;
  my ($source, $destination, $bytes) = split;
  $total_bytes{$source}{$destination} += $bytes;
  $total_bytes{$source}{$all} += $bytes;
}
```

Next, make a sorted list. This holds the names of the source machines in descending order of total transferred bytes. This list is used for the outer for loop. (Rather than using a temporary array, @sources, you might have put the sort directly into the parens of the for loop.)

```
my @sources =
  sort { $total_bytes{$b}{$all} <=> $total_bytes{$a}{$all} }
  keys %total_bytes;

for my $source (@sources) {
  my @destinations =
    sort { $total_bytes{$source}{$b} <=> $total_bytes{$source}{$a} }
    keys %{ $total_bytes{$source} };
  print "$source: $total_bytes{$source}{$all} total bytes sent\n";
  for my $destination (@destinations) {
    next if $destination eq $all;
    print "  $source => $destination:",
      " $total_bytes{$source}{$destination} bytes\n";
  }
  print "\n";
}
```

Inside the loop, print out the total number of bytes sent from that source machine, and then make a sorted list of the destination files (similar to the list in @sources). As you step through that list, use next to skip over the dummy $all item. Because that item will be at the head of the sorted list, why wasn't shift used to discard it, since that would avoid checking repeatedly for $all inside the inner loop? The answer is in this footnote.* You can simplify this program, perhaps. The subexpression $total_bytes{$source} is used many times in the large output for loop (and twice in the input loop as well). That can be replaced by a simple scalar, initialized at the top of the loop:

```
for my $source (@sources) {
  my $tb = $total_bytes{$source};
  my @destinations = sort { $tb->{$b} <=> $tb->{$a} } keys %$tb;
  print "$source: $tb->{$all} total bytes sent\n";
  for my $destination (@destinations) {
    next if $destination eq $all;
    print "  $source => $destination: $tb->{$destination} bytes\n";
  }
  print "\n";
}
```

This makes the code shorter and (likely) a bit faster as well. Give yourself extra credit if you thought to do this. Also give yourself extra credit if you thought that it might be too confusing and decided not to make the change.

Answers for Chapter 6

Exercise 1

This is similar to what you saw in Chapter 5, but now it uses Storable.

```
use Storable;

my $all       = "**all machines**";
my $data_file = "total_bytes.data";

my %total_bytes;
if (-e $data_file) {
  my $data = retrieve $data_file;
  %total_bytes = %$data;
}

while (<>) {
  next if /^#/;
  my ($source, $destination, $bytes)   = split;

  $total_bytes{$source}{$destination} += $bytes;
  $total_bytes{$source}{$all}         += $bytes;
}

store \%total_bytes, $data_file;

### remainder of program is unchanged
```

---

* Even though the dummy item will sort to the head of the sorted list, it won't necessarily be the first item in the list. If a machine sent data to just one other, that destination machine's total will be equal to the source machine's total output, so that list could sort in either order.

Near the top, put the filename into a variable. You can then retrieve the data but only if the datafile already exists.

After reading the data, use Storable again to write it back out to the same disk file.

If you chose to write the hash's data to a file the hard way, by writing your own code and your own file format, you're working too hard. More to the point, unless you're extraordinarily talented or spend way too long on this exercise, you almost certainly have bugs in your serialization routines, or at least flaws in your file format.

Exercise 2

There should probably be some checks to ensure that Storable was successful. It will catch some errors (and die), but it will simply return undef for some. See the documentation for Storable. (Of course, if you checked the return values from store and retrieve, you should give yourself extra credit on the previous exercise.)

The program should save the old datafile (if any) under a backup filename so that it's easy to revert the latest additions. In fact, it could even keep several backups, such as the last week's worth.

It might also be nice to be able to print the output without having any new input data. As it's written, this can be done by giving an empty file (such as /dev/null) as the input. However, there should be an easier way. The output functionality could be separated entirely from the updating, in fact.

Answer for Chapter 7

Exercise

```perl
sub gather_mtime_between {
  my($begin, $end) = @_;
  my @files;
  my $gatherer = sub {
    my $timestamp = (stat $_)[9];
    unless (defined $timestamp) {
      warn "Can't stat $File::Find::name: $!, skipping\n";
      return;
    }
    push @files, $File::Find::name if
      $timestamp >= $begin and $timestamp <= $end;
  };
  my $fetcher = sub { @files };
  ($gatherer, $fetcher);
}
```

This code is pretty straightforward. The main challenge is getting the item names correct. When using stat inside the callback, the filename is $_, but when returning the filename (or reporting it to the user), the name is $File::Find::name.

If the stat fails for some reason, the timestamp will be undef. (That can happen, for example, if it finds a dangling symbolic link.) In that case, the callback simply warns the user and returns early. If you omit that check, you can get warnings of an undefined value during the comparison with $begin and $end.

When you run the completed program with this subroutine, your output should show only file modification dates on the previous Monday (unless you changed the code to use a different day of the week, of course).

Answers for Chapter 8

Exercise 1

In this exercise, we have to use three different output methods: to a file, which you're already familiar with; to a scalar (and you'll need Perl 5.8 for this); or to both at the same time. The trick is to store the output channels in the same variable that you'll use for the print statement. When the filehandle is a variable, we can put anything we like in it and decide what to put in it at runtime.

```perl
#!/usr/bin/perl
use strict;

use IO::Tee;

my $fh;
my $scalar;

print "Enter type of output [Scalar/File/Tee]> ";
my $type = <STDIN>;

if( $type =~ /^s/i ) {
        open $fh, ">", \$scalar;
        }
elsif( $type =~ /^f/i ) {
        open $fh, ">", "$0.out";
        }
elsif( $type =~ /^t/i ) {
        open my $file_fh,   ">", "$0.out";
        open my $scalar_fh, ">", \$scalar;
        $fh = IO::Tee->new( $file_fh, $scalar_fh );
        }

my $date       = localtime;
my $day_of_week = (localtime)[6];
```

```
print $fh <<"HERE";
This is run $$
The date is $date
The day of the week is $day_of_week
HERE

print STDOUT <<"HERE" if $type =~ m/^[st]/i;
Scalar contains:
$scalar
HERE
```

In this program, we prompt the user for the type of output, and we want her to type either "scalar", "file", or "tee". Once we read the input, we detect which one she typed by matching on the first character (using a case-insensitive match for more flexibility).

If the user chose "scalar", we open $fh to a scalar reference. If she chose "file", we open $fh to a file, as you know from before. We name the file after the program name, stored in $0, and append .out to it. If the user chose "tee", we create filehandles for a file and a scalar, then combine both of those in an IO::Tee object that we store in $fh. No matter which method the user chose, the output channels, whether sole or multiple, end up in the same variable.

From there it's just a matter of programming, and it doesn't matter much what we actually print. For this exercise, we get the date string by using localtime in scalar context, then get the day of the week with a literal list slice.

In the string we print to $fh, we include the process ID (contained in the special variable $$), so we can tell the difference between separate runs of our program, and then the date and the day of the week.

Finally, if we choose to send the output to a scalar (either alone or with a file), we print the scalar value to STDOUT to ensure the right thing ended up there.

Exercise 2

```
use IO::File;
my %output_handles;
while (<>) {
  unless (/^(\S+):/) {
    warn "ignoring the line with missing name: $_";
    next;
  }
  my $name = lc $1;
  my $handle = $output_handles{$name} ||=
    IO::File->open(">$name.info") || die "Cannot create $name.info: $!";
  print $handle $_;
}
```

At the beginning of the while loop, use a pattern to extract the person's name from the data line, issuing a warning if that's not found.

Once you have the name, force it to lowercase so that an entry for "Maryann" will get filed in the same place as one for "MaryAnn." This is also handy for naming the files, as the next statement shows.

The first time through the loop, the filehandle must be created. Let's see how to do that. The || operator has a higher precedence than the assignment, so it is evaluated first; the program will die if the file can't be created. The ||= operator assigns the file-handle to the hash, and the = operator passes it to $handle as well.

The next time you have the same name in $name, the ||= operator kicks in. Remember that $gilligan ||= $anything is effectively like $gilligan = $gilligan || $anything. If the variable on the left is a false value (such as undef), it's replaced by the value on the right, but if it's true (such as a filehandle), the value on the right won't even be evaluated. Thus, since the hash already has a value for that person's name, the hash's value is used and assigned directly to $handle without having to (re)create the file.

It wasn't necessary to code the castaways' names into this program, because they will be read in as data. This is good because any additional castaway won't require having to rewrite the program. If someone's name is accidentally misspelled, however, it puts some of their data into a new file under the wrong name.

Exercise 3

Here's one way to do it. First, we go through the arguments in @ARGV to find out which ones don't represent directories, then print error messages for each of those.

After that, we go through @ARGV again to find the elements that are valid directories. We take the list that comes out of that grep and send it into map, where we turn each string into an IO::Dir object (ignoring error handling for the moment). The file output list ends up in @dir_hs, which we go through with the foreach loop and send to print_contents.

There is nothing fancy about print_contents, though. It simply takes its first argument and stores it in $dh, which it then uses to walk through the directory.

```
#!/usr/bin/perl -w
use strict;

use IO::Dir;

my @not_dirs = grep { ! -d } @ARGV;
foreach my $not_dir ( @not_dirs ) {
        print "$not_dir is not a directory!\n";
        }

my @dirs = grep { -d } @ARGV;

my @dir_hs = map { IO::Dir->new( $_ ) } grep { -d } @ARGV;
```

```
foreach my $dh ( @dir_hs ) { print_contents( $dh ) };

sub print_contents {
        my $dh = shift;

        while( my $file = $dh->read ) {
                next if( $file eq '.' or $file eq '..');
                print "$file\n";
                }
        };
```

Answers for Chapter 9

Exercise 1

```
my @sorted =
  map $_->[0],
  sort { $a->[1] <=> $b->[1] }
  map [$_, -s $_],
  glob "/bin/*";
```

Using the -s operator to determine the file's size is an expensive operation; by cach-
ing its value, you can save some time. How much? Let's see in the next exercise's
answer.

Exercise 2

```
use Benchmark qw(timethese);

my @files = glob "/bin/*";

timethese( -2, {
  Ordinary => q{
    my @results = sort { -s $a <=> -s $b } @files;
  },
  Schwartzian => q{
    my @sorted =
      map $_->[0],
      sort { $a->[1] <=> $b->[1] }
      map [$_, -s $_],
      @files;
  },
});
```

On the 33-element /bin on his laptop, Randal was seeing 260 iterations per second of
the Ordinary implementation and roughly 500 per second of the Schwartzian implementation, so writing the complex code saved about half of the execution time. On a
74-element /etc, the Schwartzian Transform was nearly three times as fast. In general,
the more items sorted, the more expensive the computed function, and the better you

can expect the Schwartzian Transform to perform. That doesn't even count the burden on the monkey—er, we mean the operating system.

In the previous edition of this book, we had a slight design error in this code that made the Schwartzian transform seem a lot slower. brian noticed this one day while he was teaching this exercise, then sat down to go over it in way too much detail. You can read the lengthy analysis on Perl Monks: *http://www.perlmonks.com/?node_id=393128*.

Exercise 3

```
my @dictionary_sorted =
  map $_->[0],
  sort { $a->[1] cmp $b->[1] }
  map {
    my $string = $_;
    $string =~ tr/A-Z/a-z/;
    $string =~ tr/a-z//cd;
    [ $_, $string ];
  } @input_list;
```

Inside the second map, which executes first, make a copy of $_. (If you don't, you'll mangle the data.)

Exercise 4

```
sub data_for_path {
  my $path = shift;
  if (-f $path or -l $path) {
    return undef;
  }
  if (-d $path) {
    my %directory;
    opendir PATH, $path or die "Cannot opendir $path: $!";
    my @names = readdir PATH;
    closedir PATH;
    for my $name (@names) {
      next if $name eq "." or $name eq "..";
      $directory{$name} = data_for_path("$path/$name");
    }
    return \%directory;
  }
  warn "$path is neither a file nor a directory\n";
  return undef;
}

sub dump_data_for_path {
  my $path = shift;
  my $data = shift;
  my $prefix = shift || "";
  print "$prefix$path";
```

```
    if (not defined $data) { # plain file
      print "\n";
      return;
    }
    my %directory = %$data;
    if (%directory) {
      print ", with contents of:\n";
      for (sort keys %directory) {
        dump_data_for_path($_, $directory{$_}, "$prefix  ");
      }
    } else {
      print ", an empty directory\n";
    }
  }
  dump_data_for_path(".", data_for_path("."));
```

By adding a third (prefix) parameter to the dumping subroutine, you can ask it to indent its output. By default, the prefix is empty, of course.

When the subroutine calls itself, it adds two spaces to the end of the prefix. Why the end and not the beginning? Because it's comprised of spaces, either end will work. By using trailing spaces, you can call the subroutine like this:

```
  dump data_for_path(".", data_for_path("."), ">  ");
```

This invocation quotes the entire output by prefixing each line with the given string. You can (in some hypothetical future version of this program) use such quoting to denote NFS-mounted directories or other special items.

Answers for Chapter 10

Exercise 1

Here's one way to do it. First, start with the package directive and use strict:

```
  package Oogaboogoo::date;
  use strict;
```

Then define the constant arrays to hold the mappings for day-of-week and month names:

```
  my @day = qw(ark dip wap sen pop sep kir);
  my @mon = qw(diz pod bod rod sip wax lin sen kun fiz nap dep);
```

Next, define the subroutine for day-of-week number to name. Note that this subroutine will be accessible as Ooogaboogoo::date::day:

```
  sub day {
    my $num = shift @_;
    die "$num is not a valid day number"
      unless $num >= 0 and $num <= 6;
    $day[$num];
  }
```

Similarly, you have the subroutine for the month-of-year number to name:

```
sub mon {
  my $num = shift @_;
  die "$num is not a valid month number"
    unless $num >= 0 and $num <= 11;
  $mon[$num];
}
```

Finally, the mandatory true value at the end of the package:

```
1;
```

Name this file *date.pm* within a directory of Oogaboogoo in one of the directories given in your @INC variable, such as the current directory.

Exercise 2

Here's one way to do it. Pull in the *.pm* file from a place in your @INC path:

```
use strict;
require 'Oogaboogoo/date.pm';
```

Then get the information for the current time:

```
my($sec, $min, $hour, $mday, $mon, $year, $wday) = localtime;
```

Then use the newly defined subroutines for the conversions:

```
my $day_name = Oogaboogoo::date::day($wday);
my $mon_name = Oogaboogoo::date::mon($mon);
```

The year number is offset by 1900 for historical purposes, so you need to fix that:

```
$year += 1900;
```

Finally, it's time for the output:

```
print "Today is $day_name, $mon_name $mday, $year.\n";
```

Answers for Chapter 11

Exercise 1

Here's one way to do it. First define the Animal class with a single method:

```
use strict;
{ package Animal;
  sub speak {
    my $class = shift;
    print "a $class goes ", $class->sound, "!\n";
  }
}
```

Now define each subclass with a specific sound:

```
{ package Cow;
  our @ISA = qw(Animal);
  sub sound { "moooo" }
}
{ package Horse;
  our @ISA = qw(Animal);
  sub sound { "neigh" }
}
{ package Sheep;
  our @ISA = qw(Animal);
  sub sound { "baaaah" }
}
```

The Mouse package is slightly different because of the extra quietness:

```
{ package Mouse;
  our @ISA = qw(Animal);
  sub sound { "squeak" }
  sub speak {
    my $class = shift;
    $class->SUPER::speak;
    print "[but you can barely hear it!]\n";
  }
}
```

Now, enter the interactive part of the program:

```
my @barnyard = ( );
{
  print "enter an animal (empty to finish): ";
  chomp(my $animal = <STDIN>);
  $animal = ucfirst lc $animal;                # canonicalize
  last unless $animal =~ /^(Cow|Horse|Sheep|Mouse)$/;
  push @barnyard, $animal;
  redo;
}

foreach my $beast (@barnyard) {
  $beast->speak;
}
```

This code uses a simple check, via a pattern match, to ensure that the user doesn't enter Alpaca or another unavailable animal, because doing so will crash the program. In Chapter 14, you'll learn about the isa method, which lets you check more simply whether something is an available animal, even allowing for the possibility that it is an animal that was added to the program after the check was written.

Exercise 2

Here's one way to do it. First, create the base class of LivingCreature with a single speak method:

```
use strict;
{ package LivingCreature;
```

```
    sub speak {
      my $class = shift;
      if (@_) {                    # something to say
        print "a $class goes '@_'\n";
      } else {
        print "a $class goes ", $class->sound, "\n";
      }
    }
  }
```

A person is a living creature, so define the derived class here:

```
{ package Person;
  our @ISA = qw(LivingCreature);
  sub sound { "hmmmm" }
}
```

The Animal class comes next, making appropriate sounds but unable to talk (except to Dr. Dolittle):

```
{ package Animal;
  our @ISA = qw(LivingCreature);
  sub sound { die "all Animals should define a sound" }
  sub speak {
    my $class = shift;
    die "animals can't talk!" if @_;
    $class->SUPER::speak;
  }
}
{ package Cow;
  our @ISA = qw(Animal);
  sub sound { "moooo" }
}
{ package Horse;
  our @ISA = qw(Animal);
  sub sound { "neigh" }
}
{ package Sheep;
  our @ISA = qw(Animal);
  sub sound { "baaaah" }
}
{ package Mouse;
  our @ISA = qw(Animal);
  sub sound { "squeak" }
  sub speak {
    my $class = shift;
    $class->SUPER::speak;
    print "[but you can barely hear it!]\n";
  }
}
```

Finally, have the person speak:

```
Person->speak;                   # just hmms
Person->speak("Hello, world!");
```

Notice that the main speak routine has now moved into the LivingCreature class, which means you don't need to write it again to use it in Person. In Animal, though, you need to check that to ensure an Animal won't try to speak before calling SUPER::speak.

Although it's not the way the assignment was written, you can get a similar result if you choose to make Person a subclass of Animal. (In that case, LivingCreature would presumably be needed as a parent class for an eventual Plant class.) Of course, since an Animal can't speak, how can a Person? The answer is that Person::speak would have to handle its parameters, if any, before or after (or instead of) calling SUPER::speak.

Which would be the better way to implement this? It all depends upon what classes you'll need in the future and how you'll use them. If you expect to add features to Animal that would be needed for Person, it makes sense for Person to inherit from Animal. If the two are nearly completely distinct, and nearly anything that a Person has in common with an Animal is common to all LivingCreatures, it's probably better to avoid the extra inheritance step. The ability to design a suitable inheritance structure is a crucial talent for any OOP programmer.

In fact, you may find that after developing the code one way, you'll want to "refactor" the code a different way. This is common with OOP. However, it's very important to have enough testing in place to ensure that you don't break things while you're moving them around.

Answer for Chapter 12

Exercise

First, start the Animal package:

```
use strict;
{ package Animal;
  use Carp qw(croak);
```

And now for the constructor:

```
## constructors
sub named {
  ref(my $class = shift) and croak "class name needed";
  my $name = shift;
  my $self = { Name => $name, Color => $class->default_color };
  bless $self, $class;
}
```

Now, for virtual methods: the methods that should be overridden in a subclass. Perl doesn't require virtual methods to be declared in the base class, but they're nice as a documentation item.

```
## backstops (should be overridden)
sub default_color { "brown" }
sub sound { croak "subclass must define a sound" }
```

Next comes the methods that work with either a class or an instance:

```
## class/instance methods
sub speak {
  my $either = shift;
  print $either->name, " goes ", $either->sound, "\n";
}
sub name {
  my $either = shift;
  ref $either
    ? $either->{Name}
    : "an unnamed $either";
}
sub color {
  my $either = shift;
  ref $either
    ? $either->{Color}
    : $either->default_color;
}
```

Finally, the methods that work only for the particular instance:

```
## instance-only methods
sub set_name {
  ref(my $self = shift) or croak "instance variable needed";
  $self->{Name} = shift;
}
sub set_color {
  ref(my $self = shift) or croak "instance variable needed";
  $self->{Color} = shift;
}
}
```

Now that you have your abstract base class, define some concrete classes that can have instances:

```
{ package Horse;
  our @ISA = qw(Animal);
  sub sound { "neigh" }
}
{ package Sheep;
  our @ISA = qw(Animal);
  sub color { "white" }     # override the default color
  sub sound { "baaaah" }    # no Silence of the Lambs
}
```

Finally, a few lines of code to test your classes:

```
my $tv_horse = Horse->named("Mr. Ed");
$tv_horse->set_name("Mister Ed");
$tv_horse->set_color("grey");
print $tv_horse->name, " is ", $tv_horse->color, "\n";
print Sheep->name, " colored ", Sheep->color, " goes ", Sheep->sound, "\n";
```

Answer for Chapter 13

Exercise

First, start the class:

```perl
{ package RaceHorse;
    our @ISA = qw(Horse);
```

Next, use a simple dbmopen to associate %STANDINGS with permanent storage:

```perl
dbmopen (our %STANDINGS, "standings", 0666)
    or die "Cannot access standings dbm: $!";
```

When a new RaceHorse is named, either pull the existing standings from the database or invent zeros for everything:

```perl
sub named { # class method
    my $self = shift->SUPER::named(@_);
    my $name = $self->name;
    my @standings = split ' ', $STANDINGS{$name} || "0 0 0 0";
    @$self{qw(wins places shows losses)} = @standings;
    $self;
}
```

When the RaceHorse is destroyed, the standings are updated:

```perl
sub DESTROY { # instance method, automatically invoked
    my $self = shift;
    $STANDINGS{$self->name} = "@$self{qw(wins places shows losses)}";
    $self->SUPER::DESTROY;
}
```

Finally, the instance methods are defined:

```perl
## instance methods:
sub won { shift->{wins}++; }
sub placed { shift->{places}++; }
sub showed { shift->{shows}++; }
sub lost { shift->{losses}++; }
sub standings {
    my $self = shift;
    join ", ", map "$self->{$_} $_", qw(wins places shows losses);
}
```

Answers for Chapter 14

Exercise 1

There a couple of ways to tackle this problem. In our solution, we created a MyDate package in the same file as the script. The naked block defines the scope of the package MyDate statement. Later, in our script, we can't use the module because Perl won't find a file for it. We'll have to remember to call the `import` method to get the symbols into our `main` namespace.

To make the `AUTOLOAD` subroutine work only for the right subroutines, we defined `%Allowed_methods` to hold the names of the methods that will work. Their values are their offsets in the list we get back from `localtime`. That almost solves it, but `localtime` uses 0-based numbers for the month and year. In the `@Offsets` array, we store the number to add to the corresponding entry in the `localtime` list. It seems like a lot of work now since only two values have offsets, but doing it this way eliminates two special cases.

We need a `new` method (or some constructor) to give us an object. In this example, it doesn't really matter what the object actually looks like. We just use an empty, anonymous hash blessed into the current package (that's the first thing in the argument list, so it's `$_[0]`). We also know that we'll need a `DESTROY` method, since Perl will automatically look for it when it tries to clean up the object. If we don't have it, our `AUTOLOAD` will complain about an unknown method when it tries to handle `DESTROY` on its own (comment out the `DESTROY` to see what happens).

Inside the `AUTOLOAD`, we store the method name in `$method` so we can change it. We want to strip off the package information and get just the method name. That's everything after the last `::`, so we use the substitution operator to get rid of everything up to that point. Once we have the method name, we look for its key in `%Allowed_methods`. If it's not there, we print an error with `carp`. Try calling an unknown method. For which line does Perl report the error?

If we find the method name in `%Allowed_methods`, we get the value, which is the position of the value in the `localtime` list. We store that in `$slice_index` and use it to get the value from `localtime` as well as the offset for that value. We add those two values together and return the result.

That sounds like a lot of work, but how much work would we have to do to add new methods for the hour and minute? We simply add those names to `%Allowed_methods`. Everything else already works.

```perl
#!/usr/bin/perl -w
use strict;

{
package MyDate;
use vars qw($AUTOLOAD);

use Carp;

my %Allowed_methods = qw( date 3 month 4 year 5 );
my @Offsets         = qw(0 0 0 0 1 1900 0 0 0);

sub new      { bless {}, $_[0] }
sub DESTROY  {}
```

```
sub AUTOLOAD {
        my $method = $AUTOLOAD;
        $method =~ s/.*:://;

        unless( exists $Allowed_methods{ $method } ) {
                carp "Unknown method: $AUTOLOAD";
                return;
                }

        my $slice_index = $Allowed_methods{ $method };

        return (localtime)[$slice_index] + $Offsets[$slice_index];
        }
}

MyDate->import;          # we don't use it
my $date = MyDate->new();

print "The date is "  . $date->date  . "\n";
print "The month is " . $date->month . "\n";
print "The year is "  . $date->year  . "\n";
```

Exercise 2

Our script looks the same as the previous answer with the addition of the UNIVERSAL::
debug routine. At the end of our script, we call the debug method on our $date object.
It works without changing the MyDate module.

```
MyDate->import;          # we don't use it
my $date = MyDate->new();

sub UNIVERSAL::debug {
        my $self = shift;
        print '[' . localtime . '] ' . join '|', @_
        }

print "The date is "  . $date->date  . "\n";
print "The month is " . $date->month . "\n";
print "The year is "  . $date->year  . "\n";

$date->debug( "I'm all done" );
```

How did that get past the AUTOLOAD? Remember that Perl searches through all of @ISA
and UNIVERSAL before it starts looking in any AUTOLOAD method. So, Perl finds
UNIVERSAL::debug before it has to use our AUTOLOAD magic.

Answers for Chapter 15

Exercise 1

The module Oogaboogoo/date.pm looks like this:

```
package Oogaboogoo::date;
use strict;
use Exporter;
our @ISA = qw(Exporter);
our @EXPORT = qw(day mon);

my @day = qw(ark dip wap sen pop sep kir);
my @mon = qw(diz pod bod rod sip wax lin sen kun fiz nap dep);

sub day {
  my $num = shift @_;
  die "$num is not a valid day number"
    unless $num >= 0 and $num <= 6;
  $day[$num];
}

sub mon {
  my $num = shift @_;
  die "$num is not a valid month number"
    unless $num >= 0 and $num <= 11;
  $mon[$num];
}

1;
```

The main program now looks like this:

```
use strict;
use Oogaboogoo::date qw(day mon);

my($sec, $min, $hour, $mday, $mon, $year, $wday) = localtime;
my $day_name = day($wday);
my $mon_name = mon($mon);
$year += 1900;
print "Today is $day_name, $mon_name $mday, $year.\n";
```

Exercise 2

Most of this answer is the same as the previous answer. We just need to add the parts for the export tag all.

```
our @EXPORT = qw(day mon);
our %EXPORT_TAGS = ( all => \@EXPORT );
```

Everything that we put in %EXPORT_TAGS has to also be in either @EXPORT or @EXPORT_OK. For the all tag, we use a reference to @EXPORT directly. If we don't like that, we can make a fresh copy so the two do not reference each other.

```
our @EXPORT = qw(day mon);
our %EXPORT_TAGS = ( all => [ @EXPORT ] );
```

Modify the program from the previous exercise to use the import tag by prefacing it with a colon in the import list.

The main program now starts off like this:

```
use strict;
use Oogaboogoo::date qw(:all);
```

Answer for Chapter 16

Exercise

We don't have code to show you: it's just the stuff in Chapter 12. Lift that code and put it into a distribution. Most of the work is just typing.

There are a few different approaches, though. Once you have the distribution built with your favorite tool, you can split up the classes into separate module files. You can have an *Animal.pm*, *Horse.pm*, and so on. Put all the files in the same place as the original *.pm* that the module tool created. You also need to change the *Makefile.PL* or *Build.PL* to tell it about the new module files. Just follow the example of what is already there. Finally, make sure all the right files show up in *MANIFEST*.

Once you have all of the code in place, run the *Makefile.PL*, which you'll need to do every time you change that file. When you change the module files, you'll need to run make again too, although that happens when you run make test or make dist.

When you're ready, run make dist. You should find a new archive file in the current directory. You can also call make zipdist if you want a ZIP archive. Move that archive to another directory and unpack it. When you run *Makefile.PL*, you shouldn't get any errors or warnings if you did everything right. If you get a warning, fix that (it's probably a missing file, if anything) and try again.

Answer for Chapter 17

Exercise

Let's start with the test file. We write this first, and as we write the code (which we can't run until we write the module), we get an idea of the interface that we want.

In the BEGIN block, we first test if we can use My::List::Util. This will obviously fail, since we haven't written the module yet. We'll worry about that later.

Next, we check if we've defined the sum subroutine. Once we implement the My::List::Util minimal module, the use_ok will pass but this will fail. That's Test Driven Development. You define what you want, ensure that the test fails when the infrastructure is missing, then make it pass. Getting tests to pass can be easy if we don't care if they fail when they should.

After we check for the sum routine, we test a series of sums, using different numbers of arguments and different values. We don't have to identify every special case at this point (we can always add tests later), but we want to ensure that we test several different ways to call the subroutine. We even throw in a test where we pass it a non-number and a number, then a test where we pass it two non-numbers.

We do something different for shuffle. We ensure the subroutine is defined, then define $array as a starting point, but immediately copy it to $shuffled so we don't disturb the original. Before we've written the code, we've decided to pass an array reference, and that will allow our routine to affect the data that we pass to it (rather than creating a copy).

To test this, we do something really simple. We compare the original array to the shuffled one and use cmp_ok to test that at least two positions are different. That wouldn't be a very good shuffle, but we're going to punt to you for the rest of the tests.

```perl
BEGIN{ use_ok( 'My::List::Util' ) }

use Test::More 'no_plan';

# # # # # # sum
ok( defined &sum, 'The sum() routine exists');
is( sum( 2, 2    ), 4, '2 + 2 = 4'     );
is( sum( 2, 2, 3 ), 7, '2 + 2 + 3 = 7' );
is( sum( ),           0, 'null sum is 0' );
is( sum( -1 ),       -1, '-1 = -1'       );
is( sum( -1, 1 ),     0, '-1 + 1 = 0'    );
is( sum( 'Ginger', 5 ),
        5, 'A string + 5 = 5' );
is( sum( qw(Ginger Mary-Ann) ),
        0, 'Two strings give 0' );

# # # # # # shuffle
ok( defined &shuffle, "The shuffle() routine exists");
my $array = [qw( a b c d e f )];

my $shuffled = $array;
shuffle( $shuffled );

my $same_count = 0;

foreach my $index ( 0 .. $#$array ) {
        $same_count++ if $shuffle->[$index] eq $array->[$index];
        }
```

```
        cmp_ok( $same_count, '<', $#$array - 2,
              'At least two positions are different');
```

Now that we have the tests, we write the code. As we write the code, we run the
tests. At first, most of the tests will fail, but as we add more code (and possibly debug
the code that's already there), more and more tests pass. Here's our finished module:

```
package My::List::Util;
use strict;

use base qw(Exporter);
use vars qw(@EXPORT $VERSION);

use Exporter;

$VERSION = '0.10';
@EXPORT  = qw(sum shuffle);

sub shuffle {            # Fisher-Yates shuffle from perlfaq4
        my $deck = shift;  # $deck is a reference to an array
        my $i = @$deck;
        while ($i--) {
                my $j = int rand ($i+1);
                @$deck[$i,$j] = @$deck[$j,$i];
                }
        }

sub sum {
        my @array = @_;

        my $sum = 0;

        foreach my $element ( @array ) {
                $sum += $element;
                }

        $sum;
        }

1;
```

Answers for Chapter 18

Exercise 1

Since you're starting with your distribution from the last chapter, we don't have
much code to show you. To add a POD test, create a *t/pod.t* file (or whatever you
want to call it). In there, put the code you lift for Test::Pod:

```
use Test::More;
eval "use Test::Pod 1.00";
```

```
plan skip_all => "Test::Pod 1.00 required for testing POD" if $@;
all_pod_files_ok();
```

This code is clever: it only runs tests if the user has installed Test::Pod, and doesn't cause any problems if she hasn't.

If you are especially motivated, you can do the same thing with Test::Pod::Coverage. Create a *t/pod_coverage.t* file and lift the code directly from the module documentation.

Depending on which module creation tool you used, you might already have these files, too.

Exercise 2

You could create a new distribution for your test module, but you don't have to. You can include it with the distribution that you already made. You just have to put the module file in the right place and ensure that *Makefile.PL* or *Build.PL* knows about it.

We'll just show you the code, though. This is a long way to go to test $n == $m, but we wanted to make it as uncomplicated as possible so you could focus on the Test:: Builder part. You can lift most of the code directly from the example in the chapter and then write the sum_ok function.

```
package Test::My::List::Util;
use strict;

use base qw(Exporter);
use vars qw(@EXPORT $VERSION);

use Exporter;
use Test::Builder;

my $Test = Test::Builder->new();

$VERSION = '0.10';
@EXPORT  = qw(sum_ok);

sub sum_ok {
        my( $actual, $expected ) = @_;

        if( $actual == $expected ) {
                $Test->ok( 1 )
                }
        else {
                $Test->diag(
                        "The sum is not right\n",
                        "\tGot:      $actual\n",
                        "\tExpected: $expected\n"
                        );
```

```
            $Test->ok( 0 )
          }
       }

    1;
```

Answer for Chapter 19

Exercise

Were you able to solve the halting problem? We didn't really expect you to solve this problem since, in 1936, Alan Turing proved you couldn't create a general solution. You can read about the halting problem at Wikipedia: *http://en.wikipedia.org/wiki/Halting_problem*.

There's not much we can show you as an answer to an exercise about distributions. You know about testing now, so as long as your tests pass, you know you're doing the right thing (or the tests don't work!).

We're kicking you out into the real world now. We don't have anything left to tell you in this book. Go back and read the footnotes now. Good luck!

Index

We'd like to hear your suggestions for improving our indexes. Send email to *index@oreilly.com*.

DESTROY method, 139, 144
destructors, 139, 144
Devel::Cover module, 210
direct object syntax, 145
directed graph, 38
directory handles, references to, 86
directory hierarchy, capturing
        recursively, 96–98
directory separators, 14
distributions, 1, 171
    alternate installation locations for, 184
    alternate library locations, using, 187
    contributing to CPAN, 216–219
    creating, 172–179
    embedded documentation for, 179–182
    installation, testing, 186
    make test for, 185
    Makefile.PL for, 183
    presenting at Perl conferences, 220
    testing, 186
do operator, 103–105
documentation, embedded
    format for, 179–182
    testing, 209
Dump subroutine, 56
Dumper subroutine, 55, 98
dumping data (see Data::Dumper package;
        YAML)

E

embedded documentation
    format for, 179–182
    testing, 209
encapsulation, 135
__END__ marker, 179
errors
    syntax errors, 9, 105
    trapping, 8
    warnings, 9, 105
eval operator
    code sharing using, 102
    dynamic code in, 9
    errors not trapped by, 9
    nesting, 9
    trapping errors with, 8
exercises
    solutions to, 221–247
    using, 2
@EXPORT variable, 164, 177
@EXPORT_OK variable, 164, 178
%EXPORT_TAGS variable, 165, 178
Exporter module, 164–167, 177

ExtUtils::MakeMaker module, 173, 183
ExtUtils::ModuleMaker module, 172

F

factorial function, 95
File::Basename module, 13
File::Spec module, 14
file_not_exists_ok function, 205
filehandles
    barewords for, 79
    references to
        anonymous IO::File objects as, 83
        in scalar variables, 80
        IO::File objects as, 82
        IO::Scalar objects as, 84
        IO::Tee objects as, 85
files
    included files (see libraries)
    testing, 204
filesystem hierarchy, capturing
        recursively, 96–98
filtering lists, 4–6
foy, brian d (author)
    "Get More Out of Open", 81
    cpan program, 19
    Test::File module, 205
    Test::Manifest module, 201
    Test::Pod module, 209
functional interfaces for modules, 12

G

garbage collection, 39
"Get More Out of Open" (foy), 81
getters, 135
    AUTOLOAD method for, 157
    creating, 158–160
    performance of, 136
    setters included in, 136
grep operator, 4–6, 59, 60

H

h2xs program, 172–179, 183
hashes, 21
    anonymous hash constructors, 42–44
    autovivification and, 47
    dereferencing, 30–32
    instance data in, 132, 135
    references to, 30
hierarchical data (see recursively defined
        data), 95
Hietaniemi, Jarkko (CPAN FTP site), 15

I

-I command line option, 108
import routine, 163
@INC variable, 17–18, 106–108
include path for libraries, 106–108
included files (see libraries)
indices
    indirection using, 59
    of CPAN modules, 15
    sorting with, 91
indirect object syntax, 145
indirection, 59
Ingerson, Brian (YAML), 56
inheritance, 119
    multiple inheritance, 160
    of constructors, 129
instance data
    accessing, 128
    filehandles in, 139
    in hashes, 132, 135
instance variables, 126
    filehandles in, 144
    in subclasses, 147, 148
instance-only methods, 137
instances (see objects)
IO::Dir module, 86
IO::File module, 82, 83
IO::Handle module, 82–86
IO::Scalar module, 84
IO::Tee module, 85
is function, 196, 206
isa method, 155
@ISA variable, 120, 125, 154, 160
isa_ok function, 197
isnt function, 197

K

Keenan, Jim (ExtUtils::ModuleMaker
        module), 172

L

Langworth, Ian (Perl Testing: A Developer's
        Notebook), 189
Learning Perl (Schwartz), xiii, 1
Lester, Andy (Module::Starter module), 172
lexical variables
    closures accessing, 71
    packages and, 113
lib pragma, 18

libraries
    include path for, 106–108
    including
        with do operator, 103–105
        with require operator, 105
like function, 197
lists
    creating, 4
    filtering, 4–6
    mapping, 6–8
    operators for, 4
    reversing, 4
    sorting, 4

M

make dist, 186
make disttest, 218
make install, 186
make program, 172
make test, 185, 193
make utility, 183
Makefile.PL file, 172, 183, 217
MANIFEST file, 173, 218
map operator, 6–8, 60, 61, 93, 94
marshaling data, 57, 58
Math::BigInt module, 15
member variables (see instance variables)
memory leaks, 39
META.yml file, 176
methods, 117
    abstract methods, 159
    accessors (see getters; setters)
    AUTOLOAD method, 156–158
    class-only methods, 137
    constructors, 129
    DESTROY method, 139, 144
    direct object syntax for, 145
    helper methods called from, 119
    in UNIVERSAL class, 154
    indirect object syntax for, 145
    instance-only methods, 137
    invoking, 117, 122, 124, 127, 145
        with either classes or objects, 130
        with parameters, 118, 125
    not existing, alternate method for, 156
    overriding, 121–123
    parameters for, 131
    testing existence in inheritance
        hierarchy, 156
mock objects, testing with, 208

Module::Build module, 172
Module::Starter module, 172
modules, 11
   contributing to CPAN, 216–219
   dependencies of, 19
   embedded documentation for
      format for, 179–182
      reading, 12
      testing, 209
   exporting subroutines from, 164–167
   functional interfaces for, 12
   importing subroutines from
      all subroutines, 13
      custom routines for, 168
      specific subroutines, 13
      with import routine, 163
      with use operator, 162–164
   in standard distribution, 11
   installing from CPAN, 16
   local subroutines with same names as
      subroutines in, 13
   object-oriented, 14, 177
      exporting, 166
      testing, 197–199
   presenting at Perl conferences, 220
   search path for (@INC), 17, 18, 106–108
multiple inheritance, 160

N

namespace collisions, 109–112
nested arrays, 27
nested data structures (see complex data
      structures)
numbers, sorting, 89

O

object-oriented modules, 14, 177
   exporting, 166
   testing, 197–199
object-oriented programming (see OOP)
objects, 126
   accessors for (see getters; setters)
   creating, 127, 128
   destruction of, 139, 144
      at end of program, 140
      effects of, 139
      for nested objects, 141–144
   instance data for
      accessing, 128
      filehandles in, 139
      in hashes, 132, 135

invoking methods of, 127, 130
   mock objects, testing with, 208
   setters for, 133–135
   testing membership of, 155
ok function, 195, 204
OOP (object-oriented programming), 1
   encapsulation, 135
   inheritance, 119
      multiple inheritance, 160
      of constructors, 129
   when to use, 115
   (see also classes; objects)
open statement, creating filehandle references
      in, 80, 81
operators
   list operators, 4
   (see also specific operators)
our declaration, 120

P

package variables
   closures and, 75
   scope of, 113
packages
   as namespace separators, 110–112
   lexical variables and, 113
   naming, 111
   scope of, 112
packaging code (see distributions)
patterns (see grep operator)
PAUSE (Perl Authors Upload Server)
   ID, 217
   upload page, 218
Perl
   standard distribution of, 11
   version used by this book, 11
Perl Authors Upload Server (see PAUSE)
Perl Best Practices (Conway), 80
The Perl Journal, 81, 172
Perl Modules list, 217
Perl Mongers web site, 220
Perl Monks web site, 232
Perl Testing: A Developer's Notebook
      (Langworth), 189
Perl user groups, 220
PERL5LIB environment variable, 108
perl-packrats mailing list, 15
plus sign (+)
   preceding anonymous hash
      constructor, 44
   preceding terms, 141
POD format, 180, 209

pointers (see references)
PREFIX parameter, 184, 187
PREREQ_PM setting, 184
print operator, 4
programming (see distribution; testing)

R

README file, 174, 217
recursive algorithms, 95
recursively defined data, 95
    building, 96–98
    displaying, 98
ref operator, 130
reference counting, 34
    failure of, 38–40
    garbage collection as alternative to, 39
    nested data structures and, 36–38
references, 21
    assigning to variables or data structure
        elements, 23, 34
    backslash operator for, 23, 30, 64
    copying, 23, 34
    deleting, 35
    in array elements, 36–38
    multiple, count of (see reference counting)
    multiple, to one data structure, 23, 34
    to arrays, 23
    to deleted variable, 35
    to directory handles, 86
    to filehandles
        anonymous IO::File objects as, 83
        in scalar variables, 80
        IO::File objects as, 82
        IO::Scalar objects as, 84
        IO::Tee objects as, 85
    to hashes, 30
    to subroutines, 63
        anonymous subroutines, 68
        dereferencing, 64
        for callbacks, 70
        in complex data structures, 65
        named subroutines, 63–67
        returning from subroutines, 72–75
    weak references, 150–152
    (see also dereferencing)
regression testing, 190
regular expressions (see grep operator)
release cycle, 1
require operator, 105–108, 162
REUSED_ADDRESS, in debugger, 56

reverse operator, 4
reverse sort operator, 90

S

s command, debugger, 51
scalar variables, 21
    anonymous scalar variables, 72
    directory handle references in, 86
    filehandle references in, 80
    hash references in, 43
    references in, 23, 26
Schwartz, Randal L. (author)
    Learning Perl, xiii, 1
    Schwartzian Transform, 93–95
Schwartzian Transform, 93–95
Schwern, Michael ("Perl Test Master"), 193
scope of package directive, 112
selection (see grep operator)
$self variable, 128
semicolon (:), preceding blocks, 44
setters, 135
    AUTOLOAD method for, 157
    creating, 158–160
    for objects, 133–135
    getters doubling as, 136
    performance of, 136
SKIP designation for tests, 200
sort block, 89
sort operator, 4, 89, 94
sorting
    efficiency of, 92
    in descending order, 90
    map operator and, 93
    multi-level sorting, 94
    Schwartzian Transform for, 93–95
    sort operator, 4, 89, 94
    with indices, 91
spaceship operator (<=>), 90
square brackets ([]), anonymous array
    constructors using, 40
standard distribution, 11
static local variables, closure variables as, 75
STDERR, testing, 205–207
STDOUT, testing, 205–207
Stein, Lincoln (CGI module), 168
Storable module, 57–58
strings
    eval operator on, avoiding, 9
    large, testing, 203
    sorting, 89

variables (*continued*)
    package variables
        closures and, 75
        scope of, 113
    static local variables, 75
    (see also scalar variables)

W

warnings, 9, 105
weak references, 150–152
weaken routine, 151
web site resources
    CPAN Search, 16
    PAUSE ID, obtaining, 217

The Perl Journal, 81, 172
Perl Mongers, 220
Perl Monks, 232
Williams, Ken (Module::Build module), 172
WriteMakefile subroutine, 183

X

x command, debugger, 51

Y

YAML (Yet Another Markup Language), 56

About the Author

Randal L. Schwartz is a renowned expert on the Perl programming language. In addition to writing *Learning Perl* and the first two editions of *Programming Perl*, he has been the Perl columnist for *UNIX Review*, *Web Techniques*, *Sys Admin*, and *Linux Magazine*. He has contributed to a dozen Perl books and over 200 magazine articles. Randal runs a Perl training and consulting company (Stonehenge Consulting Services) and is highly sought after as a speaker for his combination of technical skill, comedic timing, and crowd rapport. He's also a pretty good Karaoke singer.

brian d foy has been an instructor for Stonehenge Consulting Services since 1998. He founded the first Perl user group, the New York Perl Mongers, as well as the Perl advocacy nonprofit Perl Mongers, Inc., which helped form more than 200 Perl user groups across the globe. He maintains the perlfaq portions of the core Perl documentation, several modules on CPAN, and some standalone scripts. He's the publisher of *The Perl Review* and is a frequent speaker at conferences. His writings on Perl appear on The O'Reilly Network and *use.perl.org*, and in *The Perl Journal*, *Dr. Dobbs Journal*, and *The Perl Review*.

Tom Phoenix has been working in the field of education since 1982. After more than 13 years of dissections, explosions, work with interesting animals, and high-voltage sparks during his work at a science museum, he started teaching Perl for Stonehenge Consulting Services, where he's worked since 1996. As it is traditional for Perl people to have at least three other unlikely interests, Tom enjoys amateur cryptography, Esperanto, and Squeak (Smalltalk). According to rumor, he has never turned down an opportunity to play a game of Zendo. He lives in Portland, Oregon, with his wife and cats.

Colophon

The animal on the cover of *Intermediate Perl* is an alpaca (*Lama pacos*). The alpaca is a member of the South American camelid family, which is closely related to the more familiar Asian and African camels. South American camelids also include the llama, the vicuna, and the guanaco. The alpaca is smaller (36 inches at the withers) than a llama but larger than its other relations. Ninety-nine percent of the world's approximately three million alpacas are found in Peru, Bolivia, and Chile.

The evolution of the wild vicuna into the domestic alpaca began between six and seven thousand years ago. The specialized breeding of alpacas for fiber production wasn't developed until around 500 B.C. The Incas developed the alpaca into the two distinct fleece types, the Huacaya (pronounced wa-kai-ya) and the less common Suri. The main difference between the two types of alpacas is the fiber they produce. The Huacaya fleece has crimp or wave; the Suri fleece is silky and lustrous and has no crimp. Alpacas are prized for their fleece, which is as soft as cashmere and warmer, lighter, and stronger than wool. Alpaca fleece comes in more colors than that of any other fiber-producing animal (approximately 22 basic colors with many variations and blends).

The lifespan of the alpaca is about 20 years. Gestation is 11.5 months, producing one offspring, or cria, every 14 to 15 months. The alpaca is a modified ruminant, not only eating less grass than most other animals but converting it to energy very efficiently. Unlike true ruminants, they have three compartments in their stomach, not four, and can thus survive in areas unsuitable to other domesticated animals. Alpacas are gentle and don't bite or butt. Even if they did, without incisors, horns, hoofs, or claws, they would do little damage.

The cover image is a 19th-century engraving from *Animate Creations*, Volume II. The cover font is Adobe ITC Garamond. The text font is Linotype Birka; the heading font is Adobe Myriad Condensed; and the code font is LucasFont's TheSans Mono Condensed.